Tried and tested

What people across the UK are saying about the **Law Express** and **Law Express Question&Answer** series:

'Covers all the main areas in a clear and concise way, and provides some excellent advice on how to tackle exam problems and write essays.'

Gwilym Owen, Lecturer in Law, Bangor University

'Students should in this book find a useful and valuable revision guide. The Q&A format is an appropriate and effective means of enhancing students' preparation for law assessments and for improving academic performance. . .'

Dr George K. Ndi, PGR Leader, University of Huddersfield Law School

'A useful, practical and informative revision guide, which makes good use of various pedagogical features to enhance accessibility to students.'

Adam Pendlebury, Senior Lecturer in Law, Edge Hill University

'This series covers well the important techniques for identifying legal issues and applying case-law to factual scenarios.'

David Selfe, Director, School of Law, Liverpool John Moores University

'Revising with this series is like having a tutor there. . .'

Mariette Jones, Senior Lecturer in Law, Middlesex University

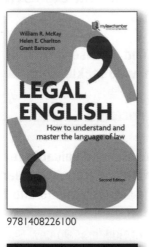

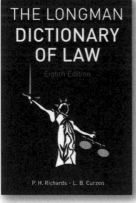
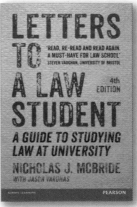

Law Express

Q&A

Question&Answer
LAND LAW

4th edition

John Duddington
Former Head of the Law School,
Worcester College of Technology

Pearson

Harlow, England • London • New York • Boston • San Francisco • Toronto • Sydney
Dubai • Singapore • Hong Kong • Tokyo • Seoul • Taipei • New Delhi
Cape Town • São Paulo • Mexico City • Madrid • Amsterdam • Munich • Paris • Milan

Pearson Education Limited
Edinburgh Gate
Harlow CM20 2JE
United Kingdom
Tel: +44 (0)1279 623623
Web: **www.pearson.com/uk**

First published 2012 (print)
Second edition published 2014 (print and electronic)
Third edition published 2016 (print and electronic)
Fourth edition published 2018 (print and electronic)

ISBN: 978-1-292-14893-9 (print)
    978-1-292-14909-7 (PDF)
    978-1-292-14917-2 (ePub)

British Library Cataloguing-in-Publication Data
A catalogue record for the print edition is available from the British Library

10 9 8 7 6 5 4 3 2 1
22 21 20 19 18 17

Print edition typeset in 10/13pt Helvetica Neue LT W1G by SPi Global
Printed and bound in Malaysia (CTP-PJB)

NOTE THAT ANY PAGE CROSS REFERENCES REFER TO THE PRINT EDITION

Contents

Acknowledgements

Author's acknowledgements

To my father, Walter Duddington, who first encouraged me to become a lawyer, and who would, I think, have enjoyed land law; to my wife, Anne, for her constant support, loyalty and technical expertise over very many years and without which my books would never begin to be written; to my daughter, Mary, for her seemingly faultless proofreading and sense of fun which keeps me going; and to my son, Christopher, for just being himself.

I would also like to thank the staff at Pearson for their encouragement, cheerfulness and practical guidance, and all the reviewers who sent in such helpful comments on preliminary drafts of this book. I have considered them all and adopted most of them. I would indeed have adopted more had space permitted.

A word to students who may think of buying a (doubtless) cheaper previous edition. Examiners often base questions on recent cases and statutes, and this book contains new questions reflecting decisions of the Supreme Court on the application of the Human Rights Act 1998 to possession actions (Chapter 1), registered land (Chapter 2) and proprietary estoppel (Chapter 5). In addition, the material in Chapter 4 on trusts of the home has been almost completely recast in the light of continued judicial activity in this area. All of these are very likely topics for examination questions and a study of the questions on them in this book will, I hope, repay your investment in it. In addition, there is new material in every chapter, whether it is incorporating new cases, the throwing of new light on old cases or looking at a topic in a new light.

I must not forget happy afternoons spent at the ground of Worcestershire County Cricket Club where, during quiet passages of play, many of the ideas for the questions in this book still come to my mind.

Finally, readers should know that this book is based on sources available to me on 12th October 2016, which also happens to be my birthday!

John Duddington

Publisher's acknowledgements

We are grateful to the following for permission to reproduce copyright material:

Text

Extract on page 4 from *Powell* v *McFarlane* (1977) 38 P & CR 452, Incorporated Council of Law Reporting; Extract on page 9 from *Leeds CC* v *Price* [2006] 2 AC 465, Incorporated Council of Law Reporting; Extract on pages 13–4 from *Botham* v *TSB Bank plc* (1997) 73 P & CR D1, Incorporated Council of Law Reporting; Extract on page 109 from *Lloyds Bank* v *Rosset* [1991] AC 107, Incorporated Council of Law Reporting; Extracts on page 122, page 124 from *Bruton* v *London and Quadrant Housing Trust* [2000] 1 AC 406, Incorporated Council of Law Reporting; Extracts on page 125, page 127 from *Mexfield Housing Co-operative Ltd* v *Berrisford* [2012] 1 AC 955, Incorporated Council of Law Reporting; Extract on page 133 from *Walsh* v *Lonsdale* (1882) 21 Ch D 9, Incorporated Council of Law Reporting; Extract on page 137 from *Warren* v *Keen* [1954] 1 QB 15, Incorporated Council of Law Reporting; Extract on page 200 from *Knightsbridge Estates* v *Byrne* [1939] Ch 441 (HC), Incorporated Council of Law Reporting; Extract on page 201 from *Kreglinger* v *New Palagonia Meat and Cold Storage Co. Ltd* [1914] AC 25, Incorporated Council of Law Reporting; Extract on page 202 from *Reeve* v *Lisle* [1902] AC 461, Incorporated Council of Law Reporting; Extract on page 209 from *Palk and Another* v *Mortgage Services Funding plc* [1993] 2 WLR 415, Incorporated Council of Law Reporting; Extract on page 209 from *Ropaigealach* v *Barclays Bank* [2000] QB 263, Incorporated Council of Law Reporting; Extract on page 218 from *Royal Bank of Scotland* v *Etridge* (No. 2) (2002) 2 AC 773, Incorporated Council of Law Reporting.

Contains public sector information licensed under the Open Government Licence v3.0.

Our thanks go to all reviewers who contributed to the development of this text, including students who participated in research and focus groups who helped to shape the series format.

Guided tour

How to use features in the book 📖 and on the companion website 🖱

📖 **What to do for every question** – Identify the key things you should look for and do in any question and answer on the subject, ensuring you give every one of your answers a great chance from the start.

📖 **How this topic might come up in exams** – Understand how to tackle any question on this topic by using the handy tips and advice relevant to both essay and problem questions. In text, symbols clearly identify each question type as they occur.

📖 **Before you begin** – Visual guides to help you confidently identify the main points covered in any question asked. You can also download them from the companion website to pin on your wall or add to your revision notes.

📖 **Answer plans and Diagram plans** – A clear and concise plan is the key to a good answer and these answer plans and diagram plans support the structuring of your answers.

📖 **Answer with accompanying guidance** – Make the most out of every question by using the guidance; recognise what makes a good answer and why. The length of the answers reflect what you could realistically achieve in an exam and show you how to gain marks quickly when under pressure.

📖 **Make your answer stand out** – Impress your examiners with these sources of further thinking and debate.

📖 **Don't be tempted to** – Spot common pitfalls and avoid losing marks.

  Try it yourself – Compare your responses with that of the answer guidance on the companion website.

Visit **www.pearsoned.co.uk/lawexpressqa** for a wealth of additional resources to support your revision, including:

All diagrams from the book to download and print. Pin them to your wall or add them to your own revision notes.

Additional Essay and Problem questions with **Diagram plans** give you more opportunity to help you to practise and hone your exam skills.

You be the marker – Evaluate sample exam answers and understand how and why an examiner awards marks.

Table of cases and statutes

■ Cases

■ Statutes

■ International conventions

What you need to do for every question in Land Law

When you first look at a question in a Land Law exam, ask yourself three questions:

1 What type of right is claimed? Is it a proprietary right or a personal right, and if it is a proprietary right then is it legal or equitable?
2 Then check whether the right claimed has been properly created.
3 Then check whether title to the land is registered or unregistered.

Here is an example from a problem question. Suppose that you are faced with a question in the exam that told you that:

> X and Y agreed in writing that Y would have a 10-year lease of a flat. Title to X's land is registered.

Now look at this, using the three steps above:

1 Identify the right. Here, we are told that it is a lease, and a lease is a proprietary right.
2 How has it been created? We are told that X and Y 'agreed in writing'. This looks like an equitable lease.
3 Is title to the land registered or unregistered? It is registered.

This gives you the bare bones of an answer, and you should always start from here, but let us go further in search of those extra marks.

- We are told that X and Y agreed on a lease. Check whether, in fact, it is really a lease.
- We are told that X and Y agreed by deed. This could be a deed and, if so, the lease would be legal but the words 'in writing' rather than 'by deed' often indicate an equitable lease. On the other hand, the writing might not satisfy all the requirements for a valid equitable lease. If so, what would be the position?

So, in problem questions in Land Law:

- Get the basic points absolutely clear.
- Then go on and ask *questions* about the facts given.

> Where the question is an essay, remember that you are not being asked just to state all that you know on a point, but are being asked to comment critically on a particular aspect of Land Law. The advice for problem questions applies here, also in that you need to be absolutely clear on the basic points, but then you must go further. Look for areas that have caused controversy or have been the subject of recent cases or of Law Commission reports. Obvious examples are trusts of the home, easements and restrictive covenants, and so you should come to your own view on controversial points in these areas before the exam.

Rights over land – the impact of the Human Rights Act: finder's titles

How this topic may come up in exams

This is an area where there are fewer reasonably standard and predictable areas for exam questions than others, and you will need to check your syllabus and past exam questions to see which topics are likely to arise. Examples are questions on fixtures and fittings and on the impact of Article 8 of the European Convention on Human Rights (ECHR) on Land Law. However, one topic that is essential for all Land Law exams is that of estates and interests in land. Even here, you may find that this area is treated only as background material and that you will require this knowledge in questions on, for example, registered and unregistered land (see Chapter 2).

■ Before you begin

It's a good idea to consider the following key themes of rights over land – the impact of the Human Rights Act 1998; finders' titles – before tackling a question on this topic.

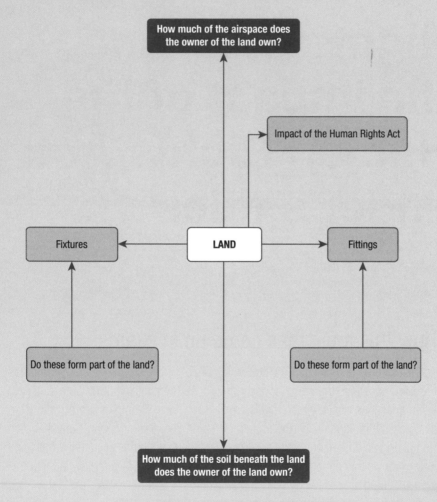

How much of the airspace does the owner of the land own?

Impact of the Human Rights Act

Fixtures

LAND

Fittings

Do these form part of the land?

Do these form part of the land?

How much of the soil beneath the land does the owner of the land own?

A printable version of this diagram is available from **www.pearsoned.co.uk/lawexpressqa**

🖋 Question 1

Do you consider that the maxim 'he who owns the land owns everything reaching up to the very heavens and down to the very depths of the earth' is still an accurate statement of the law, especially in the light of the decision in *Bocardo SA* v *Star Energy UK Onshore Ltd* [2010] UKSC 35?

Answer plan

→ What the maxim means?

→ Explain the decision in *Bocardo*.

→ Three-dimensional quality of land.

→ Evaluate the maxim in relation to the rights of landowners.

→ Different owners have rights in different strata of the land.

→ Should we concentrate on the idea of 'stratified ownership'?

Diagram plan

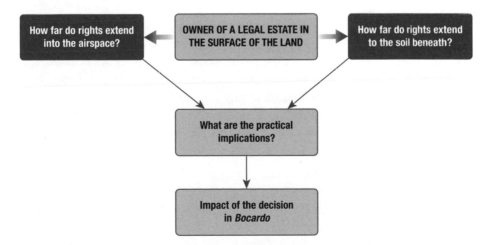

A printable version of this diagram plan is available from **www.pearsoned.co.uk/lawexpressqa**

Answer

[1] This must not be the end of your answer, but you do need to start by explaining what the maxim means.

This statement, read literally, means that whoever has a legal estate in land owns not only the surface of that land but also the airspace above it, to an unlimited extent, and the land below, also to an unlimited extent.[1]

It is an ancient maxim, dating from the 13th century or even earlier, and was most recently considered in depth by the UK courts in **Bocardo SA v Star Energy UK Onshore Ltd** [2010] UKSC 35.

Star Energy had a licence to search for, bore for and extract petroleum. Its predecessors had diagonally drilled three wells that entered the substrata below land owned by Bocardo, at depths of up to 2,900 feet below ground level. In the words of Peter Smith J in the High Court, this did not 'interfere "one iota" with Bocardo's enjoyment of its land'.

[2] There were other issues in this case, such as assessment of compensation on a compulsory purchase of land. These are not relevant, so make sure to concentrate on the point that you are asked about!

Nevertheless, Star Energy was held liable for trespass. One issue[2] was the extent to which rights of landowners extended beneath the surface. Lord Hope referred to arguments that the rights should extend to only 1,000 feet below, but he rejected any definite limit, although he observed that 'There must obviously be some stopping point, as one reaches the point at which physical features such as pressure and temperature render the concept of the strata belonging to anybody so absurd as to be not worth arguing about.' In this case, the wells were being worked and so they were 'far from being so deep as to reach the point of absurdity'.

One argument used by Star Energy was that possession, not ownership, was essential to a claim and, here, Bocardo was not in possession of the substrata 800 feet below the surface of its land. The concept of possession is important in cases where a squatter claims title on the basis of adverse possession, but, here, Bocardo was the actual owner and, as Slade J said in **Powell v McFarlane** (1977) 38 P & CR 452: 'In the absence of evidence to the contrary, the owner of land with the paper title is deemed to be in possession of the land.'[3]

[3] This is a good example of how, in Land Law, certain concepts, in this case possession, are relevant in different areas. When you study Land Law, make a note of any underlying themes like this. It will make your study easier and increase your marks. See Chapter 10 for more details of this area.

The law on rights to the airspace above the ground is different in some respects. Section 76(1) of the Civil Aviation Act 1982 provides that no action shall lie in respect of trespass or nuisance by reason only of the flight of an aircraft over any property at a height above the ground, which, having regard to wind, weather and all the circumstances of the case is reasonable. In **Lord Bernstein v Skyviews and General Ltd** [1978] QB 479, HC, the defendants took an aerial photograph of the claimant's country house and offered to sell it to him. The claimant, however, rejected the offer and instead claimed damages for trespass and/or invasion of privacy for entering the airspace above his property and taking the photograph without permission. It was held that an owner of land has rights in the airspace above his land only to such a height as is necessary for the ordinary use and enjoyment of his land and, here, the aircraft did not cause any interference with any use to which the claimant might wish to put his land. Thus, where the branches of a neighbour's tree overhang the land of an adjacent owner, then that owner is entitled to cut them down (**Lemmon v Webb** [1895] AC 1, HL). On the other hand, the limited nature of the right is shown by the fact that the adjacent owner does not own the fruit and commits the tort of conversion[4] if she takes it (**Mills v Brooker** [1919] 1 KB 555, HC). In **Kelsen v Imperial Tobacco Co** [1957] 2 QB 334, HC, the claimant, who was the lessee of a one-storey tobacconist's shop, was granted an injunction requiring the defendants to remove an advertising sign from the wall above his shop that projected into the airspace above the shop by a distance of some 8 inches.

It was argued in the *Bocardo* case[5] that, just as there are limitations on ownership of the airspace, so there should be on ownership of the strata beneath it. However, as Aikens LJ said in the Court of Appeal ([2010] Ch 100), 'it is not helpful to try to make analogies between the rights of an owner of land with regard to the airspace above it and his rights with regard to the strata beneath the surface'. As Lord Hope pointed out: 'As a general rule anything that can be touched or worked must be taken to belong to someone.' Thus, the strata beneath the land must have an owner – unlike the airspace above.

In fact, it is possible, and very common, for different owners to have rights in different strata of the land.[6] Indeed, section 205(1)(xi) of the Law of Property Act 1925 expressly recognises this possibility by providing that the term 'land' includes land held apart from the surface 'whether the division is horizontal, vertical or made in any other way'. For example, where there is a public highway maintained by a public authority, under section 263 of the Highways Act 1980 that authority has a determinable fee simple interest in the highway and so much of the airspace above and the earth beneath as is needed to enable it to carry out its statutory duties.[7] However, apart from this, the earth beneath is owned by the adjoining landowners. Another example is where the owner of the freehold might grant a lease of the cellar underneath his land, or even a cave.

6 This is where your answer will start to gain those extra marks to get you a good pass. You could have simply continued by giving yet more examples of how the maxim does or does not apply. However, you have made your point and you need to move on.

7 This is a good example and is easy to remember, as it deals with an everyday situation.

[8] Try to bring this idea of land having a three-dimensional quality into your answer. If you use this as an idea, it can bring the answer away from the rather sterile discussion of whether the maxim is strictly correct (which, of course, is not) and instead give it a more philosophical slant.

[9] Note that we are tying in our answer to the quotation in the question.

[10] This is an excellent way to end. You have not summarised the law – something that is not necessary anyway, but have suggested another way in which the law can deal with this situation. In this way, you have moved the answer away from the purely descriptive and made it more evaluative.

The maxim does have a value as an attempt to illustrate the point that land is not one-dimensional but in a sense has a three-dimensional quality,[8] in that whoever has a legal estate in the land does have certain rights in the airspace above and some rights in the land below. The question is really whether those rights are so limited as to make the general point illustrated by this maxim virtually worthless, despite Lord Hope's statement in **Bocardo SA v Star Energy UK Onshore Ltd** that the 'proposition commands general acceptance'.[9] There is a practical point here: if we are, for example, advising a client who has bought 155 High Street, Hanbury, and she asks us exactly what she has bought, what answer shall we give?

It might be better to abandon this ancient maxim and instead concentrate on the concept of 'stratified ownership'[10] by recognising that, in fact, ownership of one piece of land can be held in different ways and by different people and so it is misleading to speak of the owner as having rights upwards and downwards from the land owned.

✓ Make your answer stand out

- Consider replacing some of the cases with a more philosophical discussion on the whole concept of what ownership of land means. You could argue that this maxim is simply a way of the common law avoiding any attempt to grapple with exactly what ownership means and instead taking refuge in an ancient and misleading maxim.

- Begin by lifting the answer to a different plane by making the point that the discussion on this maxim is based on confusion between the physical aspects of land and the abstract perceptions of land. Thus, the use of the maxim refers to an abstract perception of land, but, as the answer demonstrates, the physical aspects of ownership of land conflict with it.

- Integrate into the answer a short mention of how the landowner does not even have unrestricted rights over the surface of the land, for example the need to obtain planning consent for certain types of 'development'. You need not spend long on this but it does show how the landowner, far from having unrestricted rights above and below the land, does not even have unrestricted rights on the surface.

■ Look at different ideas on how far ownership of the surface should extend to the strata beneath. See Howell, J. (2002) Subterranean Land Law: Rights below the Surface of Land. *Northern Ireland Legal Quarterly*, 53: 268.

! Don't be tempted to . . .

■ Just set out a list of cases without any attempt to relate them to the question.
■ Give too many examples that all illustrate the same point.
■ Fail to come to a conclusion that engages with the words of the question.

✎ Question 2

'The Supreme Court decision in *McDonald* v *McDonald* [2016] UKSC 28 is another instance of the generally unadventurous approach of the courts to the application of Article 8 of the ECHR in possession actions.'

Critically comment on this view.

Diagram plan

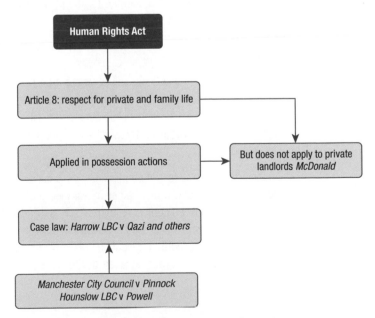

Answer plan

➜ Explain what rights Article 8 of the ECHR protects.

➜ Distinguish between the approach to be adopted by the courts to the issue of proportionality and the issue of whether Article 8 applies at all.

➜ If Article 8 does apply, examine the first issue and critically consider the decision in *Harrow LBC* v *Qazi*.

➜ Consider other cases involving possession proceedings, especially recent Supreme Court ones.

➜ Look at *Manchester City Council* v *Pinnock* and then at *McDonald* v *McDonald* on the first issue.

➜ Conclusion – referring back to the question.

Answer

[1] You could describe here how the HRA 1998 works, but, if you did, you would have less time for Land Law issues, and this is not a constitutional law essay!

[2] When you mention Article 8(1), you have to mention Article 8(2).

In answering this question, we need to be clear about what Article 8 of the ECHR covers. Article 8(1) provides for respect for family life and the home.[1] The right in Article 8(1) is qualified by Article 8(2),[2] which provides that no interference with these rights shall be justified except 'in the interests of national security, public safety or the economic well-being of the country, for the prevention of disorder or crime, for the protection of health or morals, or for the protection of the rights and freedoms of others'. In effect, this lays down a test of proportionality.

The application of Article 8 has arisen where a possession order is sought against a tenant, and it involves two issues: the approach to be adopted by the courts to the issue of proportionality and whether Article 8 applies to private landlords as well as public bodies such as local authorities.

On the first issue, the test of proportionality has been considered by the courts in the context of whether established procedures under domestic law should be subject to juridical scrutiny under the ECHR. One example of its use has been in residential possession proceedings, where it is argued that it would be disproportionate for a local authority to make an order because of the defendant's personal circumstances.

[3] Where the view of the courts on an area of the law has developed and changed over the years, you must show how this has happened, which will mean taking a historical approach, as here.

[4] It is of crucial importance to stress the debate among the judges on the application of the HRA 1998 in particular cases. A poor answer will simply say that 'the court held that . . .', but for a good mark, you need to mention, at least in outline, the main argument of the majority and, if possible, that of the minority. This is one area where you really do need to read the cases.

[5] You could add to your marks here by referring to Administrative Law principles.

[6] It is especially important to quote dissenting judgments in this question because, as we shall see, they have now been recognised in the most recent cases as representing the law. The dissenters are no longer dissenting!

[7] This is exactly the type of passage that the examiner is looking for. You have clearly contrasted the two arguments.

The courts initially limited the scope of Article 8(2) in these cases so that it had almost no effect.[3] In **Harrow LBC v Qazi** [2004] 1 AC 983, a local authority claimed possession of a council house from Qazi, who was a former joint tenant with his wife. She had given a unilateral notice to quit the premises, which had terminated Qazi's tenancy. The house held, by a majority, that the test of proportionality is irrelevant where the party claiming is, as here, already entitled to an automatic possession order against a former tenant. Lord Millett, for the majority, held that it was not for the courts to engage in 'social engineering in the housing field' and that the landlord's proprietary rights under domestic law must not be 'deflected' by some discretionary judgment based on the effect of eviction on the tenant's home life.[4]

The result was that the test of proportionality was not free standing. In **Kay v Lambeth LBC; Leeds City Council v Price** [2006] 2 AC 465, Lord Hope said that, provided that the courts consider whether 'the requirements of the laws and the procedural safeguards which it lays down for the protection of the occupier'[5] have been satisfied, there is no room for any challenge under human rights law.

However, there were dissenting voices.[6] In **Harrow LBC v Qazi**, Lord Steyn, who was in the minority, held that the approach of the majority 'emptied Article 8(1) of any or virtually any meaningful content' and held that the interpretation of Article 8(1) should not be 'coloured' by 'domestic notions of title, legal and equitable rights, and interests'. Similarly, in **Kay v Lambeth LBC**, Lord Bingham stressed the applicability of the conditions in Article 8(2) and said that individual defendants must be given the opportunity to contend that they have not been met, and the ECtHR in **McCann v United Kingdom** [2008] 2 FLR 899 endorsed this. However, Lord Nicholls said that there would be a 'colossal waste of time and money' if, in every case where possession proceedings were brought under a statutory framework, there could be a challenge under the HRA 1998.[7]

The decision of the Supreme Court in **Manchester City Council v Pinnock** [2010] UKSC 45 changed the picture. Here, the ground for possession was that some children resident at the property had been guilty of serious anti-social behaviour. The Supreme Court held that, in order for domestic law to be compatible with Article 8 in residential possession cases, the court must assess the proportionality of making the order, and so this test is now separate from the requirements

[8] This is the essential point to bring out.

of domestic law. Nevertheless, the use of the proportionality test does not mean that tenants will find it easy to resist applications for possession orders.[8] Lord Neuberger said that the proportionality of making an order for possession in favour of the local authority 'will be supported not merely by the fact that it would serve to vindicate the authority's ownership rights'. He also pointed out that a local authority has other duties, such as 'the fair allocation of its housing stock', which will often support an application for possession.

[9] Note that we have chosen to mention the issue with which *McDonald* v *McDonald* was concerned after the proportionality issue. This is because, if we had dealt with *McDonald* at the start, we would have had to explain why the proportionality point was important, This would have made it awkward to bring the other cases in. The message is to think before you start writing and to plan your answer carefully.

The second issue is whether Article 8 applies to private landlords as well as public bodies. In the leading case of **Manchester City Council v Pinnock** [2010] UKSC 45 SC, the Supreme Court expressed no view on whether Article 8 also applies to private landlords.[9] However, in **McDonald v McDonald** [2016] UKSC 28, the Supreme Court, after an extensive review of the jurisprudence of the European Court of Human Rights, concluded that courts, when considering possession proceedings brought by private landlords, cannot consider the question of proportionality. The court was prepared to accept that Article 8 might be engaged when the property was let by a private-sector landlord but held that there was no authority for holding that Article 8 rights could be invoked to justify a different order from that which was mandated by the contractual relationship between the parties, at least where there were legislative provisions, as here. Moreover, as a matter of general principle, if Article 8 was engaged, it would mean that the ECHR was directly enforceable as between private citizens, so as to alter their contractual rights and obligations, when the purpose of the Convention was to protect citizens from infringement of their rights by the state.

[10] Add in detail of cases to your answer when you can use them to emphasise a point, as we do with this case in the concluding section.

It is difficult to see how the court could have come to a different conclusion, but this was a distressing case.[10] The tenant was 45 and had had psychiatric and behavioural problems since she was five. She had been unable to hold down any employment and had lost two public-sector tenancies because of her behaviour. Her parents had bought this house for her and were her landlords, her rent being covered by housing benefit. The claim arose because her parents were in arrears with interest on the loan they took out to buy the property. A medical expert gave evidence that, if the tenant were made homeless as a result of the possession order being granted, 'she would decompensate entirely, very probably requiring admission to hospital'.

One would have thought that there was a strong case for not making an order for possession on the ground of proportionality, but it would be wrong to blame the courts for not applying Article 8, as it has always been clear that it is not intended to apply between private individuals.

In conclusion, the courts have, in recent years, shown an increasing willingness to apply Article 8(2) in possession cases, although it must be remembered that there are various detailed statutory provisions governing the rights of the parties, and the imposition of a proportionality test might upset that balance. However, there are some desperately sad cases in this area, such the one above, and perhaps the remedy lies with Parliament and society as a whole to deal more effectively with these.

✓ Make your answer stand out

- You could build your discussion around the contrasting views expressed by Lord Steyn and Lord Millett in *Harrow LBC* v *Qazi* and develop these in depth. In order to make room for this, you might have to leave out some of the discussion of later cases, but you should at least mention them, otherwise the discussion will be unbalanced.
- Look at two other cases: *Hounslow LBC* v *Powell* [2011] UKSC 8 and *Fareham BC* v *Miller* [2013] EWCA Civ 159. How do they affect the debate on Article 8?
- Do some research on the number of private-sector tenancies, where Article 8 does not apply, and the number of public-sector tenancies, where it does. This will add depth to that part of your answer dealing with *McDonald* v *McDonald*.
- Look at an article that analyses the recent Supreme Court decisions. See, for example, Cowan, D. and Hunter, C. (2012) 'Yeah but, no but' – *Pinnock* and *Powell* in the Supreme Court. *Modern Law Review*, 75(1): 75–91.
- Build on any mention of possible administrative law remedies in your answer by referring to Lovelace, I. (2014) Public Law and Art. 8 Defences in Residential Possession Proceedings. *Conv.* 78: 245, who suggests that the courts have not always distinguished between public law remedies and the application of Article 8 in these cases. See, for example, *Leicester City Council* v *Shearer* [2013] EWCA Civ 1467.

> **! Don't be tempted to . . .**
>
> - Start your answer with the details of a case without first setting the scene by explaining the relevant parts of the HRA 1998.
> - Give very full details of a case and not relate it to the argument.
> - Fail to explain the contrasting ideas and approaches of the judges.
> - Concentrate on just *Harrow LBC* v *Qazi* and fail to mention later cases.
> - Give the false impression that the law here is settled.

📝 Question 3

Meg bought a house, which has a large garden, from Jean.

(a) Would the following items, which were not specifically included in the contract, be included in the sale?

    (i) a greenhouse;

    (ii) rare shrubs planted in the garden;

    (iii) miniature trees in tubs on the patio;

    (iv) a garden seat secured to the land;

    (v) a statue of the Duke of Wellington.

(b) Just before the sale, the garden was opened to the public. Ted, a visitor, found a gold bracelet, which has been dated to 1470, together with 12 gold coins from the reign of King Harold II. Ted also found a gold ring dated 1947. He told Jean about the find of the bracelet and the coins, but he kept the gold ring. Ted's wife was concerned when he told her of what he had done and has now come forward and told Jean that Ted has the ring. Jean asks you for advice on who is entitled to these items.

Answer plan

→ Explain the distinction between fixtures and fittings and the two main tests used to decide into which category an article will fall.

→ Examine each situation in (a) and apply the tests and relevant cases.

→ Apply the law on finding of treasure to the cases of the gold bracelet and the coins.

→ Apply the law on who is entitled to property that is found to the case of the ring.

Diagram plan

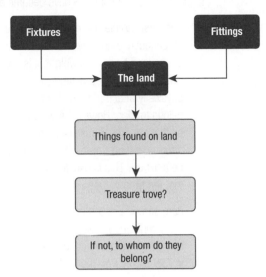

A printable version of this diagram plan is available from **www.pearsoned.co.uk/lawexpressqa**

Answer

[1] Do point this out: it is actually the normal practice in conveyancing for the contract to set out what is included in the sale.

[2] This is a vital, fundamental point. Although, in a particular case, we may be able to tell with reasonable certainty whether an article is a fixture or a fitting, there is no absolutely hard-and-fast rule to apply to these cases.

[3] Do not forget this: you will lose marks if you mention only the second test, but you should stress that the first test has less significance.

(a) All these items are either fixtures or fittings (sometimes called chattels). If they are fixtures, as the contract is silent on this point,[1] they would be transferred to Meg on the sale. If they are fittings, they will still belong to Jean. The distinction between fixtures and fittings is not clear cut,[2] but the traditional method is to consider two issues:

(i) the method of annexation and the degree of annexation;

(ii) the purpose of annexation.

(***Holland v Hodgson*** (1871–1872) LR 7 CP 328, Exch).

In general, the second test is now generally applied rather than the first, but we need to consider both.[3] Guidance on the application of the second test was given in ***Botham v TSB Bank Plc*** (1997) 73 P & CR D1, where the Court of Appeal considered whether 109 different items in a flat were fixtures or fittings. These included baths, kitchen units, sinks, refrigerators, washing machines and dishwashers. Roch LJ stated that 'if the item viewed objectively

[4] You need to mention these general points at the start, but all the others will emerge when you consider each article. If you spend too long outlining points of law in your introduction, you will not have time to apply the law to each specific point.

[5] Remember that if you do feel that it is possible to come to a conclusion, you should state what its effect will be: fixtures to Meg and fittings to Jean.

is intended to be permanent and to afford a lasting improvement to the building, the thing will have become a fixture'.[4]

(i) The first article to consider is the greenhouse. If the greenhouse is not physically attached to the land and rests on the land by its own weight, it is unlikely to be considered a fixture and so as a fitting it will belong to Jean. If it is physically attached to the land, it is likely to be a fixture and belong to Meg. However, if we apply the second test, it may be that the greenhouse is intended to be 'permanent and to afford a lasting improvement to the building' and so it will be a fixture. This is usually the case, and so it is suggested that the greenhouse will be a fixture and will pass to Meg.[5]

(ii) Rare shrubs planted in the garden are certainly annexed to the ground and are likely to be considered fixtures, especially as they are rare and as, on the basis of the test in **Botham v TSB Bank Plc**, they will afford a lasting improvement to the building, which, in this case, will include the garden.

(iii) The miniature trees are in tubs. Thus, they are not annexed to the land, as, presumably the tubs can be moved, and so it seems likely that they are fittings and belong to Jean. In **Holland v Hodgson**, Blackburne J stated that 'Articles not otherwise attached to the land than by their own weight are not to be considered as part of the land, unless the circumstances are such as to shew [sic] that they were intended to be part of the land.' In **Hulme v Brigham** [1943] KB 152, HC, a printing machine that was secured by its own weight was held to be a fitting. However, it might be argued that this was intended to serve an activity carried on the land, but the tubs are intended to enhance the land itself. However, on balance, it is likely that they are fittings.

(iv) The garden seat secured to the land could be a fixture, as it has been annexed to the land. One test is to ask whether the seat has been fixed for its more convenient use as a seat, in which case it will be a fitting, or for the more convenient use of the building, in which case it will be a fixture. In **Leigh v Taylor** [1902] AC 157, HL, a tapestry attached by tacks to wooden frames on a wall was held to be a fitting and not a fixture, as the purpose of displaying the tapestry was to enhance it rather than the building. A similar approach was taken in **Berkley v Poulett** (1976) 241 EG 911, CA, where, in addition, Scarman LJ suggested that, where an object cannot be removed without serious damage to or destruction to the realty, then it is likely to be a fixture. It is difficult to apply this test here, but it is suggested that it would not be difficult to remove the seat and so it could be considered a fitting.[6]

[6] This is a good illustration of where you would lose marks if you came to a definite conclusion.

(v) It is not clear whether the statue of the Duke of Wellington is fixed to the ground. If it is not, then the case is similar to **Berkley v Poulett**, where a white marble statue that weighed half a ton and was on a plinth was held not to be a fixture. If it is fixed, the question may depend on how difficult it is to remove it, as suggested by Scarman LJ in **Berkley v Poulett** (above).

(b) The gold bracelet that has been dated to 1470 may be treasure under the Treasure Act 1996, which provides that articles defined as treasure vest in the Crown. Section 1(1)(a) provides that treasure includes objects, excluding single coins, at least 300 years old,[7] which bear at least 10 per cent precious metal, and other specified objects at least 200 years old. In this case, the gold bracelet is over 500 years old and appears to contain at least 10 per cent precious metal, if not more. Thus, the gold bracelet belongs to the Crown, although an *ex gratia* payment is generally made to the finder. The 12 coins will also count as treasure under section 1(1)(a) of the Treasure Act 1996, as there are at least 10 of them and they are at least 300 years old. Indeed, in this case they are nearly 1,000 years old. Thus, they will also belong to the Crown.

[7] The moral here is obvious: always check the date of articles found, as this information will be crucial to your answer.

The gold ring dating from 1947 is not, of course, treasure. If the true owner can be found and it is shown that he or she has not abandoned possession of the ring, the true owner will have the best claim. If not, we must apply the fundamental principle that a person who can establish a prior possession of a chattel has a better claim to it than anyone who possessed it later (**Armory v Delamirie** (1722) 5 Str 505, KB). The question is whether Jean, as the owner of the land, had the intention to possess the gold ring.[8] It seems that the garden is not regularly open to the public, and so Jean retains possession of the land and the ring belongs to her. If it had been open regularly, it would be arguable that Ted might have a right to the ring, as in **Parker v British Airways Board** [1982] 1 QB 1004, CA.

[8] Notice here the emphasis of English Land Law on the concept of possession.

✓ Make your answer stand out

- Read Wilkinson, H. (1991) Farewell, Ladies Must We Leave You. *Conv.* 251, which is a short article on whether Greek goddesses at Woburn Abbey were considered fixtures or fittings. You could mention this in (a)(v) to add value to your answer.
- Refer to *London Borough of Tower Hamlets* v *London Borough of Bromley* [2015] EWHC 1954 Ch, HC, which concerned the classification of an ornamental object resting by its own weight as a fixture or a fitting.
- You might introduce some discussion in part (b) on the consequences of abandonment, as explored in Hudson, A. (1984) Is Divesting Abandonment Possible at Common Law? *LQR*, 100: 110.
- You could consider some of the situations in (a) together, and so make room for a discussion of the historical development of the test for annexation of objects to the ground. See Luther, P. (2004) Fixtures and Chattels: A Question of More or Less. *Oxford Journal of Legal Studies*, 24: 597.

! Don't be tempted to . . .

- Think that the law is absolutely definite in each case.
- Forget to mention that if the item is a fitting it will go to Jean, and if it is a fixture it will go to Meg.
- Forget that, in (b), the true owner, in principle, will have the best claim.

@ Try it yourself

Now take a look at the question below and attempt to answer it. You can check your response against the answer guidance available on the companion website (**www.pearsoned.co.uk/lawexpressqa**).

> 'An interest in land does not give its owner the ownership of that land but it does give a property right in that land.'
>
> Explain, with appropriate examples, what interests in land are in the light of this statement.

www.pearsoned.co.uk/lawexpressqa

 Go online to access more revision support, including additional essay and problem questions with diagram plans, and you be the marker questions, and to download all diagrams from the book.

Registered and unregistered title to land

2

How this topic may come up in exams

There are two types of question in this area, which very commonly appear in Land Law exams:

(a)   an essay on the land registration system;

(b)   a problem asking you how various rights fit into the system.

Watch out, as well, for an essay question on unregistered land, and one that asks you about both systems.

In this chapter, there are two questions, 3 and 4, which both have very similar facts but one of which deals with rights where a title is registered and the other with one where it is unregistered.

Material from other areas is also likely to be linked with material here. Examples are rights in the family home (Chapter 4) and leases (Chapter 6). Indeed, a possible question could link these areas with the registered and unregistered land systems.

■ Before you begin

It's a good idea to consider the following key themes of registered and unregistered title to land before tackling a question on this topic.

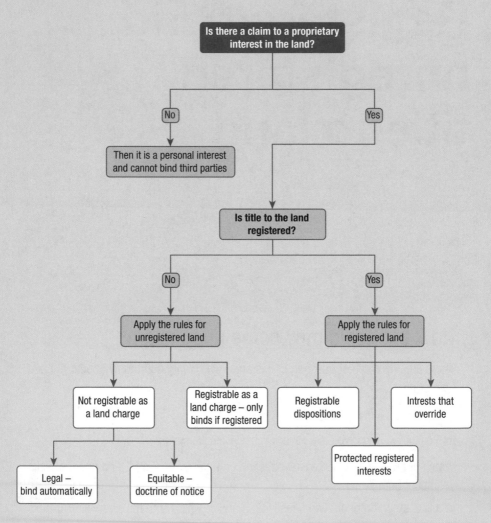

A printable version of this diagram is available from **www.pearsoned.co.uk/lawexpressqa**

Question 1

'The register provides, in effect, a fairly accurate snapshot of title (to land) at any given moment.' (Gray, K. and Gray, S.F. (2009) *Elements of Land Law*. Oxford: Oxford University Press.)

Why do the authors consider that the 'snapshot of title' is only 'fairly accurate', and could this picture be made clearer?

Answer plan

→ Outline what the land registration system is about.

→ Provide an explanation of where the register does provide an 'accurate snapshot'.

→ Consider cases where the snapshot is only 'fairly accurate' – mainly existence of overriding interests. Explanation of how overriding interests fit into the scheme of the LRA 2002 and how the LRA 2002 has reduced the scope of overriding interests. Consider whether they could be reduced further.

→ Look at other areas, such as good leasehold title.

→ Conclude by considering that, indeed, the register does provide an 'accurate snapshot' of the register.

Diagram plan

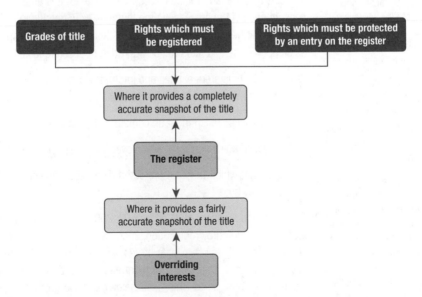

A printable version of this diagram plan is available from **www.pearsoned.co.uk/lawexpressqa**

Answer

^[1] This paragraph, and in particular the last words, is vital, as it ties your discussion into the question. Note that you could adopt a different approach and go at once to the situations where the register is not accurate, such as overriding interests. The objection is that your essay would lack balance, as it would overemphasise the cases where the register is not accurate and not explain that in most cases it is accurate.

^[2] Most students, faced with this question, would probably start with overriding interests and, indeed, might not mention anything else. However, by mentioning grades of title, which is a relevant but less obvious point, you immediately impress the examiner!

^[3] Accurate terminology is essential for a good mark. Here, we have not said 'the owner of the land' but used the accurate term 'registered proprietor'.

^[4] Note the use of the term 'fee simple' rather than 'freehold', as there are other estates of freehold, although they are not legal estates, and 'term of years' rather than lease. Accurate terminology will earn you those vital extra marks.

The reason that the authors consider that the register provides, in effect, a 'fairly accurate snapshot' of title to land at any given moment is because, despite the 'mirror principle', that the register is a reflection of title, this is not entirely true. There are situations where the register cannot be accurate because of the existence of overriding interests, which do not appear on the register at all, and where land is registered with good leasehold title. It is suggested that it is unduly harsh, however, to say that the register is, in effect, only 'fairly accurate', and in this essay I will argue that it is very largely accurate and that the changes made by the Land Registration Act 2002 (LRA 2002) have increased its accuracy.[1]

When title to land is registered, the Registrar awards a grade of title, such as absolute, possessory and qualified.[2] The result is that the register does give an accurate indication of the status of the registered proprietor's[3] title. One instance where the register is only 'fairly accurate' is where leasehold is registered with only 'good' leasehold title. This means that the freehold title has not been registered and so the Land Registry can say nothing about the freehold and, in effect, cannot give any snapshot of the freehold at all. This is not, however, a criticism of the land registration system. Instead, it is an inevitable consequence of the process of time that it takes to get title to all land registered. When this is finally achieved, this problem will disappear, as all good leasehold titles will be upgraded to absolute leasehold.

When title is registered, estates and interests existing on the land are classified into three categories by the LRA 2002:

(a) dispositions, which must be completed by registration;

(b) unregistered dispositions, which override registered dispositions;

(c) interests, which must be protected by an entry against the title that they bind.

Taking (a) first, section 27(1) of the LRA 2002 lists dispositions that must be completed by registration, such as transfers of the fee simple and also a grant of a term of years for seven years[4] from the date of the grant, together with legal easements and profits (with some exceptions, as to which see below) and the grant of a legal charge (mortgage) over the estate. Thus, if any disposition of any of the above is not completed by registration, the disposition will not take effect. By this means, the register provides a completely 'accurate snapshot' of all these rights, as the title of the question mentions.

I will deal with (c) next, as (b) will require a more extended treatment. Category (c) comprises rights that have to be protected by an entry on the register to bind a purchaser. Thus, they are treated differently from rights in (a), where the actual disposition must be registered, but the effect is the same in that when a person buys land, he or she need not be concerned about any of these rights unless they appear in the register and so, as far as they are concerned, the 'snapshot' is accurate. Examples of these are restrictive covenants, equitable easements and estate contracts.

The area that shows that the register provides only a 'fairly accurate snapshot' of title to land is overriding interests. This term is not used in the LRA 2002, but it was used in the Law of Property Act 1925 (LPA 1925) and is the most convenient short description of them. As mentioned above, they may not appear on the register but can still bind a purchaser.

[5] For some reason, some students forget to mention that the lease must be legal. Don't let it be you.

The first category is legal[5] leases not exceeding seven years. Section 118 of the LRA 2002 contains power to reduce this and it is suggested that it will eventually be reduced to three years. Under section 70(i)(k) of the Land Registration Act 1925 (LRA 1925) the term was 21 years. Legal leases granted before 13 October 2003 and that were overriding before that date continue to override.[6] The reason that these leases override is that it would be unreasonable to expect short leases to be registered and that, if they were, the register would be cluttered up by them. This exception is found in other land registration systems (see, for example, the Queensland Real Property Act 1877).[7]

[6] The extra material on the leases, which were overriding under the LRA 1925 retaining this status, is what is expected if you are aiming for at least a 2:1.

[7] A short point showing a comparative approach will gain you marks.

The second category is the interests of persons in actual occupation of the land, where these are coupled with an interest in land, and it is this category that has expanded greatly since it was introduced by the LRA 1925 and is the most controversial. It protects those who are in actual occupation under a legal or an equitable interest in the land. The familiar example is where a person is in occupation under an equitable interest arising under a trust where they have contributed to the cost of acquisition of the land, as in ***Williams & Glyn's Bank v Boland*** [1980] 2 All ER 408, HL, where a wife who had contributed to the purchase price of their home had an overriding interest against the bank to which her husband, who was the registered owner, had mortgaged it. As Denning MR put it in **Strand Securities v Caswell** [1965] Ch 373, Ch D, a person in actual occupation 'is protected from having his rights lost in the welter of registration'. The justification is that occupation by itself should be obvious to a purchaser, who should be alerted to the need to make enquiries even though the occupier's rights are on the register. Moreover, an occupier might not realise that he or she had an interest that could be registered, and in addition it is socially right that a person in the position of Mrs Boland should have priority over a lender. However, Schedule 3 to the LRA 2002 has reduced the extent to which these interests can bind a purchaser on a subsequent registration of title, so that a purchaser will not be bound if the occupation would not have been obvious on a reasonable inspection of the land at the time of the disposition.[8]

[8] Resist the temptation to go into too much detail – as here, give just enough to show the examiner that you know what you are talking about!

The third category of interests that override is a legal easement or a profit acquired by implied grant or by prescription, but Schedule 3 applies here too. It also provides that, where the easement or profit has been exercised in the year before the disposition, a purchaser will always be bound.

Finally, local land charges override, but they should be discovered by a local land charges search carried out before purchase. An example is a tree preservation order.

It should be emphasised that the LRA 2002 has substantially reduced the number and extent of overriding interests. In addition to the instances mentioned above, certain other interests, such as equitable easements, which did override under the LRA 1925, will not override if created on or after 13 October 2003. Moreover, other interests, such as chancel repair liability, ceased to override on 13 October 2013. Thus, the 'snapshot' is becoming more accurate.

[9] This type of conclusion, dealing directly with the actual words of the question and giving your view, is the hallmark of a really good answer.

Therefore, no purchaser can be confident that the register is completely accurate, as it will not include overriding interests and there is the further exception of good leasehold. However, it is not the case that the actual register is inaccurate. It would perhaps be more correct to say that it is not comprehensive, but it is slowly becoming more so.[9]

✓ **Make your answer stand out**

■ Clear, concise and appropriate use of case law to illustrate when interests of occupiers can override, for example more detail on *Wiliams and Glyn's Bank* v *Boland*.

■ Refer to the Law Commission's Reports, especially on the justification for overriding interests. See, for example, Law Commission (2001) Report, *Land Registration for the 21st Century: A Conveyancing Revolution*, No. 271. http://lawcommission.justice.gov.uk/docs/lc271_land_registration_for_the_twenty-first_century.pdf

■ Refer also to the Law Commission's Report (2016) *Updating the Land Registration Act 2002: A Consultation Paper* (No. 227). This deals mainly with the technical operation of the system, but important issues are raised – for example, title guarantee, rectification and indemnity. Look at the summary, at least.

■ Absolute clarity about which interests override, especially in the area of easements and profits.

■ Reference to the distinction between interests that override on a first registration and those that override on a subsequent registration.

■ Enhance your answer by referring to *Scott* v *Southern Pacific Mortgages Ltd* [2014] UKSC 52, where the Supreme Court emphasised the priority of registered interests in land.

! **Don't be tempted to . . .**

■ Just give lists of overriding interests.

■ Go into too much detail on one area, such as Schedule 3 to the LRA 2002 or the cases on overriding interests of occupiers.

■ Plough through the land registration system, mechanically describing it.

■ Worse still, discuss the unregistered land system.

■ Even worse, make simple errors, such as stating that all easements override.

📝 Question 2

'We are reminded that it is unwise to take positions of principle, because what counts as "actual occupation" may depend on the type of property as well as the background facts.' (Dixon M. (2016) Mortgages, co-owners and priority: some basics. *Conveyancer and Property Lawyer* 80:81

Critically examine this statement in the light of case law under both the Land Registration Act 2002 (LRA 2002) and the Land Registration Act 1925 (LRA 1925).

Answer plan

→ Set out the relevant statutory provisions in both the LRA 2002 and the LRA 1925.

→ Now set the issue in context: the policy of the LRA 2002 to reduce the number of occasions when an interest can override and the apparent extension by the courts of the concept of actual occupation.

→ Now look at cases involving claims to be actual occupation, emphasising the point in the question: that this is a fact-sensitive area.

→ Make sure to use more recent cases decided under the LRA 2002, where possible.

→ End by returning to the point in the question: that we need to look at the type of property and the background facts.

Diagram plan

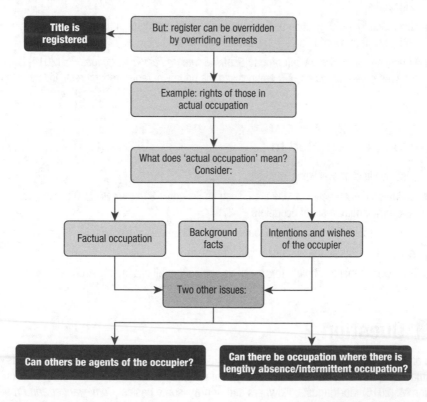

A printable version of this diagram plan is available from **www.pearsoned.co.uk/lawexpressqa**

Answer

The quotation in the question concerns the issue of when a party is in actual occupation for the purposes of Schedule 3, Paragraph 2 to the Land Registration Act 2002 (LRA 2002). This has become one of fundamental importance particularly because of the number of cases involving a claim by a person who alleges that he or she has a beneficial interest in property of which he or she is in actual occupation. In this answer, we are not concerned with whether a person has an interest but purely with what is meant by the term 'actual occupation'.[1]

Schedule 3, Paragraph 2 deals with when a purchaser can be bound by the overriding interest of an occupier,[2] and there are two conditions that must be met: the occupier must have an interest in the land and must be in occupation under that interest. However, the interest will not override if the occupation would not have been obvious on a reasonable inspection of the land, nor will it if the occupier failed to disclose his rights over the property when he could reasonably have been expected to do so. The predecessor of Schedule 3, Paragraph 2, which was section 70(1)(g) of the LRA 1925, similarly referred to 'actual occupation',[3] but instead of the two cases under Schedule 3, Paragraph 2 where an interest will not override, referred to one: where enquiries were made of the person and the interest was not revealed.

Bogusz (2011)[4] notes that in the Law Commission Consultation Paper, *Land Registration for the Twenty-first Century*, No. 254, which led to the passage of the LRA 2002, 'there was a discernable policy bias towards the protection of the disponee from potentially binding undiscoverable rights'.[5] This is why, in Schedule 3, Paragraph 2(c)(i), a disponee (i.e. usually the buyer) is bound only if the occupation is obvious on a reasonably careful inspection. She then argues that, as what she calls 'an antidote to the potential harshness of this rule', the judiciary has been prepared to move away from actual occupation in the physical sense only to looking at 'the parties' intentions and wishes'. Thus, as Dixon (2016) points out, we have to look at both the type of property and the background facts.

The starting point is **Williams & Glyn's Bank v Boland** [1980] 2 All ER 408, HL. Lord Wilberforce said that 'actual', in the phrase 'actual occupation', merely emphasised that what was required was physical presence. This does not always get us very far. What, for

[1] It is vital that you set the answer in context but that then you focus on the one issue that you have to address: that of occupation.

[2] Although you will need to set out the relevant case law in detail, this will not make sense unless you have set the statutory provisions out first. This is what this paragraph aims to do.

[3] As we need to refer to case law under the previous law, we need to say exactly what that law was. Here is a good example of boosting your marks, as many students will not have learned this.

[4] Rather than plunge in to the cases, we are setting them in a wider context.

[5] Do emphasise this point, which applies in other areas too: the general tightening up under the LRA 2002 so that a disponee (i.e. any transferee) is bound by fewer unregistered interests.

25

[6] It is vital not to just set out a list of cases on an area but to group them by themes.

example, if the occupier was not physically present but was only absent because the property was occupied by builders engaged on renovation work?[6] Could they be regarded as agents of the occupier and so their occupation be regarded as that of the occupier? This point was recognised in **Lloyds Bank Plc v Rosset** [1989] 1 Ch 350, where Nichols LJ regarded the builders as agents of the wife.

Similarly, in **Thomas v Clydesdale Bank Plc** [2010] EWHC 2755 (QB), the owners were absent because of the renovation of the house when the bank's interest arose. The court held that the degree of occupation had to take into account the fact that the house was not being used as a residence on the date of disposition, which fits in with Dixon's point about the relevance of the type of property.

In both **Lloyds Bank Plc v Rosset** and **Thomas v Clydesdale Bank Plc**, the owners frequently visited the property; in **Thomas v Clydesdale Bank Plc**, they were there almost every other day and Ramsey J pointed out that 'the degree of occupation must take into account the fact that the house was not being used as a residence'. This supports the contention of Bogusz (2011) that the courts, in addition to examining the objective factual evidence, have been prepared to consider a person's 'intentions and wishes'. In both of these cases there was little evidence of factual occupation as such, but there was ample evidence of their intentions to occupy once the renovations were completed.

[7] Note how we are returning to the point made by the quotation in the question.

However, although we need to take into account 'background facts', there needs to be some actual evidence of occupation, as Schedule 3, Paragraph 2 provides that the interest will not override if the occupation would not have been obvious on a reasonable inspection of the land.[7] This point was picked up in **Thomas v Clydesdale Bank Plc**, where Ramsey J referred to the need for 'relevant visible signs of occupation upon which a person who asserts an interest by actual occupation relies' and one of these signs in that case was the visits of the occupier.

[8] A reference to the question again.

The need to look at the type of property[8] as well as all the facts is emphasised by **AIB Group (UK) Plc v Turner** [2015] EWHC 3994 (Ch), where the occupier of a cottage in the UK was living semi-permanently in Barbados and was absent from the cottage for significant periods of time. Was she in occupation of the cottage as a second home? Although she returned there occasionally, her son stayed there in school holidays and she left personal possessions there and so she was held not to be in in actual occupation. On the facts, she had moved to Barbados. This reinforces the point, made above, that there needs to be some evidence of actual occupation. In some cases the temporary absence of an occupier has been used by the legal owner as the opportunity to sell the property and deprive the occupier of their home.[9] Thus, in **Chhokar v Chhokar** [1984] FLR 313, HC, the wife, who had an equitable interest in the matrimonial home, was in hospital when her husband took the opportunity to sell it, intending to deprive her of her rights in the property. However, this ruse failed, as it was held that she was still in occupation.

[9] Here is another theme.

In **Link Lending Ltd v Bustard** [2010] EWCA Civ 424,[10] the claimant was held to be in actual occupation, even though she was involuntarily detained under the Mental Health Act 1983, as she intended to return to the property when it was possible. Also, her possessions were still there. Mummery LJ laid down factors to be considered on this issue: 'The degree of permanence and continuity of presence of the person concerned, the intentions and wishes of that person, the length of absence from the property and the reason for it and the nature of the property and personal circumstances of the person are among the relevant factors.' Was the court, as may have happened in **Chhokar v Chhokar**, influenced by the fact that Mrs Bustard had been fraudulently persuaded to transfer the property to another for no consideration and it was a mortgagee from that person who sought possession?

[10] This is a particularly useful case on what is meant by 'occupation', especially as Mummery LJ laid down a list of relevant factors in considering whether there has been actual occupation. Therefore, it should be mentioned in any answer on this topic.

The concept of actual occupation cannot be pushed too far.[11] In **Strand Securities Ltd v Caswell** [1965] Ch 373, Ch D, it was held that the mere presence of some of the claimant's furniture will not usually count as actual occupation, and in **Chaudhary v Yavuz** [2011] EWCA Civ 1314, the claim was based on an equitable easement allowing use of a staircase giving access to the upper floors of a flat via a balcony. However, the Court of Appeal was unwilling to accept that walking up, down or along a staircase or balcony amounted to occupation of such a structure.

[11] You do need some cases showing where there was insufficient occupation.

There is no doubt that Dixon is right in arguing that, in deciding what amounts to actual occupation, the matter is, in effect, fact sensitive rather than a matter of law, with the type of property being relevant. However, as we are dealing with a basic human right to occupy a place to live, that is surely correct.

✓ **Make your answer stand out**

- Read the article by Bogusz referred to in the question, looking carefully at the policy issues.
- Read the article by Dixon referred to in the question itself.
- Read another article by Bogusz, B. (2011) – this is especially good on the case law.
- See Law Commission (1998, No.254, Para. 5.58). This will help you to see the policy issues in the LRA 2002.
- Read Lewison J. in *Thompson* v *Foy* [2009] EWHC 1076 (Ch), on what is meant by 'occupation'.
- Draw your answer together by asking whether there are actually two issues: intention to occupy and an actual manifestation of that intention.

❗ **Don't be tempted to . . .**

- Go straight to the cases without first setting out both the relevant statute law and the policy considerations.
- Discuss other issues – for example the general nature of overriding interests, the facts of cases such as *Williams & Glyn's Bank* v *Boland* etc. Concentrate on actual occupation in the context of the LRA 1925 and the LRA 2002.
- Just set out facts of cases without linking them to the theme of whether there is actual occupation.

❓ Question 3

Six months ago, Tim bought a freehold factory building, together with adjoining land, from Fred. The property was correctly registered at HM Land Registry with absolute title. Since the purchase was completed, the following matters have come to light:

(a) Quick Money Ltd claims that it has a legal mortgage over the land, granted by Fred three years ago. It says that, as instalments are now considerably in arrears, it wishes to enforce its security.

(b) Eileen has produced a letter, signed by both her and Fred, in which Fred agreed to allow her to graze her goats over the land.

(c) Albert, who owns adjoining land, has produced an old deed that prevents any industrial activities taking place on Tim's land.

(d) Aidan, another adjoining landowner, says that he and his predecessors in title have used a path across Tim's land for at least the last 100 years and that he has evidence to prove this.

(e) Teresa claims that Fred allowed her to sit on the land to paint, and she hopes that Tim will continue to do so.

Advise Tim on whether he is bound by any of these claims.

Answer plan

→ Provide a short introduction – explain the significance of registered title and that it is absolute. Also mention that this is a subsequent registration.

→ In each question, assume that none of the matters appeared on the title and make this clear in your answer.

→ For each question, identify the right claimed and then explain where it fits in the registered land system.

→ Then decide whether Tim is bound.

Diagram plan

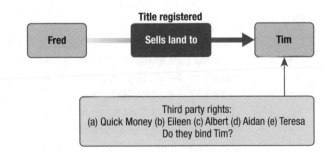

A printable version of this diagram plan is available from **www.pearsoned.co.uk/lawexpressqa**

Answer

[1] Do make sure that, at the start of any problem question on registered or unregistered land, you address these three points. They are straightforward and usually easily answered and will get your answer off to a good start.

There are three points to note at the start of this answer: first, that Tim holds the freehold; secondly, that title is registered and so we must apply the land registration rules applicable on a subsequent registration; and, thirdly, that it is registered with title absolute, which is the best grade of title.[1] The assumption from the question is that none of the matters mentioned appeared on the register.

[2] It is much better always to follow the structure of the question and not to write a general answer. Often, marks are allocated to each section.

[3] Note that we have gone straight into the issues and have not given a general description of the land registration system. There is no time for this and it is not required. In addition, there is no need to go back to the law of contract and discuss what 'valuable consideration' means.

[4] We are told that there was a letter, but this may not contain a contract. You will gain marks by highlighting the areas of uncertainty rather than just making an assumption that there is a contract.

(a) Quick Money claims that it has a legal mortgage,[2] but there was no mention of this on the register when Tim purchased. A legal mortgage is required, by section 27(2)(f) of the LRA 2002, to be registered as a legal charge over the land. If it is not, as is the case here, by section 29(1) of the LRA 2002, it will not bind a purchaser for valuable consideration. Tim did provide valuable consideration, as he bought the property, and so, applying section 29(1), he is not bound by Quick Money's mortgage and they cannot enforce it against him.[3]

(b) Eileen's claim to graze her goats over Tim's land is a claim to a profit à prendre, as she is claiming the right to enter Tim's land and take something from it. A profit can be created by deed, in which case it will be a legal profit, but here it has been created by a letter and so it will be equitable provided that it satisfies the requirements of section 2 of the Law of Property (Miscellaneous Provisions) Act 1989. This provides that a contract for the sale or other disposition of an interest in land, which includes a profit, must be in writing, signed by the parties, and the writing must incorporate all the terms agreed by the parties. We do not know that there was a contract,[4] but, if there was, it was in writing and signed by both Fred and Eileen. However, we do not know whether it incorporated all the terms. If the requirements of section 2 are satisfied, Eileen has a valid equitable profit, but, to bind Tim, it must be protected on the register, as provided by section 32 of the LRA 2002, and, if so, section 29 of the LRA 2002 provides that it will have priority over any later disposition of the land. Thus, if Eileen had protected her interest by a notice, it would have bound Tim but, as she has not, he is not bound.

(c) The old deed produced by Albert contains a restrictive covenant. We can assume that it is valid and that it applies to Tim's land. However, restrictive covenants are equitable interests in land and, although they do not have to be substantively registered, they must be protected by a notice on the register, as for the equitable profit in (b) above. As it has not been protected, Tim will not be bound.

(d) Aidan's claim is to an easement, as he is claiming the right to use the land of another. We can assume that it satisfies the requirements for a valid easement, as laid down in *Re Ellenborough*

[5] There is no need to go into detail on the requirements for an easement, as the question does not lead us in this direction by giving any further information. However, a mention, as above, is essential.

[6] Watch for this point: if Aidan and his predecessors had used the path for, say, 100 years but had not used it at all for the period of two years immediately before the action was brought, there could not be a claim under section 2.

[7] There is no case law on this point and so there is no harm in using your common sense to predict what the courts might do.

Park [1955] 3 All ER 667.[5] A valid easement can be created by prescription, that is long use and, under section 2 of the Prescription Act 1832, a claim to an easement except one of light may be made on the basis of 20 years' continuous use for the period immediately before the action on the easement. However, if the easement was enjoyed by the permission of the owner of the land, the period is 40 years unless the permission was in writing, in which case no easement by prescription can be claimed. Thus, oral permission will still allow a claim based on 40 years' continuous use. It seems that Aidan has a valid claim to an easement by prescription. There appears to be no evidence that permission was ever given for Aidan or his predecessors in title to use the path and, even if it was oral, the use here was for 100 years. Thus, it seems that a legal[6] easement by prescription can be claimed. If so, this is an overriding interest under Schedule 3, Paragraph 3 to the LRA 2002 and so Tim may be bound even though it does not appear on the register. However, we need to look more closely at the conditions set out in Schedule 3, Paragraph 3. Paragraph 3(2) provides that, if the easement has been exercised in the period of one year ending with the day of the disposition, Tim will be bound. Thus, if Aidan can show that he used the path in the year before Tim bought the land, Tim will be bound even though, when he purchased, he had no knowledge of the easement. If Aidan had not used the path in this time, Tim will not be bound if he can show that when he bought he had no actual knowledge of the existence of the easement and it would not have been obvious on a reasonably careful inspection of the land at the time of the disposition. This is a question of fact, on which we cannot come to a conclusion, but if a path had been used for 100 years, it is likely that there would be evidence of it,[7] and so Tim would not be able to say that it would not have been obvious on a reasonably careful inspection. Thus, it is likely that Tim will be bound by Aidan's claim.

(e) Teresa's claim can only be to a licence. In *Thomas v Sorrell* (1673) Vaugh 330, Exch, Vaughan CJ held that: 'a licence properly passes no interest not alters or transfers property in any thing'. The effect is that a licence does not create an interest in land and so it cannot bind a third party nor appear on the register. Thus, in *King v David Allen & Sons Billposting Ltd*

[1916] 2 AC 54, HL, a licence to fix advertisements to the wall of a cinema did not bind a lessee of the cinema. Nor could Teresa claim that her sitting on the land amounted to occupation so as to give her an overriding interest and, in any event, any occupation must be under an interest in the land, which she does not have. If Tim wishes to allow her to continue to sit on his land, he may do so, but he does not have to.

✓ Make your answer stand out

- Mention *Barclays Bank Plc* v *Zaroovabli* [1997] Ch 321, Ch D, where a bank that had failed to register a mortgage was bound by a tenancy created after the date of the mortgage.
- Clear analysis of Eileen's letter.
- Clear analysis in Aidan's claim of how Schedule 3, Paragraph 3 to the LRA 2002 applies to the situation.
- Possible mention, in the case of Teresa, of cases where a licence might bind a purchaser, but point out that they will not apply here.

! Don't be tempted to . . .

- Include an introduction dealing with the issues in general.
- Discuss whether the claimed easement by Aidan satisfies the requirements for a valid easement.
- Speculate on whether Teresa's claim could be anything other than a licence. It clearly is not, for example, an easement, as it is purely personal and neither is it a profit, as she is not taking anything from the land.

? Question 4

In 2012, Alf bought a disused farm building, together with adjoining land, from Anita. Title to the property was not registered. Since the purchase was completed, the following matters have come to light:

(a) Cheeploans Ltd claims that it has a legal mortgage over the land granted by Anita three years ago. It says that, as instalments are now considerably in arrears, it wishes to enforce its security.

(b) Roger has produced a letter, signed by both him and Anita, in which Anita agreed to allow him to graze his sheep over the land.

(c) Aaron, who owns adjoining land, has produced an old deed that prevents any industrial activities taking place on the land that Alf has bought.

(d) Liz, another adjoining landowner, says that she and her predecessors in title have used a path across Alf's land for at least the last 200 years and that she has evidence to prove this.

(e) Sam claims that Anita allowed him to sit on the land to sketch and he hopes that Alf will continue to do so.

Advise Alf on whether he is bound by any of these claims.

Answer plan

→ Provide a short introduction – explain the significance of unregistered title as contrasted with registered title.

→ For each question, identify the right claimed and then explain where it fits in the unregistered land system. Does it have to be registered as a land charge?

→ Distinguish clearly between legal and equitable interests in cases where the interest does not have to be registered as a land charge.

→ Then decide whether Alf is bound.

Diagram plan

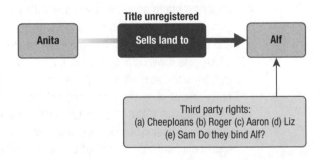

A printable version of this diagram plan is available from **www.pearsoned.co.uk/lawexpressqa**

Answer

The fact that title was unregistered when Alf bought the property means that we must consider in each case whether the right was registrable as a land charge and, if not, whether the right is a legal or an equitable interest in land, and the rules applicable in each of these cases.[1]

(a) A legal mortgage is a legal interest in land under section 1(2) of the LPA 1925. If the mortgagee (Cheeploans Ltd) had taken possession of the title deeds, this would have been a trigger to title to the land being registered. This is because a mortgage by deposit of title deeds is a protected legal mortgage by section 4(8) of the LRA 2002 and, by the operation of section 4(1)(g), it will trigger registration of the title. However, we are told that the title has not been registered in this case and so this must be a second or subsequent legal mortgage (a puisne mortgage)[2] and, as such, it requires protection as a Class C(i) land charge. If this is not done, as seems to be the case here, by virtue of section 4(5) of the Land Charges Act 1972, it is void against a purchaser of the land such as Alf. Furthermore, section 199(l)(i) of the LPA 1925 provides that a purchaser is not prejudicially affected by notice of it, so, even if Alf did have notice of the mortgage before he purchased, he would not be bound by it.

[2] This analysis, although it may seem complex, is vital. The essential point is that you cannot assume that the mortgage is either a first or subsequent mortgage.

(b) Roger's claim to graze his sheep over Alf's land is a claim to a profit à prendre, as he is claiming the right to enter Alf's land and take something from it. A profit can be created by deed, in which case it will be a legal profit, but here it has been created by a letter and so it will be equitable provided that it satisfies the requirements of section 2 of the Law of Property (Miscellaneous Provisions) Act 1989. This provides that a contract for the sale or other disposition of an interest in land, which includes a profit, must be in writing, and signed by the parties, and the writing must incorporate all the terms agreed by the parties. We do not know that there was a contract,[3] but if there was, it was in writing and signed by both Roger and Anita. However, we do not know whether it incorporated all the terms. If the requirements of section 2 are satisfied, Roger has a valid equitable profit, but as it was created on or after 1 January 1926,[4] it must be protected

[3] You must not assume that there is a contract. You will gain extra marks if you follow this approach.

[4] In a question on unregistered land, check whether you are told the date of creation of the equitable profit (or equitable easement or restrictive covenant, as the rules are the same). If you are not, you must examine the possibilities on the basis that it was created either on or after 1 January 1926 or, alternatively, before this date.

as a Class D(iii) land charge to bind Alf. If not, by section 4(6) of the Land Charges Act 1972, it is void against a purchaser for money or money's worth and we are told that Alf purchased the land, which means that he gave money for it. Therefore, he is not bound by Roger's claimed profit, even if he had notice of it (s. 199(l)(i) of the LPA 1925).

(c) The old deed produced by Aaron contains a restrictive covenant. We can assume that it is valid and that it applies to Alf's land.[5] Restrictive covenants are equitable interests in land and the answer depends on the date when the covenant was originally entered into. If this was on or after 1 January 1926, the covenant must be registered as a Class D(ii) land charge, otherwise it will not bind a purchaser of the land for money or money's worth, such as Alf. If, however, this date was before 1 January 1926,[6] the covenant is not registrable as a land charge and whether Alf is bound depends, instead, on the rules governing equitable interests. Alf will be bound unless he is a bona fide purchaser of the land for value without notice of the interest. Alf certainly gave value for the land, as he purchased it, and there is no reason to suspect that he is not bona fide – but did he have notice of it? It is clear that he did not have actual notice, as we are told that the matter came to light after he purchased the land – but did he have constructive notice? On the facts, it is impossible to be certain. In **Hunt v Luck** [1901] Ch 45 Ch D, it was held that a purchaser is bound by all matters that would be revealed by an examination of the land,[7] but it is likely that no inspection of the land would have revealed the existence of this covenant. Nor does it seem that the deeds made any reference to it, because, as pointed out above, the matter only came to light after the purchase. Thus, it is likely that Alf will not be bound by the covenant.

(d) Liz's claim is to an easement, as she is claiming the right to use the land of another. We can assume that it satisfies the requirements for a valid easement as laid down in **Re Ellenborough Park** [1955] 3 All ER 667, CA.[8] A valid easement can be created by prescription, that is long use and, under section 2 of the Prescription Act 1832, a claim to an easement except one of light may be made on the basis of 20 years' continuous use for the period immediately before the action on the easement. However, if the easement was enjoyed by the permission of the

[5] Show the examiner that you are aware of the requirement that the covenant must apply to the land benefited, but there is no need, or time, for detail on this.

[6] Note that you must not just say that a restrictive covenant must be registered as a land charge in order to bind a purchaser: it depends on the date of its creation.

[7] This is a crucial point in unregistered land.

[8] We have no information on any matter that would enable us to decide whether the requirements in *Re Ellenborough Park* have been met, so this is a sure indication that the examiner does not expect us to discuss this.

owner of the land, the period is 40 years unless the permission was in writing, in which case no easement by prescription can be claimed. Thus, oral permission will still allow a claim based on 40 years' continuous use. There appears to be no evidence that permission was ever given for Liz or her predecessors in title to use the path and, even if it was oral, the use here was for 200 years. Thus, it seems that a legal easement by prescription can be claimed. A legal easement does not require registration as a land charge to bind a purchaser and so Alf will be bound on the fundamental principle that a legal interest in land binds all the world.

[9] This is a straightforward point and so you need not discuss it in detail.

(e) Sam's claim can only be to a licence.[9] In ***Thomas v Sorrell*** (1673) Vaugh 330, HC, Vaughan CJ held that: 'a licence properly passes no interest not alters or transfers property in any thing'. The effect is that a licence does not create an interest in land and so it cannot bind a third party such as Alf, nor appear on the register. Thus, in ***King v David Allen & Sons Billposting Ltd*** [1916] 2 AC 54, HL, a licence to fix advertisements to the wall of a cinema did not bind a lessee of the cinema.

✓ Make your answer stand out

- Clear explanation of rules where title is unregistered – do not mention registered land.
- Clear analysis of the position regarding the mortgage.
- Appreciation of the significance of the fact that, in (c), we do not know the date of the restrictive covenant.
- Application of the rule in *Hunt* v *Luck* to the question of the restrictive covenant.

! Don't be tempted to . . .

- Include an introduction dealing with the issues in general.
- Leave out a clear explanation of how the Land Charges Act 1972 works.
- Forget that, if a claim is to a proprietary right which is not registrable as a land charge, then you must ask whether it is a legal or an equitable interest and apply the appropriate law.

❓ Question 5

Maureen bought 'The Laurels', a freehold detached house, for herself and her partner, Oliver, to live in. The purchase price was £300,000. Oliver paid the 10 per cent deposit and the balance of the price was funded by a mortgage taken out by Maureen with the Easypay Bank. The property was registered in Maureen's name. The purchase was completed in January 2013 and the property, together with the bank's charge to secure the mortgage, was registered in February 2013.

In January 2015, Maureen needed extra funds to pay for the care of her mother and so she took out a loan of £20,000, funded by a mortgage with the Shark Finance Co., secured by a another charge on 'The Laurels'. At this date, 'The Laurels' was unoccupied, as it was being renovated, and Maureen and Oliver moved back in April 2015.

Maureen is now in financial difficulties and she cannot meet the repayments on either mortgage. Oliver asks your advice on whether he has any interest in the property that binds:

(a) the Easypay Bank;

(b) the Shark Finance Co.

Answer plan

→ Does Oliver have an interest in the property?

→ What is his position regarding the acquisition mortgage?

→ What is his position regarding the second mortgage?

→ Detailed discussion of what is meant by 'actual occupation'.

→ Application of Schedule 3, Paragraph 2 to the LRA 2002.

Diagram plan

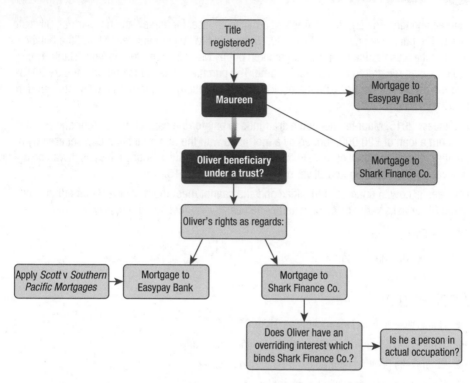

A printable version of this diagram plan is available from **www.pearsoned.co.uk/lawexpressqa**

Answer

[1] This must be your starting point. If Oliver does not have a beneficial interest, he has no rights in the property at all.

The first question is whether Oliver has an interest in 'The Laurels'.[1] The property is registered in Maureen's sole name and an interest of Oliver's can be equitable only on the basis that, by virtue of his payment of the deposit, Maureen holds the property for herself and him under a trust, thus giving him a beneficial interest in it. As Oliver's interest arose by way of contributions to the purchase price, there is certainly a resulting trust (***Dyer v Dyer*** (1788) 2 Cox Eq Cas 92 Exch). Moreover, there may be a constructive trust under the principles laid down in ***Capehorn v Harris*** [2015] EWCA Civ 955, CA, where Slade LJ held that 'the person claiming the beneficial interest must show that there was an agreement that he should have a beneficial interest

[2] It could be argued that any discussion of the extent of Oliver's beneficial interest is irrelevant, as we are asked only whether he has an interest at all. However, an examiner may expect some reference to this issue, but a long discussion is clearly not required, as we do not have enough information. If the question went into detail on the respective contributions of the parties, it would be relevant to discuss beneficial interests in more detail.

[3] This must be your next point.

[4] This is a point almost universally missed by students, and so, if you include it, you should certainly add to your marks.

in the property owned by his partner'. The payment of 10 per cent of the price is evidence of this. The advantage of a constructive trust is that Oliver's beneficial interest in the property will not be limited to the extent of his contribution to the purchase price, but the court can take into account other factors; and, in **Jones v Kernott** [2011] UKSC 53, SC, Lord Walker and Lady Hale said that reliance on contributions alone would be rare in a domestic context.[2] However, we are asked simply whether Oliver has an interest in the property, and the answer is that he does.

The next question is whether his interest binds the Easypay Bank,[3] which provided the finance to acquire the property and which therefore has an acquisition mortgage over it. Oliver's claim will be that, as title to the property is registered, he has an overriding interest under Schedule 3, Paragraph 2 to the LRA 2002. It should be noted that, as the property is already registered, this is the applicable schedule rather than Schedule 1, which applies on applications for first registration.[4]

In fact, Oliver's claim will not have priority over that of the bank. In **Abbey National Building Society v Cann** [1990] 1 All ER 1085, HL, the House of Lords held that, in order to bind a purchaser, there must be occupation under an interest in the land at the time of the disposition, which here means the time of the creation of the rights of the lender. This will have been at completion of the purchase, as, in **Abbey National Building Society v Cann**, it was held that, on an acquisition mortgage, as here, the conveyance and mortgage are treated as occurring simultaneously. Oliver's right to occupy arises only after completion, as his rights depended on Maureen holding the property on trust for him, and she could not do this until title had been transferred to her following completion. This was recently confirmed by the Supreme Court in **Scott v Southern Pacific Mortgages Ltd** [2014] UKSC 52, where it was held that, even if a person has equitable rights, as Oliver has, those rights become proprietary interests, and so capable of taking priority over a mortgage, only after completion. The same result, but by a different route, is reached by following the decision in **Paddington Building Society v Mendelsohn** (1985) 50 P & CR 244, HC, holding that Oliver had, by implication, consented to the mortgage, as he must have known that a mortgage was needed to complete the purchase.

5 Note that this is a crucial distinction. Watch for subsequent mortgages in questions of this kind.

[5] Note that this is a crucial distinction. Watch for subsequent mortgages in questions of this kind.

[6] This phrase is still usually taken as the starting point of any discussion.

[7] There have been a number of recent cases on overriding interests of occupiers, of which this is one. Make sure that you keep up to date with them.

[8] This is the crucial link: if he is not in actual occupation, there is no point in applying Schedule 3, Paragraph 2.

The position is different with regard to the second mortgage, with the Shark Finance Co. as this was a post-acquisition mortgage.[5] We need to distinguish between the question of whether Oliver was in actual occupation when the bank's interest was created; and whether, assuming that he was in occupation, the Shark Finance Co. can successfully argue that it is not bound by his overriding interest. Was Oliver in occupation when the bank's interest was created? If he was, he will have an overriding interest. However, Oliver (and Maureen) were not physically present at the property when the mortgage was taken out, as the house was being renovated and was unoccupied. In *Williams & Glyn's Bank* v *Boland* [1980] 2 All ER 408, HL, Lord Wilberforce said that 'actual' in the phrase 'actual occupation' merely emphasised that what was required was physical presence.[6] Although Oliver was not physically present, the builders engaged in renovation could be regarded as in actual occupation; so, if they can be regarded as agents of Oliver, can their occupation be regarded as that of Oliver? In *Lloyds Bank Plc* v *Rosset* [1989] 1 Ch 350, Nichols LJ regarded the builders as agents of the wife, who was in Oliver's position.

This is supported by *Thomas* v *Clydesdale Bank Plc* [2010] EWHC 2755 (QB),[7] where, as here, the owners were absent because of the renovation of the house when the bank's interest arose. The court held that the degree of occupation had to take into account the fact that the house was not being used as a residence on the date of disposition.

In both *Lloyds Bank Plc* v *Rosset* and *Thomas* v *Clydesdale Bank Plc*, the owners frequently visited the property; in *Thomas* v *Clydesdale Bank Plc*, they were there almost every other day and Ramsey J pointed out that 'the degree of occupation must take into account the fact that the house was not being used as a residence'.

We are not told whether Oliver visited the property when it was being renovated, but, even if he did not, it is submitted that the occupation by the builders would be regarded as his and so he was in actual occupation when the bank's interest was created.

If Oliver is in actual occupation, we must apply Schedule 3, Paragraph 2 to the LRA 2002,[8] which deals with when a purchaser can be bound by the overriding interest of an occupier. A purchaser, here the Shark Finance Co., will not be bound by the interest of Oliver as an occupier in two cases:

(a) If his occupation would not have been obvious on a reasonable inspection of the land. Here, it is suggested that the presence or not of Oliver assumes particular significance. Schedule 3, Paragraph 2 refers specifically to 'his' occupation, and so it is the occupation of Oliver that must be obvious. In **Thomas v Clydesdale Bank Plc**, Ramsey J referred to the need for 'relevant visible signs of occupation upon which a person who asserts an interest by actual occupation relies', and one of these signs in that case was the visits of the occupier. In **Thomas v Clydesdale Bank Plc**, Ramsey J was unwilling to add a requirement that the person inspecting should make reasonable enquiries, which might have revealed Oliver's occupation. In conclusion, it could be argued that a reasonable inspection would not have revealed Oliver's occupation and so Shark Finance Co. would not be bound. However, it is not possible to come to a definite conclusion.[9]

[9] Avoid giving dogmatic conclusions unless the answer is really clear. Here, it is not, and so a dogmatic conclusion would lose marks.

(b) If he failed to disclose his rights over the property when he could reasonably have been expected to do so. There is no evidence that the Shark Finance Co. ever asked Oliver whether he had an interest in the property, and indeed that it knew he even existed, and so this will not apply.

✓ Make your answer stand out

- Start with a clear (but not too detailed) analysis of whether Oliver has an interest in the property at all. If he does not, he cannot have an overriding interest.
- Some reference to academic debate on, for example, the question of when a constructive trust, as opposed to a resulting trust, can arise, and the distinction between them.
- Clear analysis that goes from beneficial interest – occupation – Schedule 3, Paragraph 2 of the LRA 2002.
- Make sure that you are up to date with the developing case law on Schedule 3, Paragraph 2 of the LRA 2002. Look at the article by Bogusz, B. (2011) Defining the Scope of Actual Occupation under the LRA 2002: Some Recent Judicial Clarification. *Conv.* 75: 268 and at Mummery LJ's judgment in *Link Lending* v *Bustard* (2010) EWCA Civ 424, CA.
- Look carefully at the Supreme Court decision in *Scott* v *Southern Pacific Mortgages* and whether, in all cases on an acquisition mortgage, the conveyance and mortgage are treated as occurring simultaneously. Note Lady Hale's view, and see Televantos T. and Maniscalco M. (2015).

! Don't be tempted to . . .

- Ignore the initial question of whether Oliver has an interest in the property at all. If he does not, he cannot have an overriding interest and so there would be no point in answering the rest of the question.

- Forget to include an analysis of how the operation of Schedule 3, Paragraph 2 of the LRA 2002 affects the claim. This is a crucial issue and if you ignore this your marks will be reduced considerably – so do learn this area!

- Include cases on overriding interests that do not bear directly on the question.

- Give a very dogmatic answer to the question. There isn't one!

@ Try it yourself

Now take a look at the question below and attempt to answer it. You can check your response against the answer guidance available on the companion website (**www.pearsoned.co.uk/lawexpressqa**).

Moyra was the registered owner of 'The Ark', a small cottage where she lived with her sister Connie, who had contributed 10 per cent of the purchase price. Moyra was having financial problems and, having discussed these with Connie, it was agreed that Moyra should borrow £5,000 to be secured by a charge on the house. In fact, Moyra borrowed £25,000 from Hanbury Finance Co. She told the finance company that she lived alone. No-one was at home when the finance company's surveyor called to inspect the property and so the valuation was confirmed without any further inspection. The loan was secured by a legal charge on 'The Ark', which was completed while Connie was away visiting relatives.

Now Moyra's financial problems have worsened and she can no longer afford to pay the mortgage.

Advise Connie as to her position in relation to the Hanbury Finance Co.

www.pearsoned.co.uk/lawexpressqa

Go *online* to access more revision support, including additional essay and problem questions with diagram plans, and you be the marker questions, and to download all diagrams from the book.

Co-ownership
of land

3

How this topic may come up in exams

The standard question in this area is a problem that asks you to consider various methods of severance of a joint tenancy. This may be linked with a question on the Trusts of Land and Appointment of Trustees Act 1996 (TLATA), or a TLATA question may appear separately.

Essay questions may ask you about the historical basis of the law on trusts of land, dealing with trusts for sale and strict settlements, and also about the debate on whether it should no longer be possible for an equitable joint tenancy to exist and in all cases of joint ownership there should be a tenancy in common.

■ Before you begin

It's a good idea to consider the following key themes of co-ownership of land before tackling a question on this topic.

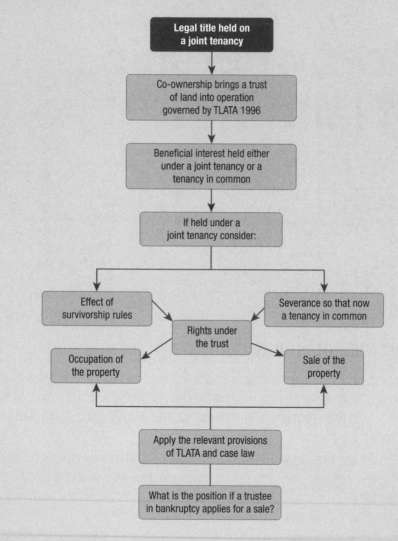

A printable version of this diagram is available from **www.pearsoned.co.uk/lawexpressqa**

❓ Question 1

In 2010, Jim and his wife, Amy, who had separated, bought a restaurant for £600,000. Their finances were, of course, kept separate and they each contributed equally to the price. The property was held in their joint names but the transfer did not record the beneficial interests.

The business ran successfully but, later, the strain of working with her estranged husband proved too much for Amy and she left. She then wrote to Jim, saying that she would like to have the business sold so that she could realise her share of it, especially as she now had a son by her new partner, Don, and she wished to make provision for him. Jim was reluctant to agree to this, as he felt that the business was doing well.

Advise Amy on whether she has an interest in the restaurant and, if so, in what share. In addition, you are asked to advise her on any procedures that she would need to follow in order to enforce a sale if Jim persists in refusing to agree to one.

Answer plan

→ Decide whether the beneficial interest is held as joint tenants or as tenants in common. Do this by looking at all the relevant factors – not forgetting to apply the reasoning of the majority in *Stack* v *Dowden* [2007] UKHL 17.

→ If it is held as joint tenants, consider whether Amy has severed her interest and then identify and apply the relevant method of severance.

→ Explain the law on applications to the court for a sale, and the principles to be applied.

→ End by outlining what Amy could do if her application for a share were to be refused.

Diagram plan

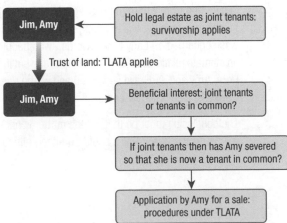

Answer

[1] An answer on co-ownership should always start by identifying this point. The beneficial interests should be dealt with only after you have dealt with the legal estate.

[2] This is vital: see whether you are told what the actual transfer says about the beneficial interests. It may say that the parties are to hold as joint tenants and, if so, this is really telling you that this will almost certainly be a question on severance of that joint tenancy. Here, the question is less straightforward, as we shall see.

[3] This type of approach always picks up marks. You are carefully looking at the issue from two different angles: here, the argument in favour of a tenancy in common and then that of a joint tenancy.

[4] You will certainly pick up marks by mentioning *Stack* v *Dowden* but, equally, you will also pick them up by quickly spotting that in this scenario it will not apply.

[5] You could come to the opposite conclusion on this point, although this one seems the more likely.

Under section 34(2) of the Law of Property Act 1925 (LPA 1925), where land is conveyed to co-owners who are of full age they must be joint tenants, and so Jim and Amy will hold the legal estate as joint tenants.[1] The question is then whether they hold the beneficial interests in equity as joint tenants or as tenants in common. If they hold as joint tenants, then neither will have a separate share and survivorship will apply so that, on the death of the first, the beneficial interest will pass automatically to the survivor. If they are tenants in common then they do have separate shares that can, for instance, be sold and that will form part of their estate when they die.

We are told that the transfer did not record the beneficial interests and so we must turn to equitable principles.[2] There are no words of severance indicating a separate share, and so a tenancy in common, but we are told that Jim and Amy, although still married, were separated when they bought the restaurant. There is an equitable presumption against a joint tenancy where there is a relationship of a commercial character, such as partnership property (**Re Fuller** [1933] Ch 652 Ch D) and it is suggested that, as Jim and Amy are separated, their relationship is commercial and not domestic and so they will be tenants in common and have a separate share. On the other hand, they contributed equally to the purchase price, which in itself indicates a joint tenancy.[3] The decision in **Stack v Dowden** [2007] UKHL 17, which held that the courts could hold that there is beneficial a tenancy in common even where there is a declaration that they hold the legal title as joint tenants, will not apply here,[4] as it was made clear that it was concerned, in Lady Hale's words, 'with people living together in an intimate relationship' and not with, as she put it, 'commercial men'. Here, Amy and Jim have separated and so the relationship should be viewed in a commercial context.[5]

The conclusion must be that, as the matter is uncertain, this answer will be on the basis that it could be either, although my view is still

[6] This is a crucial sentence, on which the rest of the answer hangs: you have spotted that there could be either a joint tenancy or a tenancy in common and so you are going to answer on the basis of both possibilities. A poor answer would plump for one of these and so lose lots of marks. Always be confident enough to say, as here, that the application of the law to the facts is uncertain and so consider more than one possibility.

[7] Beware here: it would be easy to slip into saying 'shares' but if you do so, you would lose marks, as we have not made up our minds whether, indeed, it is a joint tenancy (no separate shares) or a tenancy in common (separate shares).

[8] The significant words, which you could quote, are that Amy 'would like to have the business sold' – not that she wants to have it sold.

[9] This is a basic point on applications for a sale and should be mentioned at the start.

that a tenancy in common is the more likely.[6] Whichever it is, there seems no reason why their beneficial interests[7] should not be equal.

Here, Amy has written to Jim, saying that she would like to have the business sold, and the question is whether this amounts to a severance of any joint tenancy. If Amy holds as a tenant in common with Jim then, of course, there is nothing to sever, as she already has a separate share. However, if the property is held as joint tenants then the question is whether Amy has severed her interest by her letter saying that she would like to have the business sold so that she could realise her share of it. By section 36(2) of the LPA 1925, a joint tenancy in equity can be severed by a notice in writing to the other joint tenants and, by section 196(3) of the LPA 1925, a notice is sufficiently served if it is left at the last-known place of abode of the person to be served. This looks more like the opening of negotiations between them than an actual notice of severance[8] and so Amy would be well advised to serve on Jim a formal notice of severance that complies with section 196(3) of the LPA 1925. This would safeguard her position in the event, for example, of Jim dying before negotiations were concluded.

The question is then what procedures Amy would have to follow to force a sale in the event of Jim not agreeing to one, as Jim feels that the business is doing well. Amy has no right to insist on a sale and all that she can do is to apply to the court, which has a discretion.[9]

Section 14 of the Trusts of Land and Appointment of Trustees Act 1996 (TLATA) allows any person interested in the trust to apply to the court for an order, which could be, for example, for a sale or authorising what would otherwise be a breach of trust. The term 'any person interested' includes trustees, beneficiaries, remaindermen and secured creditors of beneficiaries and so, here, it clearly includes Amy as a trustee and also a beneficiary.

Section 15 sets out the following criteria, to which the courts must have regard when settling disputes:

(a) the intentions of the settlor;

(b) the purposes for which the property is held on trust;

(c) the welfare of any minor who either occupies, or might reasonably be expected to occupy, the land as his or her home;

(d) the interests of any secured creditor of any beneficiary.

[10] Although this criterion turns out not to be relevant, you should mention it, as we are told that Amy has a son and so it could have been relevant!

It should be noted that these criteria are not in any order of importance. Of them, (c) is not relevant here as, although Amy has a son, who presumably is a minor, there seems to be no intention that he should occupy the land as his home, especially as there appears to be no living accommodation.[10] Nor is a sale sought by a creditor such as a mortgagee, which would have involved (d). Thus, the only relevant criteria are (a) and (b), which amount to the same because Amy and Jim are the settlors, as they created the trust and they also decided why the property was to be held on trust – in this case, for it to be run as a restaurant.

In *Re Buchanan-Wollaston's Conveyance* [1939] Ch 738, CA, land was bought by four co-owners to prevent it from being built on. One later wished to sell, but the others did not. As the original purpose remained, the court refused to order a sale. On this basis, Jim would have a strong case to resist an application by Amy for a sale, as the restaurant, according to him, is doing well and so there is no reason to sell it. This decision pre-dates the TLATA and was based on its predecessor, section 30 of the LPA 1925,[11] but it is submitted that, as section 15 of the TLATA does specifically refer to the purposes for which the property was acquired, this decision is still good law and can be applied in this case.

[11] You will lose marks if you quote pre-1996 cases in a question on the TLATA, unless you show, as here, that they can still be relevant.

If Amy cannot force a sale then she still remains a joint tenant in law with Jim and so her consent will be needed to a sale and she will be able to ensure that she receives her entitlement at that point. If she does not want to wait that long, she could sever her joint tenancy (if that is what she has) in equity by a sale to another, including Jim, as this is one of the equitable methods of severance set out in *Williams v Hensman* (1861) 1 John & H 546, QB, and receive the proceeds of sale.

✓ Make your answer stand out

- Note this quote from Lady Hale in *Stack v Dowden:* 'Parties may not intend survivorship, even if they do intend their shares to be equal.' You could use this to bolster your argument that the parties are tenants in common.

- More detail on what can constitute severance. See Garner, J. (1977) Severance of a Joint Tenancy. *Conv.* : 77.

- Look at the facts of *Burgess v Rawnsley* [1975] Ch 429, CA and contrast with those in this problem.

- Read the judgment of Greene MR in *Re Buchanan-Wollaston's Conveyance* [1939] Ch 738, at 747, on the principles that should govern the exercise of the court's discretion in applications for a sale. Although this, of course, pre-dates the TLATA, his remarks are still relevant.

! Don't be tempted to . . .

- Assume at the start that there is either a joint tenancy or a tenancy in common and fail to spot that there is a doubt.
- Forget to mention *Stack* v *Dowden* – as the latest decision of the highest court on this area, it must be considered.

? Question 2

Sam, Ben, Ed and Sue, who worked at a firm of City of London solicitors as litigators, bought 'The Nest' in 2012 to provide a home for themselves while they were working at the firm. They remembered their Land Law and were registered as joint owners of the property in law and equity. A restriction was entered on the register, at the insistence of Sam, providing that 'The Nest' could not be sold without his written consent.

In 2013, Ben was short of money and so he sold his interest in 'The Nest' to Sue. Ben later died, leaving 'all my rights' in 'The Nest' to his girlfriend, Nesta.

Later that year, Ed decided to leave the firm and work for a country firm of solicitors as a conveyancer, which he thought would be less stressful. He orally agreed with Sam and Sue that Emma, a mutual friend, would 'take my place' but Ed died before the agreement could be formalised. Ed died intestate, leaving only a brother as a close relative.

It is now 2017 and Emma has moved into 'The Nest'. Sam and Emma have quarrelled and Sam says that Emma should leave the property. Meanwhile, Emma, Nesta and Sue all want the property to be sold but Sam refuses his consent. Advise the remaining parties on:

(a) Who now holds the legal title to the property;

(b) Who now has a beneficial interest in the property;

(c) Whether Emma can be required to leave the property;

(d) Whether Emma, Nesta and Sue can insist that the property is sold.

Answer plan

→ Explain how the legal title will be held.

→ Move on to decide how the beneficial interests will be held.

→ Assuming that they are held as joint tenants, have they been severed so that they are now held as tenants in common? Identify and apply the relevant law.

→ Now explain how the law on the rights of occupation of beneficiaries can apply to this question.

→ Outline the position regarding the restriction on the register.

→ End by considering the law on applications to the court for a sale.

Diagram plan

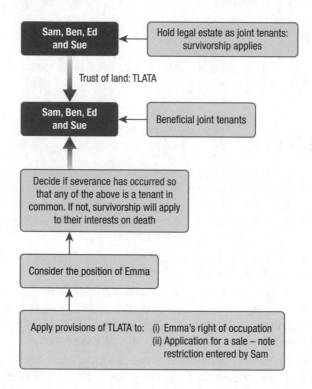

Sam, Ben, Ed and Sue → Hold legal estate as joint tenants: survivorship applies

Trust of land: TLATA

Sam, Ben, Ed and Sue → Beneficial joint tenants

Decide if severance has occurred so that any of the above is a tenant in common. If not, survivorship will apply to their interests on death

Consider the position of Emma

Apply provisions of TLATA to: (i) Emma's right of occupation
(ii) Application for a sale – note restriction entered by Sam

A printable version of this diagram plan is available from **www.pearsoned.co.uk/lawexpressqa**

Answer

[1] Do remember that where there are co-owners, there *cannot* be a tenancy in common of the legal estate and the legal estate must always be held on a joint tenancy. If you make a mistake on this, it will throw the rest of your answer out and lose you a lot of marks.

[2] Note that the term 'beneficial interests' means the same as equitable interests, i.e. the interests of the beneficiaries.

Under section 34(2) of the LPA 1925, where land is conveyed to co-owners who are of full age, they must be joint tenants[1] and there cannot be more than four. Thus, the legal title to 'The Nest' will vest in Sam, Ben, Ed and Sue and clearly they are of full age, as a minor cannot hold a legal estate in land (s. 1(6) LPA 1925).

As the land is held by joint tenants, by section 36(2) of the LPA 1925, it must be held on trust, which now means a trust of land governed by the Trusts of Land and Appointment of Trustees Act 1996 (TLATA).

We next need to decide how the beneficial interests[2] under the trust will be held. The choice is between joint tenancy and tenants

[3] The choice between a joint tenancy and a tenancy in common *only applies* to the beneficial interest. This is another of those vital turning points in an answer on co-ownership: it is not difficult, but get it wrong and you could lose a lot of marks.

in common.[3] The property was conveyed to them with a declaration that they were joint tenants, in both law and equity, and this is decisive. It seems that they had not remembered their Land Law revision very well: a tenancy in common would have been more appropriate here, as there is no apparent connection between them apart from work. The result is that the doctrine of survivorship will apply to the legal estate, which is inevitable, and also to the beneficial interest, which need not have happened.

The restriction entered on the register, that the property cannot be sold without Sam's consent, has been entered under section 40(2) of the LRA 2002, which provides that a restriction can prohibit the making of an entry in respect of any disposition. Thus, if the property is sold without Sam's consent, the actual transfer will be valid[4] but the new owners will not be able to be registered as such and the effect is to prevent any transfer without Sam's consent.

[4] Note carefully exactly what the effect of a restriction is. A clear and accurate explanation will earn you much credit, as this is not a straightforward point.

In 2013, Ben sold his interest in 'The Nest' to Sue, thereby effecting a severance of his interest in equity under one of the rules set out in **Williams v Hensman** (1861) 1 John & H 546, QB, that a joint tenancy can be severed in equity by the act of one joint tenant 'operating on his own share', as this destroys one of the four unities – that of title. Although, technically, he has no share, it seems that the very act of sale or other disposition brings about a severance. The curious position is that Sue is now a tenant in common of the share acquired from Ben but a joint tenant with regard to her interest, which she holds as a joint tenant with Sam and Ed. However, Ben's legal joint tenancy is not affected and will pass by survivorship on his death to the remaining joint tenants, Sam, Sue and Ed. His will leaving 'all his rights' in the property to Nesta has no effect, as section 3(4) of the Administration of Estates Act 1925 provides that the interest of a joint tenant ceases at death and so Ben has no 'rights' to leave.

[5] This is the point to pick up on. If there was a written formalised agreement then the answer would be easy, as there would be severance. However, here you need to think whether an oral agreement will suffice.

Ed has orally[5] agreed with Sam and Sue that Emma will 'take his place'. Even though the agreement is not formalised, it is likely that Ed has severed his beneficial joint tenancy (**Williams v Hensman**), as the agreement does not have to be a specifically enforceable contract (**Burgess v Rawnsley** [1975] Ch 429, CA). Thus, Emma takes Ed's share as a tenant in common and when Ed dies his interest in the legal estate goes to Sam and Sue by survivorship.

The next question is whether Emma can be required to leave the property.

[6] Here, you need to refer back to the start of the question and remind yourself of the reason why the property was purchased. Students often forget to do this. Remember to make a note, right at the start of your answer, of why the property was purchased (to remind you to refer back to it later).

[7] This is important and often forgotten. It gives protection from eviction not only to those who are entitled to occupy under section 12 of the TLATA (i.e. beneficiaries under the trust) but also to any others in occupation.

[8] Note this point, especially, of course, where there are more than two trustees. The reason for requiring the consent of at least two is to enable overreaching to take place. Check that you are clear on what overreaching means.

Section 12 of the TLATA 1996 gives a right of occupation to beneficiaries who are entitled to an interest in possession in the land, provided that the trust so allows, but no right of occupation arises if the land is either unavailable or unsuitable for occupation by the beneficiary in question. The property was originally purchased as a home for the original four joint tenants while they were working at the same firm in London, but all we know of Emma is that she is a 'mutual friend'. So it could be argued that the land is in this sense unsuitable for occupation by her.[6]

Even if she continues to live there, section 13 of the TLATA allows the trustees to exclude or restrict her right to occupy, but the power must not be exercised unreasonably. Section 13(4) sets out matters to which the trustees must have regard when exercising their powers to restrict or exclude the right to occupy, and a relevant one here is the purposes for which the land is held on trust, which, as mentioned above, does not seem to include occupation by Emma. So there seems no reason why the trustees could not exclude her from occupation, but section 13(7) provides that a person in occupation of the land, whether or not in occupation under section 12, shall not be evicted except with their consent or a court order.[7] The court, when deciding whether to evict, may, by section 13(8), have regard to the matters set out in section 13(4).

If Emma is to be allowed to stay, or at least pending a court order that she must leave, conditions may be imposed on occupation, and section 13(5) sets out examples: paying outgoings and complying with obligations, for example ensuring that any planning permission is complied with. Thus, Emma could, for example, be obliged to contribute towards gas and electricity bills and council tax.

Finally, under section 10(2) of the TLATA, the consent of any two trustees of land[8] to a disposition of the land is sufficient in favour of a purchaser, and here there are only two remaining: Sam and Sue. In deciding whether to sell, section 11 of the TLATA provides that all the beneficiaries have a right to be consulted by the trustees, who should give effect to the wishes of the majority. However, if Sam still refuses to consent, then, as the restriction entered on the register means that any disposition requires his consent, an application to the court under section 14 of the TLATA is needed. An application can be made by any person interested in the trust and the term 'any person interested' includes trustees and beneficiaries. This includes Sue, Sam and Emma but not Nesta, who has no interest in the property.

Section 15 of the TLATA sets out criteria to which the courts must have regard when settling disputes, and the relevant one here is (b): the purposes for which the property is held on trust. It is suggested that, as only one of the original four owners, Sam, still wishes the property to be held for its original purpose, then, using the analogy with section 11 and giving effect to the wishes of the majority, the property should be sold, but it must be emphasised that this will be in the discretion of the court.

✓ Make your answer stand out

- Include further discussion of the principles on which the court can order a sale under section 15 of the TLATA, as set out in the cases.
- Mention section 15(3) of the TLATA: the court must have regard to the wishes of the beneficiaries of full age, and in cases of dispute the wishes of the majority according to the value of their combined interests. Thus, there is a kind of majority rule – not by numbers but by the value of interests.
- Look at the article by Hopkins, N. (1996) The Trusts of Land and the Appointment of Trustees Act 1996. *Conv.* : 267, which was written when this Act was passed and contains a valuable survey of its provisions, although, obviously, it needs to be looked at in the light of developments since then.
- Explain exactly what overreaching means in the context of section 10(2) of the TLATA.

! Don't be tempted to . . .

- Plunge in without first setting out how both the legal title and the beneficial interests are held.
- Ignore the effect of the restriction.
- Spend too long on either section: devote roughly equal time to the question of how the interests are held and then the question of rights under the TLATA of occupation and sale.
- Fail to apply each of the relevant provisions of section 13 of the TLATA to this question.

📝 Question 3

Critically consider the view that beneficial joint tenancies should be abolished and that where there is a legal joint tenancy, the beneficial interests should be held as tenants in common.

Answer plan

→ Explain why the existence of a joint tenancy can cause problems: survivorship, undivided shares.

→ Point out the differences between joint tenancies and tenancies in common.

→ Explain and seek to justify the rule that the legal title should be held as joint tenants.

→ Now move on to look at the argument that beneficial interests should always be held under a tenancy in common – separate shares and no survivorship.

→ Look at problems caused where parties think that they have severed but have not.

→ End by referring to *Stack* v *Dowden* in the context of this debate.

Diagram plan

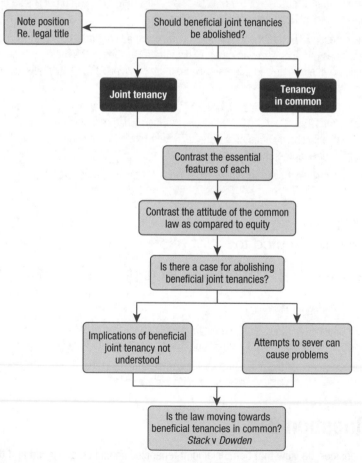

A printable version of this diagram plan is available from **www.pearsoned.co.uk/lawexpressqa**

Answer

[1] At once we have engaged
with the question posed.
A poor answer would have
begun: 'There are the
following differences between
joint tenancies and tenancies
in common . . . '.

[2] This is the essential point to
make clear.

[3] Just a reminder: where there
is a joint tenancy, we refer to
'interests'; with tenancies in
common it is 'shares'.

[4] Although the question is
primarily about beneficial
interests, in order to give a
complete picture you need
to mention why the legal
title is always held on a joint
tenancy.

The view that joint tenancies should be abolished has been advocated for a long time. The fundamental objection to them is that they 'take a choice away'.[1] The essential feature of all joint tenants is that they are co-owners who are not regarded as having separate shares but together own all.[2]

Where there is a joint tenancy, you have no choice as to who will receive your interest on death. Instead, this is decided by survivorship: as joint tenants own an undivided share, their interest[3] ceases on death (s. 3(4) Administration of Estates Act 1925) and so they cannot leave any part of their joint tenancy by will, nor does it pass under the intestacy rules. Instead, it passes to the surviving joint tenants under the right of survivorship – *jus accrescendi*. Where the deaths of joint tenants occur in circumstances making it uncertain which died first, then the younger is to be deemed to have survived the elder (s. 184 LPA 1925). This was applied in **Hickman v Peacey** [1945] AC 304, HL, where deaths occurred simultaneously in a bomb blast.

The alternative, tenancy in common, means that the beneficial owners have undivided shares and survivorship does not apply. Instead, they can decide who will have their share on death and this will not be decided by the accident of who dies first.

As the question recognises, a different approach may be justified where the legal title is concerned, as this is always held on a joint tenancy. [4] This is for practical reasons. Suppose that title to land is held by tenants in common. There are no restrictions on how many can do this and so very many people could hold shares in the legal title to, for example, a small house. As the consent of all of them would be needed to a sale, it could be practically impossible to sell. Instead, by section 34(2) of the Law of Property Act 1925 (LPA 1925), where land is conveyed to co-owners who are of full age, they must be joint tenants and there cannot be no more than four. So if title to 'Blackacre' was originally held by X, Y, Z and W but, when it came to be sold, all except X had died, then X would have the right to sell. He could show that the others had died by producing their death certificates.

However, although this makes sense with the legal title, it is less easy to justify with the beneficial interests.

[5] This is an absolutely basic point and you do need to be clear on it.

There is, however, a choice with regard to the beneficial interests: they can be held as joint tenants or as tenants in common[5] where, as we saw, survivorship does not apply. Suppose that Richard and Amanda are legal and beneficial joint tenants but Amanda has children by a previous marriage. If Amanda dies first, then, by survivorship, all her interest in the house will go to Richard, as we saw above. However, Amanda can protect the interests of her children by ensuring that she and Richard hold the beneficial interest as tenants in common. As we noted above, with a tenancy in common the right of survivorship does not apply as each is entitled to a separate share and can dispose of it either during life or on death.[6] This is why it could be to Amanda's advantage to have a tenancy in common.

[6] Note the clear comparison between the two types.

How does Amanda ensure that there is now a tenancy in common? She does so by severing the beneficial joint tenancy so that she and Richard become tenants in common. This will work if the parties realise the implications of a joint tenancy, especially where one has contributed more to the purchase than the other, but there is evidence that often people do not know this. Thus, they would not be aware of the potential problem and so be unable to take the action that Amanda took.

[7] This is absolutely crucial in gaining those extra marks. An average answer would have just set out the survivorship rule and how it works. This answer has gone further and backed this up with a reference to a case which is, in fact, not very well known and so needed some research to find it. Perfect!

An example of the problems caused by a beneficial joint tenancy is ***Campbell v Griffin*** [2001] EWCA Civ 990,[7] where Campbell was a lodger in a house and had taken care of the owners, an elderly couple. The husband executed a codicil to his will, leaving Campbell a life interest in the house, but, as the house was held by the couple as legal and beneficial joint tenants, the gift failed by survivorship. In fact, the situation was rescued by applying proprietary estoppel to give Campbell a charge over the property. However, if the couple had had a beneficial tenancy in common, the husband would have been able to leave what would then have been his share to Campbell and this expensive litigation would have been avoided. As Bandali, S.M. (1977) puts it: 'when used in relation to beneficial ownership its effect is to produce fortuitous and intended enrichment of a surviving joint tenant'.

[8] It is important to bring in this extra argument too. You will then need to refer to the law on what constitutes severance, but not in too much detail.

In addition to the argument that many co-owners do not understand that survivorship will apply and so do not take action to prevent this happening, attempts to sever a joint tenancy so that it becomes a tenancy in common can be problematic.[8] Severance can be by written notice addressed to all the other joint tenants (s. 196 LPA 1925). Alternatively, severance in equity can be effected by agreement with

[9] A small point of detail but one that shows that there are views on this.

[10] A mention of this decision, in addition to being relevant, will add to your marks, as *Stack* v *Dowden* is usually studied in the area of trusts of the home and not here. So a mention of this case will show the examiner that you can think laterally across the subject: always a plus point. You could also add in some references to the debate on this case.

[11] You could, of course, take the opposite view and gain an equally good mark. It is quite reasonable to argue that beneficial joint tenancies should survive. What matters, of course, is how you justify your view.

all the other joint tenants (**Williams v Hensman** (1861) 1 John & H 546, QB). The agreement does not have to be a specifically enforceable contract (**Burgess v Rawnsley** [1975] Ch 429, CA) but in **Slater v Slater** (1987) 4 BPR 9431, CA it was held that there must be an intention to sever 'irrespective of the outcome of the negotiations'. What is not acceptable is an oral declaration by one joint tenant that she wishes to sever, despite the suggestion that it would be by Denning MR in **Burgess v Rawnsley**.[9] This makes perfect legal sense, as, if severance by oral declaration were possible, there would be no need for the provisions of section 196 of the LPA 1925, governing severance by written notice. Thus, if Amanda simply says to Richard, 'From now on our interests will be held as tenants in common', this achieves nothing. If there was always a tenancy in common, there would be no need for severance.

It could be said that the law is moving in favour of a tenancy in common anyway. In **Stack v Dowden** [2007] UKHL 17 it was held that there can be a tenancy in common even where there is a declaration that the parties hold the legal title as joint tenants.[10] While this is true, it does not do away with the situation where the parties have expressly declared that they hold the beneficial interests as joint tenants but then wish to sever. It is suggested that the end of beneficial joint tenancies would be a very useful reform of our law.[11]

✓ **Make your answer stand out**

- There has been a great deal of academic debate on the question of whether beneficial joint tenancies should continue to exist. Start with Bandali (1977) and then move on to Thompson, M.P. (1987) Beneficial Joint Tenancies. *Conv.* : 29, which agrees with Bandali. For a contrary view, see Pritchard, A.M. (1987) Beneficial Joint Tenancies: A Riposte. *Conv.* : 273.

- Refer to Douglas, G.F., Pearce, J. and Woodward, H. (2008) on the evidence that people are often unaware of the consequences of a beneficial tenancy in common.

- Add some references to the debate on *Stack* v *Dowden* and *Jones* v *Kernott* [2011] UKSC 53 – see Chapter 4.

- Look at *Bindra* v *Chopra* [2009] EWCA Civ 203 – an interesting angle on this area, where the Court of Appeal upheld an arrangement whereby a tenancy in common in life was to become a joint tenancy of the proceeds of sale of the property on death. Inclusion of this case will add depth to your answer.

> **! Don't be tempted to . . .**
>
> - Just list the ways in which joint tenancies can be severed – integrate the methods of severance into your answer and you will give your marks a real boost.
> - Ignore the point that legal title to land must always be held on a joint tennacy.
> - Spend too long on the first area and neglect the more challenging issue raised by the second part of the question.

📷 Question 4

Dixon (2014a) considers that case law on section 15 of the Trusts of Land and Appointment of Trustees Act 1996 has 'not been consistent in those cases . . . in which the rights of creditors are in contest with the rights of co-owners'.

Critically consider this view.

Answer plan

→ Set out the criteria in section 15 and explain how they are exercised on an application under section 14.

→ Briefly mention the previous law to evaluate whether and, if so, how the law has changed.

→ Consider *Mortgage Corporation* v *Shaire* and in particular Neuberger J's views on the application of section 15.

→ Evaluate how subsequent courts have dealt with applications under section 15: consider each decision and contrast the approaches taken by each court.

→ Emphasise that the approach has to be flexible and so the statement in the question is not, in fact, a criticism of the law.

Diagram plan

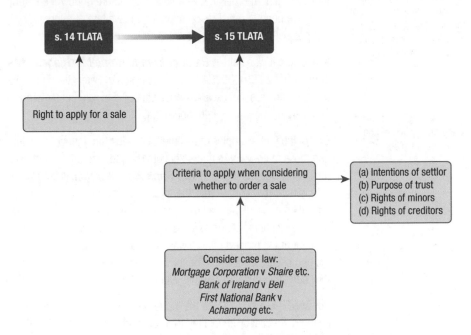

A printable version of this diagram plan is available from **www.pearsoned.co.uk/lawexpressqa**

Answer

Section 15(1) of the Trusts of Land and Appointment of Trustees Act 1996 (TLATA) sets out criteria to which the courts must have regard when settling disputes over whether land should be sold, together with other disputes. The use of section 15(1) is triggered by an application for sale under section 14 of the TLATA. The criteria are as follows:

(a) the intentions of the settlor;

(b) the purposes for which the property is held on trust;

(c) the welfare of any minor who either occupies, or might reasonably be expected to occupy, the land as his or her home;

(d) the interests of any secured creditor of any beneficiary.

These criteria are not ranked in order of importance and so the fact that the rights of creditors are placed below those of co owners does

[1] This is a good point: you have shown that you are *thinking about* the words of the question and relating them to the actual criteria under section 15(1) of the TLATA.

[2] This point is not usually made and so you will gain credit for doing so!

[3] This is one of those areas where an outline (but no more) of the previous law does add depth to your answer, as, here, there has been more of a change in emphasis in the law rather than a radical alteration.

not say anything about their relative importance. It is also worth stressing that, in order to give a complete picture of how the criteria work, we need to consider criterion (c), the welfare of minors. Thus, it is not just a tug between creditors and co-owners.[1]

In addition, it was held in **Bank of Ireland Home Mortgages Ltd v Bell** [2001] 2 FLR 809, CA that, in the words of Peter Gibson LJ, the above criteria are 'not exclusive but inclusive' and so other factors can be taken into account where appropriate.[2]

One of the first examples of a contest between the rights of creditors and those of co-owners under section 15(1) to reach the courts was the County Court decision in **TSB Bank Plc v Marshall** [1998] 2 FLR 769, where it was held that the interest of the chargee in a matrimonial home would prevail over the interests of an innocent spouse, save in exceptional circumstances. Here, although there were children resident at the property, there was no clear evidence to suggest that the purpose to provide a home for them was intended to survive once they became adults, which they all now were.

However, it is arguable that the judge here was influenced too much by the predecessor to section 15(1) of the TLATA, section 30 of the LPA 1925, which gave a wide discretion to the courts and did not set out any criteria.[3] Instead, as the judge put it in **TSB Bank Plc v Marshall**: 'section 30 enabled the court to do what was equitable, fair and just'.

The first detailed consideration of section 15(1) by the higher courts was in **Mortgage Corporation v Shaire** [2001] Ch 743, HC. The house was held by X and Y as joint tenants. It was bought to provide a home for them and Y's son by a previous marriage. X owned a 25 per cent share in equity and Y a 75 per cent share. X mortgaged the house by forging Y's signature and after X's death the mortgagee sought a sale. The court refused. Here, Neuberger J emphasised that the law had changed under the TLATA and that, by comparison with section 30 of the LPA 1925, Parliament, in section 15(1) of the TLATA, had intended to 'tip the scales more in favour of families and against banks and other chargees'. Neuberger J also made this obvious but necessary point: if the law was to stay the same, then why had it been necessary to pass the TLATA? Pascoe, S. (2000) Section 15 and the Trusts of Land and Appointment of Trustees Act 1996 – A Change in the Law? *Conv.* : 315 has described the approach of Neuberger J in this case as 'wiping the slate clean and starting afresh with secured creditors as the likely casualties of the new approach'.

[4] In this question we have a line of cases none of which differs from each other radically but all of which show subtle differences of approach. This means that you will gain marks by paying very close attention to the actual facts and how the decision in each case depended partly on its facts and partly on a different approach.

However, in **Bank of Ireland Home Mortgages Plc v Bell** the Court of Appeal, while apparently approving of Neuberger J's approach in the above case, did not follow the same bold reasoning.[4] The family home was owned jointly by the husband (H) and wife (W) in law but the wife had only a 10 per cent beneficial interest. H forged W's signature on a mortgage and then left W. She remained in the house with their son for 10 years after H stopped making mortgage repayments and, when the bank sought possession, W was in poor health. The mortgage debt was now £300,000. The court recognised that the law had now changed, as the courts were now required to have regard to particular factors set out in section 15, but nevertheless it held that a sale would be ordered here as a 'powerful consideration' was 'whether the creditor is receiving proper recompense for being kept out of his money'. This was clearly not the case. This case appears to show that, as the quotation in the question points out, the case law has apparently not been consistent. However, another way of putting it would be to say that the courts, being given a set of criteria, all of equal importance, are obviously going to reach decisions on the facts of each case.[5]

[5] These two sentences do two things: first, they remind the examiner that you have not forgotten what the question is asking you about and, secondly, they make a new point which you now need to follow through in your answer.

First National Bank Plc v Achampong [2003] EWCA Civ 487 shows the way in which the courts try to balance the interests of the different parties in applying the factors under section 15(1) of the TLATA when the creditor applies for a sale. The house was purchased as the matrimonial home, but, at the time of the application, the marriage had broken down and the parties had not been in contact for many years. Thus, the court held that the purpose for which the property was acquired (s. 15(1)(b)) was no longer relevant. One child of the marriage was grown up and no longer in occupation but the other child had a mental disability and, although an adult, still lived at the house. However, there was no clear evidence that her disability meant that she had to continue to live there. There were infant grandchildren in occupation and the court was prepared to regard this as relevant but it was not clear how their interests would be adversely affected if an order for sale was made.[6] Therefore, the court held that it would order a sale, bearing in mind that, if it did not, the bank 'will be kept waiting indefinitely' for its share of the property.

[6] As section 15(1) of the TLATA sets out a number of criteria for the courts to apply, if you are to score highly you need to really research these cases. This passage shows that the cases have been read in detail.

In **Edwards v Lloyds TSB Bank Plc** [2004] EWHC 1745 (Ch), the court dealt with an application by the creditors for a sale of the matrimonial home by granting a postponed order for sale that allowed the wife to continue living in the house until the youngest child reached full age.

[7] Notice how we have referred to the views in an article and then go on to link this to a case. This approach will really impress your examiner. So many students just pick out a quote from an article, mention it and do not show how it is relevant. Do not be one of them!

Omar, P. (2006) Security over Co-owned Property and the Creditor's Paramount Status in Recovery Proceedings. *Conv.* 70: 157 says that disputes between owners and creditors still tend to be resolved in the creditor's favour. However, the decision in **Edwards v Lloyds TSB Bank Plc** certainly took account of the needs of the family[7] and that in **First National Bank Plc v Achampong** might have been different if more evidence had been produced to the court on the situation of members of the family.

[8] It is important that a conclusion brings the arguments together in a succinct way.

It is submitted that Omar's view is too pessimistic and that, although the statement in the question is true, it is not a criticism that the courts have 'not been consistent in those cases . . . in which the rights of creditors are in contest with the rights of co-owners', but simply a recognition that there is no one right answer in these cases but instead a number of factors that have to be balanced.[8]

✓ Make your answer stand out

- It is interesting that in several of the cases (*Bank of Ireland Home Mortgages Plc v Bell* and *First National Bank Plc v Achampong*) the County Court judge had held very strongly that no order for sale should be made, and this was reversed by the Court of Appeal. Consider at least one of these County Court judgments and contrast it with the approach of the Court of Appeal.

- Mention that, in *Mortgage Corporation v Shaire*, Neuberger J referred to the Law Commission (1989) Transfer of Land, Trusts of Land, No. 181. www.bailii.org/ew/other/EWLC/1989/181.pdf which had led to the passage of the TLATA, and referred to Paragraph 12.9, which stated that its aim was not only to consolidate the law but also to rationalise it.

- Note that where one of the co-owners is bankrupt then his estate vests in the trustee in bankruptcy (s. 306 Insolvency Act 1986) and he may apply for a sale under section 14 of the TLATA. Mention briefly at the end how this might affect the position – see, e.g., *Re Citro* [1991] Ch 142, CA.

- Note *Bagum v Hafiz* [2015] EWCA Civ 801 – an interesting application of section 14 of the TLATA.

- Possible application of the Human Rights Act – Article 8: Respect for Private and Family Life – see *Barca* v *Mears* [2004] EWHC 2170 (Ch).
- Note *Bank of Baroda* v *Dhillon* [1998] 1 FLR 524, CA, which deals with the relationship between section 14 and section 15 of the TLATA and overriding interests.

! Don't be tempted to . . .

- Just set out a list of cases on section 15(1) of the TLATA and say nothing on the principles.
- Spend too much time on the facts of the cases and not relate them to principles and in particular the criteria in section 15(1) of the TLATA.
- Leave out a mention of what the law was before the TLATA.

? Question 5

John and Jane are cohabitees and are joint tenants in law and equity of 'Southlands', a detached house. They have one child, Amy, who has a learning difficulty and cannot live independently.

Jane ran a hairdressers' business but, due to some rash expansion plans failing in the recession, she was declared bankrupt in July 2016 and her assets have vested in her trustee in bankruptcy.

It is now May 2017 and Jane has heard that the trustee in bankruptcy is applying for a sale of 'Southlands'.

Advise John and Jane on the likelihood of the trustee in bankruptcy being able to force a sale.

Answer plan

→ Identify ownership of the legal and beneficial interests in the property.

→ Explain the relevant provisions of the Insolvency Act 1986 and apply them to the facts.

→ Stress the different provisions that apply where there is an application for a sale more than one year after the bankruptcy.

→ Consider the possible application of Article 8 of the ECHR.

Diagram plan

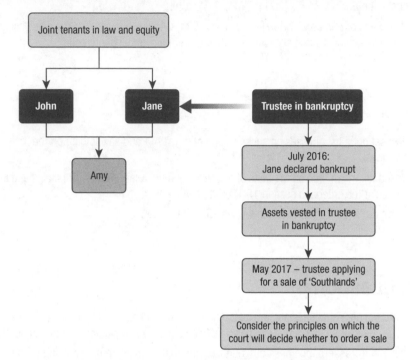

A printable version of this diagram plan is available from **www.pearsoned.co.uk/lawexpressqa**

[1] You will not be expected to examine the extent of Jane's beneficial interest in the property but in this opening paragraph you simply need to explain clearly where Jane's assets are in the property.

[2] The point is that as this is not a dispute between the two co-owners, we do not need to decide the extent of their respective beneficial interests.

[3] This is an important point and you will lose marks for omitting it: it is obviously sensible to see whether a sale can be negotiated before going to court.

Answer

The first stage is to identify what assets Jane has in the property.[1] She is a legal joint tenant with John and also a joint tenant in equity. An equitable joint tenancy implies that the beneficial interest is in equal shares but, since **Stack v Dowden** [2007] UKHL 17, it is possible to displace this presumption in certain cases. However, in this question we are simply required to identify that she has assets.[2] The trustee in bankruptcy has a duty to realise Jane's assets in order to pay off her creditors.

The first step will be that the trustee will see whether Jane and John are opposed to a sale.[3] We assume that they will be, as if there is a sale, they will lose their home and they also have their daughter to consider. if so, the trustee in bankruptcy will have to apply for a sale under section 14 of the Trusts of Land and Appointment of Trustees Act 1996 (TLATA), which provides that any person who has an interest in property subject to a trust of land may make an application to the court for an order under this section and, as the assets of Jane have vested in the trustee in bankruptcy, they will count as such a person.

On applications for a sale of property, the considerations to which the court must have regard are set out in section 335A(2) of the Insolvency Act 1986, which was inserted into this Act by the TLATA. This provides that, on such an application, the court is to make such order as it thinks just and reasonable, and it then sets out a number of factors that involve trying to balance the needs of the creditors, the bankrupt and others who may be affected by a sale. The factors to which the court must have regard differ depending on whether the parties are married or civil partners or not, and, here, John and Jane are not married.[4] In all cases, by section 335A(2)(a), the court must naturally have regard to the interests of the bankrupt's creditors. Section 335A(2)(b) does not apply here, as it applies only where the application is made in respect of land which includes a dwelling house which is or has been the home of the bankrupt or the bankrupt's spouse or civil partner or former spouse or former civil partner. Here, the parties are cohabitees. If section 335A(2)(b) had applied, then the court could have had regard to a number of factors including the conduct of the parties and the needs and financial resources of the parties and their children. And, here, the parties have a child, Amy. It would be astonishing and grossly unfair if Amy's needs were not considered, and it is suggested that they would be under section 335A(2)(c), which allows the court to consider all the circumstances of the case other than the needs of the bankrupt.[5] Moreover, in **Re Citro** [1991] Ch 142, CA, it was held that the predecessor to section 335A(2), section 336(3) of the Insolvency Act 1986, did apply to unmarried couples.

The general principle, as laid down in **Re Solomon** [1967] Ch 573, Ch D, was that in these cases 'the voice of the trustee in bankruptcy is one which ought to prevail' (Goff J). Here, it should be noted that Jane was declared bankrupt in July 2016 and it is now May 2017. It seems unlikely that the trustee in bankruptcy will apply for a sale within a year of the bankruptcy.[6] If he does not, then section 335A(3) applies and the court will assume, unless the circumstances of the case are exceptional, that the interests of the bankrupt's creditors outweigh all

[4] This is a typical point that arises in these questions. Check, at the very start of your answer, whether the parties are married/civil partners or not.

[5] This is another familiar point in these questions.

[6] Do make a note of when the bankruptcy occurred and the date of the question so that you can see whether this point applies. In practice, it is generally the case that the application is made after a year of the bankruptcy.

other considerations. Thus, the principle laid down in **Re Solomon** is in effect applied even more strongly.

[7] It is vital that you identify this point and show how it has been applied in the case law.

The question is then what are exceptional circumstances.[7] In **Dean v Stout** [2004] EWHC 3315 (Ch) it was held that, typically, these related to the personal circumstances of one of the owners, such as a medical or mental condition. However, exceptional circumstances were not to be categorised and the court was to make a value judgement after looking at the circumstances. Thus, it would not be an exceptional circumstance for a wife with children to be faced with eviction in circumstances where the realisation of her beneficial interest would not produce enough to buy a comparable home. The problem is that, although this tells us what will not be exceptional, it does not tell us what will be exceptional.

[8] This does need to be stressed, even if you do not agree!

[9] This is a very useful quotation to include, especially as it relates to the possible application of Article 8 of the ECHR, as explained below.

In this case the fact that the parties will lose their home is clearly not exceptional.[8] As Nourse LJ put it in **Re Citro**, such cases are 'the melancholy consequences of debt and improvidence with which every civilised society has been familiar'.[9] One arguably exceptional circumstance is that Jane and John have a daughter, Amy, who has a learning difficulty and cannot live independently. The nearest parallel is **Barca v Mears** [2004] EWHC 2170 (Ch), where it was argued that a sale should be postponed where the parties had a son with special educational needs. In this case the son was, however, able to live independently and the issue was whether a sale of the house would require him to leave his present school. On the facts, it would not and indeed a sale was ordered. In this case there is no evidence, unlike in **Barca v Mears**, that the relationship between John and Jane has broken down, and it may be that they have sufficient capital to enable them to obtain another home and live as a family. If this was not so and John and Jane would be homeless then this might well count as an exceptional circumstance, as Amy then would have to live apart from them, presumably in residential accommodation, and

[10] This is one of the few cases where the Human Rights Act has had an impact on Land Law. You must mention this point in any answer on this topic. However, you should first state the relevant domestic law before turning to the ECHR.

be separated from her parents.

The case against a sale will be strengthened if it can be argued that, under the Human Rights Act 1998, Article 8 of the European Convention on Human Rights 1950 (ECHR) applies.[10] This provides that 'Everyone has the right to have respect for his private and family life, his home and his correspondence'. In **Barca v Mears**, the court held that the approach of the courts to the effect on a sale on family life might not be compatible with Article 8. Thus, a shift in emphasis in the interpretation of sections 335A, 336 and 337 of the Insolvency Act 1986 might be necessary to achieve compatibility with a bankrupt's rights under the ECHR. The effect would be that eviction from the family home might sometimes be relied on under the Insolvency Act as exceptional circumstances.

✓ Make your answer stand out

- Clear identification of the crucial statutory provisions and an ability to show how these have been applied in the case law.
- Mention *Re Holliday* [1981] Ch 405, CA, which is one of the very few cases where a sale has not been ordered in an application by a trustee in bankruptcy in this type of case.
- Refer to the Cork Committee (1982) *Insolvency Law and Practice*. Cmnd. 8558, especially Paragraphs 1114–1123, and consider whether the attitude of the committee is reflected in the provisions of the Insolvency Act 1986 and in the case law.
- Instead of giving details of the facts in *Barca* v *Mears*, just give the decision, which is obviously vital, and then mention other cases which have considered the possible application of the ECHR in these cases. An example is *Nicholls* v *Lan* [2007] 1 FLR 744 Ch D.

! Don't be tempted to . . .

- Ignore the significance of the application for a sale being likely to be more than a year after the bankruptcy.
- Fail to mention the provisions of the Insolvency Act before you deal with the cases.
- Forget that the cases are applying the statute law.
- Mention too many cases on this area without explaining the principles.

@ Try it yourself

Now take a look at the question below and attempt to answer it. You can check your response against the answer guidance available on the companion website (**www.pearsoned.co.uk/lawexpressqa**).

Jo, Mike, Alf, Tom and Sue purchased a house with registered title, to live in while they studied law at Hanbury University. The property was conveyed to them with a declaration that they were joint tenants, in both law and equity.

In January, Jo died, leaving all her property to Battersea Dogs Home. During March, Mike decided to sever his joint tenancy in the property and sent a notice of severance to the others by registered post. When Alf, who was the only one in at the time, took delivery of it, he was so annoyed that he threw it away. Three weeks later, Mike was killed in a riding accident, leaving all his property to his friend, Kate. In July, Tom was told that he had failed his Land Law exam and so he sold his share in the property to Ned. In August, Alf decided to move out in order to live with his partner, Larry. He discussed with Sue the possibility of selling his interest in the house and they had almost reached an agreement on a price when Alf had a heart attack and died. Alf's will left all his property to Larry.

You are asked to advise on the devolution of the legal and equitable interests in the property.

---

www.pearsoned.co.uk/lawexpressqa

Go online to access more revision support, including additional essay and problem questions with diagram plans, and you be the marker questions, and to download all diagrams from the book.

Trusts and the home

4

Before you begin

It's a good idea to consider the following key themes of trusts and the home before tackling
a question on this topic.

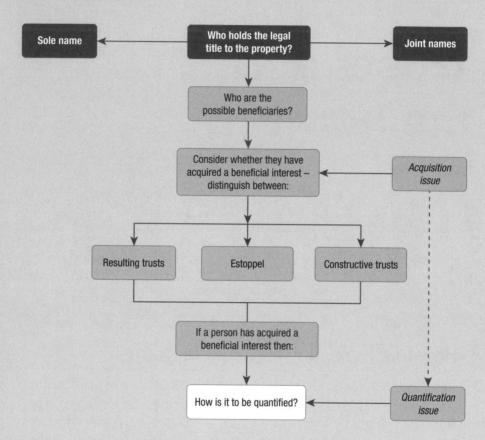

A printable version of this diagram is available from **www.pearsoned.co.uk/lawexpressqa**

![icon] Question 1

'Where an asset is owned in law by one person but another claims to share a beneficial interest in it a two-stage analysis is called for to determine whether a common intention constructive trust arises.'

Slade LJ in *Capehorn* v *Harris* [2015] EWCA Civ 955

Critically comment on this statement of the law and, in your answer, consider also whether the present law works fairly in the interests of all the parties.

Diagram plan

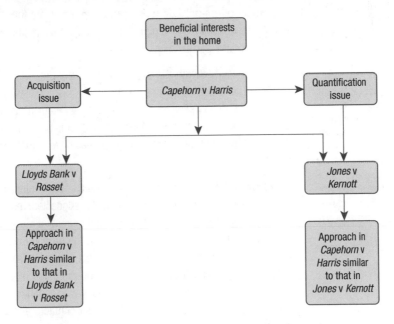

A printable version of this diagram plan is available from **www.pearsoned.co.uk/lawexpressqa**

Answer plan

→ Explain when this issue is relevant.

→ Distinguish between acquisition of a beneficial interest and quantification of a beneficial interest.

→ Explain the decision of the Court of Appeal in *Capehorn* v *Harris*, setting it in the context of other cases.

→ Contrast *Capehorn* v *Harris* with *Lloyds Bank* v *Rosset* on the acquisition issue, and assess the relative merits of the judgments in each case on particular points.

→ Then look at what *Capehorn* v *Harris* said on the quantification issue, and note the similarities with *Jones* v *Kernott*.

→ Mention that imputed intention can become the imposition by the courts of what they consider to be a fair decision.

→ Consider how the law might develop in the future: is legislation the answer?

Answer

[1] This may seem a complicated start, but it is vital to clear the ground at the start and make clear exactly when this issue is relevant.

This question relates to claims to a beneficial interest in property in what are known as sole name cases, either where the parties are unmarried, or are not in a civil partnership, or where they may be but the issue is not a claim to property arising on the break-up of the marriage or civil partnership.[1]

[2] It is important that you make this clear at the start – students often get confused between the law where the title is in a sole name and the law where it is in joint names.

It is not concerned with the situation where the property is in joint names.[2] This is because Slade LJ was distinguishing between what is known as the acquisition issue, deciding whether a party has a beneficial interest at all, and the quantification issue,[3] which determines the extent of the share that the parties have in that beneficial interest.

[3] This terminology is very useful and saves you time so as to be able to make other points that will earn you marks. Try to use it.

Capehorn* v *Harris [2015] EWCA Civ 955, CA, is the latest in a long line of cases in this area and the decision, it is suggested, represents a welcome clarification. The property was in the name of Mrs Capehorn (C) and the claim to a beneficial interest in the property was by her partner, Mr Harris (H) with whom she had cohabited for many years. C had paid the deposit and also funded the mortgage repayments. After H was declared bankrupt, his business was continued by C as a sole trader, but H had the main business contacts and was the dominant force in running it.

[4] Although you would not normally say much about the decision of a lower court in a case, here it is useful as the lower court fell into the error that the CA is trying to prevent.

The district judge found that there was no actual agreement, but the extent of H's contribution to the business 'should be sufficient to impute an intention to the parties that he should acquire a beneficial interest not only in the business but also in the property'.[4]

The Court of Appeal held that this was in error, as the judge had imputed an intention to the parties at the acquisition stage, whereas any question of imputation arose only at the quantification stage. Instead, Slade LJ, with whom the other judges agreed, applied the two-stage analysis referred to in the question. He held that in deciding whether a beneficial interest existed at all (the acquisition issue): 'the person claiming the beneficial interest must show that there was an agreement that he should have a beneficial interest in the property owned by his partner'. If this was so, then, at the quantification stage, if there is no agreement as to the extent of the interest, 'the court may impute an intention that the person was to have a fair beneficial share in the asset and may assess the quantum of the fair share in the light of all the circumstances'.

The judgment is notably concise on the law and avoids detailed analysis of earlier authorities. Slade LJ is clear that, when he refers to an agreement, this means not only an express agreement but also cases where one can 'be inferred from conduct in an appropriate case'. Thus, of the three types of intention, express or inferred intention is needed to establish a beneficial interest but, in addition to these, imputed intention will also suffice to establish the extent of the interest.

[5] Although *Lloyds Bank v Rosset* is not the main authority today, it is still used, as we shall see, and, in addition, to achieve a good mark in this essay, you need to set the law in context.

On the quantification issue, this approach is similar to that of Lord Bridge in **Lloyds Bank Plc v Rosset** [1991] 1 AC 107, HL,[5] who said that there were two ways in which a party could claim a beneficial interest, both resting on what he called the common intentions of the parties.[6] One was whether there was any agreement, arrangement or understanding between the parties that the property was to be shared beneficially. If so, the party claiming must show that they have acted to their detriment in relying on this. In effect, the notion of estoppel was used. In the absence of express discussions, the court must rely on conduct to support the inference of a common intention and, said Lord Bridge, in nearly every case the only relevant conduct is direct contributions to the purchase price.

[6] Note that we have summarised what these two ways are, because *Lloyds Bank v Rosset* principles can still be important.

[7] This is the approach that earns you marks: you are adopting a clear analytical approach to the judgments in the two cases.

However, there seem to be three differences between the approaches of Slade LJ in **Capehorn** and Lord Bridge in **Rosset**.[7] First, Slade LJ refers to 'an agreement' albeit that this can be inferred, whereas Lord Bridge speaks of 'common intention'. It is suggested that 'common intention' is to be preferred, as finding an actual agreement can be difficult here. As Waite J said in **Hammond v Mitchell** [1992] 2 All ER 109, Fam D: the parties were 'too much in love at this time either to count the pennies or pay attention to who was providing them'.[8] Thus, it is likely that in most cases intention will have to be inferred

[8] This is a nice vivid quote and easily remembered!

from conduct, and this leaves open the question of whether this is the same as imputing an intention, as there may be a fine line between them.

Secondly, Slade LJ did not mention Lord Bridge's often-criticised statement that, in the absence of direct contributions, 'it is at least extremely doubtful if anything less will do'. In fact, Slade LJ's reference to inferring an agreement from conduct seems similar to the approach in *Le Foe* v *Le Foe* [2001] 2 FLR 970, HC, where the wife contributed to the family economy by paying for general outgoings while the husband made the mortgage payments, and this in itself gave her a beneficial interest, the value of which was increased by her later mortgage repayments. This is welcome. Thirdly, Slade LJ did not use the analogy with estoppel favoured by Lord Bridge. This, in itself, may make it easier to establish a claim, as it will not be necessary to show detrimental reliance on a common intention.

[9] Although most of the interest in *Capehorn* v *Harris* is in the acquisition issue, do not forget the quantification issue.

When the court comes to assessing the share of the beneficial interest,[9] Slade LJ is adopting the approach of the Supreme Court in the joint names case of *Jones* v *Kernott* [2011] UKSC 53, where Lady Hale and Lord Walker said that the fallback position was that 'if the courts cannot deduce exactly what shares were intended, it may have no alternative but to ask what their intentions as reasonable and just people would have been had they thought about it at the time'. However, is this just a cover for the court to impose what it considers a just solution? Lord Wilson thought so when he said in *Jones* v *Kernott*, 'Where equity is driven to impute the common intention, how can it do so other than by a search for the result which the court itself considers fair?' Have we then reached the stage where the court is simply deciding what a fair result is?

[10] Do not forget that the question is asking you whether the law works fairly and so, in addition to adopting a critical approach to the present law, you should look at alternatives.

The basing of rights to a beneficial interest in the home on the intentions of the parties has bedevilled this area of law.[10] Would it be better to abandon it and replace it with searching for a fair result? Alternatively, is the solution legislation? In 2007, the Law Commission (Report (2007) No. 307) proposed a scheme whereby parties to a relationship could claim a share in property on the basis of economic advantage or disadvantage. The effect would have been to widen the net for possible claimants, but the Government has shown little interest in its implementation.

✓ **Make your answer stand out**

- Keep an eye out for *Curran* v *Collins* [2015] EWCA Civ 404, CA – a sole name case that may be going to the Supreme Court.

- If you have studied Family Law, or can research it, then why not see how the courts deal with distribution of assets on a divorce or at the end of a civil partnership? Have we reached the same stage with cohabitees and, if not, should we? Look at *White* v *White* [2001] 1 AC 596, HL. It is arguable that Lady Hale, in particular, with her background in family law, is attempting to introduce a similar regime in cases involving cohabitees. Do you consider that this is right?

- Note the Privy Council decision in *Abbott* v *Abbott* [2007] UKPC 53, which seemed to adopt the broader principles on acquisition of a beneficial interest set out by Lady Hale in *Stack* v *Dowden*. Ask whether the law is going back to a more rigid approach.

- Refer in more detail to the Law Commission (2007) Report, *Cohabitation: The Financial Consequences of Relationship Breakdown*, No. 307. http://lawcommission.justice.gov .uk/docs/lc307_Cohabitation.pdf for a possible solution.

! **Don't be tempted to. . .**

- Just give an account of the cases – go for the underlying principles.
- Fail to make your own judgements on the state of the law.
- Fail to make a clear distinction between acquisition and quantification issues and sole name and joint name cases.
- End without considering whether the present law works fairly, as mentioned in the question. Avoid generalities here – mention specific points, if only briefly.

❓ Question 2

Ted bought 'The Laurels' as a home for himself and his partner, Mel. The house was registered in Ted's name and the mortgage was in Ted's name also, as he was the wage earner. It was agreed that, as the house was only barely habitable, Mel would stay at home and organise the repairs. The other household bills would be paid partly out of Ted's income and partly out of Mel's savings. It was the intention of both of them that, when the repairs were completed, Mel would start work and her income would then go to help paying the household bills and perhaps the mortgage.

The relationship between Ted and Mel has broken down and Mel wishes to leave 'The Laurels' and find another home.

Advise Mel on whether she has any interest in 'The Laurels' and, if so, on any principles that could be used to determine its extent.

How, if at all, would your answer differ if 'The Laurels' was registered in the joint names of Ted and Mel?

Diagram plan

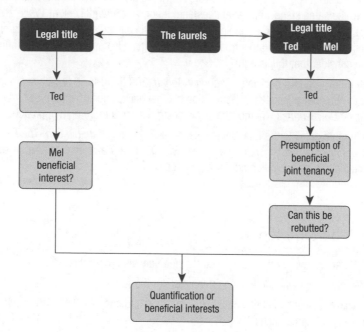

A printable version of this diagram plan is available from **www.pearsoned.co.uk/lawexpressqa**

Answer plan

➜ Note that the property is registered in Ted's name only and so Mel, the claimant, can have only a beneficial interest in the property.

➜ Mel's claim: first, the acquisition issue. Does she have a beneficial interest at all?

➜ Remember here, and in the rest of this answer, to make clear distinctions among express, inferred and imputed intentions.

➜ Assuming that Mel does have a beneficial interest, next move on to the quantification issue: the extent of that beneficial interest.

➜ If the property is registered in joint names, the acquisition issue does not arise.

➜ However, the quantification issue does, and you need to apply the case law, starting with Lady Hale's principles in *Stack* v *Dowden*.

Answer

As the parties are unmarried,[1] any claim will be under trusts law, whereas, if they were married, it would be under the Matrimonial Causes Act 1973. 'The Laurels' is registered in Ted's name only and so any claim by Mel can be only to a beneficial interest under a trust.[2] There is no express declaration of trust[3] and, if there was, it would need to be in writing or evidenced in writing to satisfy section 53(1)(c) of the Law of Property Act 1925 (LPA 1925).[4] As there is no express trust, any trust will be implied and, by section 53(2) of the LPA 1925 resulting, implied or constructive trusts are exempted from the requirement of writing.[5]

Thus, in this case it is permissible to look for evidence of a trust other than in written documents. The principles in **Stack v Dowden** [2007] UKHL 17 appear to apply to cases where the property is in joint names, and the only issue is how the extent of the beneficial interest should be quantified. Where it is a sole name case and the issue is whether a beneficial interest has been acquired at all, then different principles apply.[6] In **Jones v Kernott** [2011] UKSC 53, Lady Hale and Lord Walker recognised this by saying that although a 'common intention' trust is of central importance to 'joint names' as well as 'single names' cases, 'it is important to point out that the starting point for analysis is different in the two situations'.

So, as this is a sole name case, we must take the starting point as **Lloyds Bank v Rosset** [1991] 1 AC 107[7] and then the recent decision in **Capehorn v Harris** [2015] EWCA Civ 955, CA. Lord Bridge laid down in **Rosset** that a beneficial interest can be acquired either though a common intention supported by detrimental reliance on this or by direct contributions to the purchase price. In this case, Mel did not make any contributions to the cost of acquisition nor did she make any contribution to the repayment of the mortgage, but she may be able to establish a common intention. This idea of common intention was, as saw above, approved in **Jones v Kernott**. In **Capehorn v Harris**, Slade LJ stated that 'the person claiming the beneficial interest must show that there was an agreement that he should have a beneficial interest in the property owned by his partner'. This looks like common intention, but, in addition, Slade LJ held that this agreement could 'be inferred from conduct in an appropriate case'.

---

[1] This will usually be the case in a trusts question, but you will gain credit for pointing it out.

[2] This must be your first point in any question on trusts of the home: identify who holds the legal title and, when you have done this, you will be able to see where any trusts will exist.

[3] Almost certainly, there will not be an express trust, but, logically, you should first check whether there is, and you will lose marks if you do not.

[4] This should always be your next one.

[5] And this is the fifth one. This opening paragraph ticks five boxes and, in just over 100 words, you have mentioned five good points and not only earned a lot of marks but neatly cleared the ground for the discussion that follows.

[6] This has been the source of some confusion and so it is vital to make this point clear.

[7] Although there may at one time have been some doubt on this, it is clear from more recent cases that where there is a sole name case then *Rosset* remains good law on the acquisition issue.

[8] This is an essential link in your answer. First, ask whether there is express intention and then move on to whether intention can be inferred.

Here, there is no express agreement, so Mel's claim must rest on inferred intention.[8] Ted and Mel intended 'The Laurels' to be a home for them both, as it was agreed that Mel would stay at home and see to the repairs to make the house habitable. Moreover, they agreed about payment of the household bills, which shows that the parties arranged their finances together. In addition, they both intended that, when the repairs were completed, Mel would start work and her income would then help paying the household bills and perhaps the mortgage. It is suggested that this is enough for an intention to be inferred that Mel should have a beneficial interest. It is not clear whether detrimental reliance on the common intention leading to an estoppel is still required,[9] although, in the recent case of ***Curran v Collins*** [2015] EWCA Civ 404, CA, this was treated as an essential requirement. If so, then it is suggested that their agreement that Mel would stay at home and organise the repairs to make the house habitable would amount to detrimental reliance by Mel on an agreement that she should have a beneficial interest.

[9] The estoppel point is worth raising in these types of questions.

[10] A clear structure is essential in this complicated area, so do make it clear that this is now a question of assessing the extent of the beneficial interest and we have moved on from deciding whether one exists at all.

If she does have a beneficial interest, its extent is quantified[10] by the principles laid down in ***Stack v Dowden*** and ***Jones v Kernott***. In ***Stack***, Lady Hale held that the search is 'for the result which reflects what the parties must, in the light of their conduct, be taken to have intended' and she emphasised that it is not for the court to impose 'its own view of what is fair upon the situation'. However, in ***Jones v Kernott***, Lady Hale and Lord Walker, in a joint judgment, recognised that it may be impossible 'to divine a common intention'. In this case, they said that 'the court is driven to impute an intention to the parties which they may never have had'.

In ***Aspden v Elvy*** [2012] EWHC 1387 (Ch), the court based its assessment on the financial contributions made by each party to the property and here we could look at Mel's contribution by paying the household bills and undertaking the repairs to make the house habitable. We cannot, on this evidence, make an exact quantification and the court may use another standpoint, because, as Lady Hale said in ***Stack v Dowden***: 'context is everything'.[11]

[11] There is a trap here: trying to make an exact calculation of the extent of Mel's beneficial interest. We can only set out the principles and also point out that the starting point that we have chosen is only one possibility.

If 'The Laurels' is held in the joint names of Ted and Mel, of course the acquisition issue does not apply, as Mel already has acquired the legal title by virtue of her and Ted's holding it as joint tenants. However, there are still two issues: whether the parties intended to vary the beneficial ownership and, if so, what the shares should be. As with sole name ownership, the first issue must be decided by looking at the intentions of the parties, whether express or inferred (***Barnes* v *Philips*** [2015] EWCA Civ 1056, CA).

[12] Do make this clear, as students often get this wrong: your first stage is to ask what the transfer said. Only if this is silent do you consider what Lady Hale and others have said.

If they are registered as beneficial joint tenants, this will be conclusive and the beneficial interest will be shared jointly, 50:50 (***Goodman* v *Gallant*** [1986] Fam 106). If there is no declaration that they are beneficial joint tenants, the principles set out in ***Stack* v *Dowden*** and ***Jones* v *Kernott*** will apply.[12] In ***Stack* v *Dowden***, Lade Hale said that 'a conveyance into joint names indicates both legal and beneficial joint tenancies, unless and until the contrary is proved'. So we start from the presumption of shared beneficial interest. Lady Hale then said that 'Cases in which the joint legal owners were to be taken to have intended that their beneficial interests should be different from their legal interests would be very unusual.'

[13] This is an example of where close analysis of the facts really helps. It would be easy to say that, as Mel has been the claimant so far, she will in effect be so here but that is probably not so.

Thus, in ***Stack* v *Dowden*** itself, a 65:35 split was decided on. Here, the court will first decide whether the presumption of shared beneficial ownership is rebutted and then, if it is, what the shares should be. We note that Mel has not contributed to the cost of acquisition and so shared ownership would probably be in her favour. So Ted might try to rebut the presumption of shared beneficial interests by showing that a split in his favour was intended and that they should hold the property otherwise than as joint beneficial tenants.[13] It is very difficult, on the evidence, to come to a conclusion. However, if the court decides that there was an intention not to share the beneficial interest jointly, when considering quantification of their interests the court can if necessary impute an intention where one cannot be found or inferred. Here, an intention would have to be imputed, as there seems to be no evidence of an express or inferred intention. As with the sole name situation, the court might emphasise financial contributions and/or other factors.

✓ Make your answer stand out

- Remember to separate the issues very clearly: sole name and joint name; acquisition issue and assessment issue.
- Remember that, even where it is a joint names case, there are two separate issues.

▶

- Refer to the factors listed by Lady Hale in *Stack* v *Dowden* for deciding on the quantification of the beneficial interest.
- Refer to the judgments of Lords Kerr and Wilson in *Jones* v *Kernott*, whose reasoning differed from that of the majority.
- Read and refer to Gardner S. and Davidson K. (2011) 'The Future of Stack v Dowden'. 127 *Law Quarterly Review* 13. This is a very valuable and clear article and is also not too long! It was referred to with approval by Lady Hale and Lord Walker in their joint judgment in *Jones* v *Kernott*.
- Read and refer to Hayward (2015) on the recent case of *Barnes v Phillips*.

! Don't be tempted to . . .

- Although the factors listed by Lady Hale in *Stack* v *Dowden* are useful, if you do refer to them, do not list them mechanically.
- Fail to separate the issues clearly – this is absolutely essential in a question like this.
- Remember that in sole name cases, your approach will differ from that in joint name ones.
- Ignore the question of the quantification of the beneficial interests.

◤ Question 3

Critically evaluate the different directions that English law on beneficial interests in the family home might take in the future.

Answer plan

→ Evaluate possible developments along the lines of *Stack* v *Dowden*.

→ Consider, by contrast, a possible return to the resulting trust idea.

→ Evaluate the possibility of statute law taking over from the law of trusts: look at the proposals of the Law Commission (2007) Report, *Cohabitation: The Financial Consequences of Relationship Breakdown*, No. 307. http://lawcommission.justice.gov.uk/docs/lc307_Cohabitation.pdf.

→ Evaluate how other jurisdictions deal with this – Canada, Australia and New Zealand.

→ Summing up.

Diagram plan

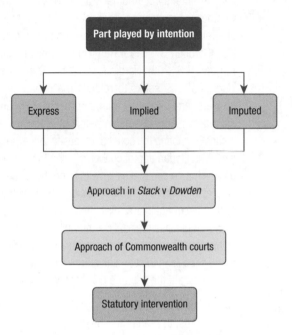

A printable version of this diagram plan is available from **www.pearsoned.co.uk/lawexpressqa**

Answer

[1] Although some may object
that we should, in this
question, be looking to the
future and not the past, it is,
of course, impossible to do
this without saying something
about the problems that the
law has had in this area. If
there had been no problems,
this question would probably
not have been asked!

There is no doubt that English law has found it extremely difficult to
find a satisfactory way of dealing with claims to a beneficial interest
in the home. The search began over 40 years ago[1] with the decisions
of the House of Lords in ***Pettit v Pettit*** [1970] AC 777, HL, and
Gissing v Gissing [1971] AC 886, HL, and then continued through a
restatement of the law, again by the House of Lords, in ***Lloyds Bank
Plc v Rosset*** [1991] 1 AC 107, HL, and then to the decision, also by
the House of Lords, in ***Stack v Dowden*** [2007] UKHL 17, followed
by that of the Supreme Court in ***Jones v Kernott*** [2011] UKSC 53.
Yet there is still debate.

The fault lines are really between those who would argue for an
approach based on the intentions of the parties, whether express

[2] A poor answer would at once take refuge in a recital of cases, but if you are aiming for a really good pass, you need to first sketch in the general background to the debate, and this paragraph seeks to do that. You then have a structure for your answer, as you can look at the cases through the prism of the two approaches set out here.

[3] Note that we have not set out the facts of *Stack* v *Dowden*, as they would not assist the argument. Instead, we have picked out what seems to be the *ratio* of Lady Hale's speech, but then, later in the same paragraph, pointed out that, elsewhere, she said something that seemed to indicate a different *ratio*. This analytical approach will gain you marks, so adopt it whenever you can.

[4] Do not just say that the law is unclear, but give evidence for this view, as here.

[5] This question is clearly asking you to look at what approach is used in other jurisdictions. Although it is only possible to give a snapshot, this answer has selected three jurisdictions and in each case selected a leading case and, most importantly, the principle of law that is applied.

or implied, and an approach based on wider considerations such as imputed intention.[2] Another way of looking at the debate is to ask whether the law should be founded in rewarding the consequences of a relationship or should be based on the intentions of the parties. (See Gardner, S. (1993) Rethinking Family Property. *Law Quarterly Review*, 109: 263). Harding, M. (2009) Defending *Stack* v *Dowden*. *Conv.* 73: 309 seeks to refocus the debate around the concepts of liberal and communitarian approaches. He argues that a liberal approach means upholding personal autonomy and in this context means promoting the concept of reasonable expectation. By contrast, a communitarian approach would mean that, as he puts it, 'the basis on which a person makes a claim to her home against her cohabiting partner is different from the basis on which such a person may make such a claim against a stranger'. Thus, a communitarian approach would emphasise precisely community. In terms of the law of trusts, an approach based on the intentions of the parties would indicate the use of a resulting trust and an approach based on wider considerations would indicate the use of a constructive trust.

The present approach, set out by Lady Hale in **Stack v Dowden**, is, in her words, to search 'for the result which reflects what the parties must, in the light of their conduct, be taken to have intended' and she emphasised that it is not for the court to impose 'its own view of what is fair upon the situation'.[3] This looks like an approach based on intention or, as Harding would put it, a liberal approach. However, it is not clear that this is so, as Lady Hale also said earlier: 'The search is to ascertain the parties' shared intentions, actual, inferred or imputed, with respect to the property in the light of their whole course of conduct in relation to it.' The use of the word 'imputed' seems to give power to the courts to impute an intention to the parties that they may not have had. This point was made by Lords Kerr and Wilson in the subsequent Supreme Court decision in **Jones v Kernott** and the result is that the present law in England is unclear.[4] Are we, in fact, moving towards a jurisdiction based on fairness, and is the talk of 'imputed intention' just a cover for this?

To decide where the law might go in future, we can turn to Canada,[5] where the leading case is **Pettkus v Becker** (1980) 117 DLR (3rd) 257 SC Can, where a farm had been bought out of the owner's savings but this was possible only because his partner had paid all their living expenses out of their joint earnings and had also contributed to the running of the farm. Dickson J, who delivered the majority judgment, held that 'The principle of unjust enrichment lies at the heart of the constructive trust.' In this context, he was referring to the remedial constructive trust based on a general power of the court to 'achieve a result consonant with good conscience' (**Rathwell v Rathwell** (1978) 83 DLR (3rd) 289 SC Can). A later case (**Peter v Beblow** (1993) 101 DLR (4th) 621 SC Can) shows the application of this principle to the provision of domestic services by the woman as 'housekeeper, homemaker and stepmother' and the court ordered that, as these services were an enrichment to the man, the home should be transferred into the woman's name.

In the Australian case of **Baumgartner v Baumgartner** (1987) 62 ALJR 29, Ans HC, an unmarried couple pooled incomes to meet their living expenses and the purchase of a house that was put in the man's name. They separated and the court held that the woman was entitled to a 45 per cent share, corresponding to the amount of pooled income that she had contributed. The *ratio* of the decision was unconscionability and the court referred to **Muchinski v Dodds** (1985) 160 CLR 583, Ans HC, where Deane J referred to the principle of joint endeavour: this means that where there is a joint endeavour that has failed and one party has contributed money or other property to the endeavour that it was not intended that the other should retain, equity will not permit him to do so. The New Zealand decision in **Gilles v Keogh** [1989] 2 NZLR 327, NZ CA, is based on the concept of meeting the reasonable expectations of the parties reinforced by evidence of direct or indirect contributions of either a monetary or a non-monetary kind.

[6] At this stage, you need to sum up the approaches of the courts in other jurisdictions and then relate this to the question.

In all these cases, there is a much wider approach than has been adopted by the courts in England, with the relationship of the parties as the starting point rather than a narrow search for what they intended. This is therefore one direction in which English law might develop.[6]

[7] The examiner is obviously expecting you to deal with statute law also, especially as some statutory regulation of this area still remains a possibility in England.

The other possibility is that statute law might eventually take over from case law.[7] There are precedents for this – for example, the De Facto Relationships Act, a New South Wales statute of 1984, provides that the basis of the jurisdiction of the courts is whether it would be just and equitable to make an order adjusting the interests of de facto partners in property.

Legislation did at one time, seem likely in England, following the Law Commission Report (2007) No. 307. This proposed a scheme whereby parties to a relationship could claim a share in property on the basis of economic advantage or disadvantage.

[8]The decision in *Stack* v *Dowden* has also made it less likely that there will be legislation, on the basis that if the courts are developing the law satisfactorily, why bother with legislation?

The effect would have been to widen the net for possible claimants but the Government announced that it was delaying any implementation of the scheme until it had assessed research findings on the effect of the Family Law (Scotland) Act 2006, which has similar provisions.[8]

What is clear is that none of these schemes, whether statutory or based on case law, uses the intention approach as a model. The conclusion must be that the law is likely to develop in a broadly based direction, with the relationship of the parties at its centre.

✓ Make your answer stand out

There have been many academic articles on this area. There is obviously not the time to include references to all of them in this answer but here are some suggestions for how to make your answer stand out:

■ Look at Gardner (1993). Although the law has moved on a great deal since then, this article does provide an excellent analysis of the law as at that date, and in particular of Commonwealth decisions.

■ See Rotherham, C. (2004) The Property Rights of Unmarried Co-habitees: A Case for Reform. *Conv.* 268. You could follow the article by Gardner with this one. It was written when the idea of statutory intervention in this area was much more likely than it is now.

■ Law Commission Report (2007) No. 307 must be looked at if you want to be prepared to attempt this type of question. The summary is a good place to start – but not to end!

■ Etherton, T. (2008) Constructive Trusts: A New Model for Equity and Unjust Enrichment. *CLJ,* 265 and Etherton, T. (2009) Constructive Trusts and Proprietary Estoppel: The Search for Clarity and Principle. *Conv.* 73: 104 are both essential for a good mark. These look at how these types of cases should be classified and at their relationship with resulting trusts, constructive trusts, proprietary estoppel and unjust enrichment.

■ Harding (2009) has some excellent material on Australian decisions, especially the important one of *Cummins* v *Cummins* (2006) CLR 278, which you could integrate into your answer.

! Don't be tempted to . . .

- Plunge into an account of the present law without setting the scene.
- Forget to mention the Law Commission Report (2007) No. 307.
- Omit discussion of the theoretical issues. Instead, you should try to integrate them into your answer.
- Forget to give the facts of some (but not all) of the cases you mention to show how the law works.

@ Try it yourself

Now take a look at the question below and attempt to answer it. You can check your response against the answer guidance available on the companion website (**www.pearsoned.co.uk/lawexpressqa**).

John and his partner, Meg, bought a house, 15 Barnes Avenue, and were registered as joint tenants in law and equity. John contributed £50,000 of the purchase price, Meg £200,000 and the remainder was by a mortgage secured by a legal charge on the property. The mortgage repayments were made from a joint account into which their salaries were paid. John earned around £25,000 a year and Meg £50,000. The following year, they had a child, Amy, but they both continued working.

The relationship between John and Meg has ended. They have agreed to sell the house and John argues that the beneficial interest should be split 50:50 between them. Meg, however, feels that she is entitled to a larger share.

Advise Meg on her chances of success in claiming this.

www.pearsoned.co.uk/lawexpressqa

Go online to access more revision support, including additional essay and problem questions with diagram plans, and you be the marker questions, and to download all diagrams from the book.

Licences
and estoppel

How this topic may come up in exams

There have been two very important House of Lords decisions on estoppel, so you should be prepared for either or both essay or problem questions on this. A problem question on estoppel will involve a discussion of the concept of detriment, as well as other points, and detriment can also appear as a topic on its own for an essay question.

Licences lend themselves to an essay on the extent to which licences are interests in land, and on the extent to which they can be enforced against third parties. Licences and estoppel can, of course, appear in the same question.

Before you begin

It's a good idea to consider the following key themes of licences and estoppel before tackling a question on this topic.

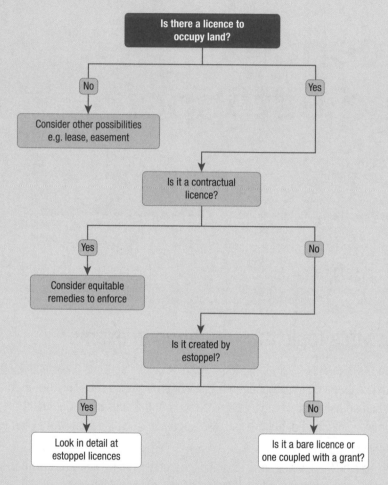

A printable version of this diagram is available from **www.pearsoned.co.uk/lawexpressqa**

? Question 1

John runs a car breaker's yard, and in 2009 he was given a licence by Steve to use part of Steve's land to store cars. The licence was in writing and was stated to run for 10 years at an annual fee of £1,000. John then erected a shed to store some of the cars. Steve saw the shed and said: 'That looks a nice building.'

In 2017, Steve decided that he needed the land as he was expanding his own business, and he told John that he would need to vacate the land in three months.

John wishes to remain and asks your advice.

Would your answer differ if Steve had sold the land to Roger in 2009 and it was Roger who wished to terminate the licence?

Answer plan

→ Identify the main features of licences and mention the possibility of a lease.

→ Outline the rules on termination of a licence and assess the equitable remedies to restrain a breach.

→ Is there the possibility of estoppel?

→ Explain why the licence does not bind Roger.

→ Conclusion.

Diagram plan

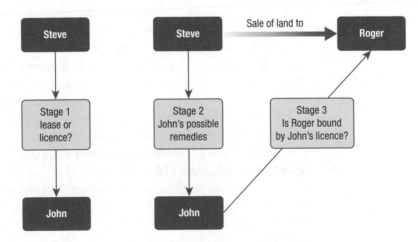

A printable version of this diagram plan is available from **www.pearsoned.co.uk/lawexpressqa**

Answer

Steve has granted John a licence but it is worth checking first whether it could amount to a lease.[1] However, John's licence only extends to part of the land and so John does not have exclusive possession. In **Street v Mountford** [1985] AC 809, HL, this was identified as one of the essential indications of a lease and so it is submitted that John has only a licence. This is important, as a licence confers only a personal right in the land and not, as in the case of a lease, a proprietary right. Exceptions are where the licence is coupled with a grant – for example, if John had been granted a profit, which does not apply here, or where a licence arises by estoppel,[2] which is a possibility here and which will be considered later. At the moment, we will proceed on the basis that John has a contractual licence, as his consideration is the payment of an annual fee of £1,000.[3]

In 2017, Steve told John to vacate the land in three months, although the licence is due to expire in 2019, having been granted in 2009 for 10 years. This is obviously in breach of the licence, but what remedies does John have? As a licence does not confer a proprietary interest, John has no interest in the land itself and so his remedies must be contractual. In **Wood v Leadbitter** (1845) 13 M & W 838, HC, it was held that, at common law, a licence can be revoked at any time even though this is in breach of the licence. Thus, Steve, on this basis, need not give John three months' notice. If Steve did actually eject John, John would have no right to claim for damages for assault as this was the claim that failed in **Wood v Leadbitter**. However, John would be able to claim damages for breach of contract (**Kerrison v Smith** [1897] 2 QB 445, HC). These would be assessed on the normal basis for contractual damages, as laid down in **Hadley v Baxendale** (1854) 9 Exch 341, Exch.[4] Moreover, he is entitled to reasonable packing up time[5] and so does not become a trespasser at once. (See Lord MacDermott in **Winter Garden Theatre (London) Ltd v Millennium Productions Ltd** [1948] AC 173, HL.) Thus, if Steve tries to eject John without giving him any time to remove his property and, possibly, make alternative arrangements for their storage, John will have a claim against him in tort, for, for example, assault if Steve tries to forcibly eject him.

However, John may be able to remain on the land until 2019 if he is able to utilise equitable remedies. The status of a contractual licensee

[1] A mention of the possibility of a lease shows the kind of intelligent lateral thinking that will earn you extra marks. It is best to mention it at the start, as it enables you to bring out the essential feature of a licence, which you need to mention for your answer, and contrast it with a lease.

[2] It is worth raising these two possibilities, if only briefly, as, if a licence fell into either of these categories, the answer would be different. As it is, point out now that estoppel could be relevant, but leave it till later.

[3] A small point: if you just say 'John has a contractual licence', the examiner will ask 'Why?'– a mark lost. So say why!

[4] Rather than speculate unprofitably on just what damages John might claim on the facts (we do not have enough information), gain marks by referring to another area of law – in this case, contract – which you have probably studied.

[5] This point is often missed by students, so a mention of it will certainly improve your marks!

has improved with the availability of equitable remedies in all courts following the Judicature Acts 1873–5. In ***Winter Garden Theatre (London) Ltd v Millennium Productions Ltd*** it was recognised that, at common law, there can be an implied term that a licence will not be revoked until the end of the specified period unless the licensee is in breach of the licence. Thus, if the licence is wrongfully revoked, the court can restrain this by the grant of an injunction.[6] This term was not implied in the ***Winter Gardens Theatre (London) Ltd v Millennium Productions Ltd*** case as there was an express term allowing termination on one month's notice, which the court regarded as reasonable. Here, there seems to be no express term allowing revocation on notice and so, as there is no evidence of breach by John, he can seek an injunction to restrain the termination of the licence by Steve until 2019. The court does have discretion as to whether to grant an injunction; it did not do so, for example, in ***Thompson v Park*** [1944] KB 408, HC,[7] where breach of a personal sharing arrangement was not restrained by injunction, but this is a commercial arrangement and there seems no reason why one would not be granted. Specific performance is also available (***Verrall v Great Yarmouth Council*** [1981] QB 202, HC) but this would be more appropriate where, for example, Steve had made the agreement to grant the licence but had not carried it out. There would also be the possibility of equitable damages in lieu of an injunction (Chancery Amendment Act 1858).

If Steve had sold the land to Roger, the law on termination of the licence is the same but there is the preliminary question of whether the licence binds Roger. As we mentioned above, contractual licences do not create a proprietary interest in land and so, in general, they are not binding on third parties. An example is ***King v David Allen & Sons Billposting Ltd*** [1916] 2 AC 54, HL, where a licence to place advertisements on the wall of a cinema did not bind a third party. In ***Errington v Errington*** [1952] 1 All ER 149, CA, it was held by Denning LJ that where, in that case, a person took land with notice of a contractual licence, he or she could be bound by it in equity. But the decision on that point[8] has been held to be wrong. John may have more success if he relies on authority, starting with ***Bannister v Bannister*** [1948] 2 All ER 133, CA and continued by ***Binions v Evans*** [1972] Ch 359, CA, that equity may impose a constructive trust if he can show that, on the sale of the land by Steve to Roger, there was a clear intention that Roger should give effect to John's licence[9]

---

[6] It is vital to link these two points: the courts cannot simply grant an injunction. There must be evidence, in this context, of an actual or threatened breach of contract. The development of the implied term supplies this.

[7] This point is often forgotten by students, especially if they are not studying equity. If you mention equitable remedies at any point, you will lose marks if you do not also mention that they are discretionary. The addition of a case here, which is relevant but in fact not well known, will boost your marks.

[8] Where there is more than one issue in a case, it is important to single out the one that applies to your answer and to deal only with that, as we have done here.

[9] There is no need to mention the reasoning of Denning MR in *Binions* v *Evans,* as this was disapproved by the Court of Appeal in *Ashburn.* Instead, a good student will mention the explanation of the decision in *Binions* v *Evans* by Fox LJ in *Ashburn,* as this represents the law.

[10] The facts of *Binions* v *Evans* are not needed – just this point.

(see Fox LJ in ***Ashburn Anstalt v Arnold*** [1988] 2 All ER 147, CA). It would help John if Roger paid a reduced price for the land, as happened in ***Binions v Evans***, precisely because part of it was occupied by John.[10] If equity does impose a constructive trust, John could argue that, if title to the land is registered, he has an overriding interest as he is an occupier who has an equitable interest in the land. If title is unregistered, he could argue that Roger is bound by his equitable interest, as he is a purchaser for value with notice.

[11] A quick reading of the question will show you that an estoppel claim is very unlikely to succeed, but the mention of the building of the shed by John is enough to show that you are expected to mention it.

[12] It would be tempting to refer to section 116 in more detail, but time is likely to be lacking! At least show that you are aware of the position concerning registered and unregistered land.

Finally, there is the question of whether John can claim that he has a licence by proprietary estoppel.[11] Estoppel requires persons claiming it to show that they acted on a representation by the other party to their detriment. Although John built a shed on the land and Steve saw it and approved of it, there is no evidence that he was in any way encouraged to build it by Steve, and so John did not act on any representation by Steve. It is submitted that estoppel does not apply. If it did, and if title is registered and John is in occupation, he could claim that Roger is bound by the estoppel under section 116 of the LRA 2002, as he has an overriding interest. If title is unregistered, John would claim that Roger is bound if he purchased with notice.[12]

Accordingly, John may claim damages for revocation of his licence by Steve and may be able to claim an injunction to prevent its revocation at all. Whether Roger is bound will depend on establishing the existence of a constructive trust.

✓ **Make your answer stand out**

- Discuss exclusive possession as a requirement for a valid lease.
- Clearly discuss the current law as stated in *Ashburn Anstalt* v *Arnold*.
- Discuss the need for a representation in estoppel in the light of *Thorner* v *Major* [2009] UKHL 18, HL.
- Include the possibility of future developments that might lead to an occupational contractual licence having the status of a proprietary interest.
- Read the judgment of Fox LJ in *Ashburn Anstalt* v *Arnold,* where you will see that he thought that the decision in *Errington* v *Errington* could be justified on three other possible grounds. There is no need at this stage to examine these but you will increase your marks if you show that you are at least aware of this.

> ! **Don't be tempted to . . .**
>
> ■ Confuse the right of the licensee to reasonable packing-up time with a right to reasonable notice of termination of the actual licence.
>
> ■ Discuss *Hurst* v *Picture Theatres Ltd* [1915] 1 KB 1, CA, which tried to use the idea of a licence coupled with a grant to extend the status of contractual licences. This is no longer good law.
>
> ■ Mix up common law remedies with equitable ones.
>
> ■ Divert your answer into a discussion of the facts and detailed reasoning in *Binions* v *Evans*.
>
> ■ Overlook the different rules that apply if title to the land is registered or unregistered and estoppel is claimed.
>
> ■ Miss out estoppel altogether or spend too long on it.

✒ Question 2

'Just how proprietary is the modern licence? There is no entirely clear or complete answer to this controversial question.' Gray, K. and Gray, S.F. (2005) *Elements of Land Law* (4th edn). Oxford: Oxford University Press.

With reference to decided cases, discuss the principles of law governing the extent to which a licence may be considered to be a proprietary interest in land.

Diagram plan

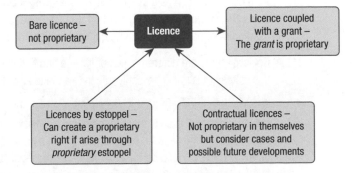

A printable version of this diagram plan is available from **www.pearsoned.co.uk/lawexpressqa**

Answer plan

→ Explain the traditional view that a licence is not an interest in land.

→ Contractual licences – can they be an interest in land?

→ Explore the cases where licences have been enforced through the mechanism of a constructive trust.

→ Explain how section 116 of the LRA 2002 affects estoppel licences.

→ Conclusion – can a licence ever be an interest in land?

Answer

[1] The effect of granting proprietary status would be that the right bound third parties. The main area where this is significant is contractual licences, where there is a right of occupation.

The fundamental point is that English law arrived at a list of proprietary interests in land many years ago and is reluctant to add to that list. This explains why licences are not regarded as proprietary despite many attempts to make them so. In this essay I will argue that this reluctance of English law should be overcome and that some types of licences should have the status of proprietary interests in land.[1] A proprietary interest in land has the capacity to bind a purchaser of the land, but, by contrast, a mere personal interest cannot do so. Thus, a right arising only by contract is personal. The argument is then that, in some circumstances, a licence should be capable of binding a purchaser.

The traditional view is that this is not so (***Thomas v Sorrell*** (1673) Vaugh 330, HC). In ***Street v Mountford*** [1985] 2 All ER 289, HL, Lord Templeman said 'A licence does not create an estate in the land to which it relates but only makes an act lawful which would otherwise be unlawful'. The effect is that a licence simply prevents the licensee from being regarded as a trespasser. Thus, in ***King v David Allen & Sons Billposting Ltd*** [1916] 2 AC 54, HL, a licence to place advertisements on the wall of a cinema did not bind a third party.

However, there are different types of licence and it is submitted that this statement is not necessarily true in relation to all of them.

It is true that bare licences cannot confer any proprietary interest in the land. A bare licence is merely a personal permission of the owner of land to enter the land to, for example, attend a party, and it would be extraordinary if it conferred any proprietary interest. On the other hand, a licence coupled with the grant of an interest in the land, such as a licence to enter on land to exercise a profit à prendre, certainly does have a proprietary character, but this arises because of its link

[2] It would be easy here to simply plough through the categories of licences and say in each case whether it amounted to a proprietary interest. This would be a waste of time that could be better spent on gaining marks in discussing the cases where there is the possibility of a licence amounting to a proprietary interest. So in this paragraph we have quickly disposed of two categories where the position needs little discussion.

[3] Do not leave the examiner guessing. Show that your answer is thought out by flagging up that you know what to write later on.

[4] Concentrate on the essential point that the licence bound a third party, i.e. the mother.

with a recognised proprietary right rather than because of its status as a licence. The question is really concerned with two other types of licence: a contractual licence and a licence arising by estoppel.[2]

A contractual licence arises where the right to enter land arises by contract. The rights of a contractual licensee have gradually increased as a result of the availability of equitable remedies since the Judicature Acts (1873–5). In *Wood v Leadbitter* (1845) 13 M & W 838, HC, it was held that, at common law, a contractual licence could be revoked at any time and the licensee had no remedy, but in *Verrall v Great Yarmouth Council* [1981] QB 202, HC, the equitable remedy of specific performance was granted to restrain the decision of the council to cancel the licence of a hall. Although this development does not mean that licences have a proprietary status, it does show how equity can intervene to improve the rights of a licensee, and we will return to this point later.[3]

At the same time, there have been attempts to argue that a contractual licence should have proprietary status. In *Errington v Errington* [1952] 1 All ER 149, CA, a daughter and son-in-law occupied a house under a contractual licence where the father promised that, if they paid off the mortgage on it, he would transfer it to them. After his death, the daughter continued to occupy the house and her licence was held binding on the mother who had inherited the house.[4] Denning LJ held that the couple had 'a contractual right, or at any rate, an equitable right, to occupy the house and remain as long as they paid the instalments'. Thus, he lifted contractual rights into equitable rights, which, of course, can create an interest in land. As title in the house was unregistered and the mother had notice of their equitable right, it followed that it bound her.

This decision was disapproved by the Court of Appeal in *Ashburn Anstalt v Arnold* [1988] 2 All ER 147 and in *Camden LBC v Shortlife Community Housing Ltd* (1992) 90 LGR 358, CA, Millett LJ considered the idea that a contractual licence could bind third parties as 'heretical'. Thus, it can be concluded that a contractual licence in itself does not confer a proprietary interest in the land.

In *Binions v Evans* [1972] Ch 359, CA, Denning MR tried the different argument that a contractual licence could be held subject to a constructive trust so as to create a proprietary interest and bind third parties. Here, Mrs Evans had been allowed to occupy a house under a contractual licence but it was then sold, although the buyers paid

[5] Try to bring out the distinction between Denning MR's reasoning that, in effect, the starting point is the need to enforce a contractual licence (unorthodox) and the general principle that a constructive trust may be imposed where there has been unconscionable conduct (orthodox). If you are clear on this, it will certainly add to your marks.

[6] Note that we always come back to the phrase 'proprietary interest' – this is the phrase in the question and so we must continually link our answer to it.

[7] Note that we have not said 'will' bind a purchaser, as this will depend on the operation of Schedule 3, Paragraph 2 to the LRA 2002. (See Chapter 2.) A small point, but one that an examiner will pick up on!

[8] This kind of point will certainly impress the examiner. You are showing that you have researched this area and also you are demonstrating the capacity to think laterally across the syllabus by mentioning another area.

[9] Do not forget to end with a reference to the words of the question.

a reduced price as they took subject to her licence. This payment of a lower price meant that Denning MR's decision was considered correct on the facts by Fox LJ in **Ashburn Anstalt v Arnold** on the general basis that equity can impose a constructive trust to prevent unconscionable conduct, but the use of a constructive trust to elevate a contractual licence to a proprietary interest has been disapproved.[5]

The one area where a licence can be said to create a proprietary interest[6] is where that licence arises through proprietary estoppel as in **Inwards v Baker** [1965] 1 All ER 446, CA. This has added significance where title to the land is registered. Section 116 of the LRA 2002 provides that, where the court determines that an estoppel has arisen, it takes effect from the moment it arises and so, if a person is in occupation under a licence, they may have an overriding interest that can[7] bind a purchaser. This confirms that, in this situation, estoppel licences can be regarded as having a proprietary nature. However, whether equity by estoppel exists is in the discretion of the court (see, e.g., **Jennings v Rice** [2002] EWCA Civ 159) and it is open to a court to hold that a licence cannot be enforced against a third party.

The conclusion must be that this is an unsatisfactory area of the law. There is the possibility that, in time, a contractual licence may evolve into a proprietary interest in the same way as restrictive covenants did with the decision in **Tulk v Moxhay** (1848) 1 H & Tw 105, HC.[8] We have already seen that the law has extended the rights of contractual licensees to the grant of equitable remedies to prevent the revocation of a licence in breach of contract. Could the law now go further and provide that where the licence gives rights of occupation it confers a proprietary interest in the land?

At the moment the quotation in the question is correct. There is no 'clear or complete answer' to the question of whether a licence creates a proprietary interest in land.[9]

✓ Make your answer stand out

■ Refer to academic discussion on the enforceability of licences and their status as proprietary interests. An excellent article is that by Dewar, J. (1986) Licences and Land Law: An Alternative View. *Modern Law Review*, 741.

- Discuss the significance of section 116 of the LRA 2002 in asserting the proprietary character of estoppel licences – see Law Commission (2001) Report, Land Registration for the 21st Century: A Conveyancing Revolution, No. 271. **http://lawcommission .justice.gov.uk/docs/lc271_land_registration_for_the_twenty-first_century.pdf** (Paras. 5.29–5.32) and also *Scott* v *Southern Pacific Mortgages Ltd* [2014] UKSC 52, SC.
- Consider statute law, which treats a contractual licence, especially one to occupy, on the same level as a lease, e.g. section 3(2A) and (2B) of the Protection from Eviction Act 1977.
- Emphasise the contribution of equity and the availability of equitable remedies in all courts in improving the position of licensees.
- Mention possible use of Article 8(1) of the ECHR (right to respect for the home) by a contractual licensee whose residential licence is terminated without notice.

! Don't be tempted to . . .

- Give a list of types of licence without discussion of the underlying issue.
- Start without explaining exactly what is meant by a 'proprietary interest'.
- Fail to distinguish between the extent to which types of licences can create a proprietary interest.
- Assume that the decisions in all the cases still represent the law. If you read the answer, you will see that they may not, e.g. *Errington* v *Errington*. Make this clear.
- Leave out a reference to the significance of section 116 of the LRA 2002.

? Question 3

Chris worked for over 45 years as a housekeeper/companion for Robert, who had a physical disability and needed considerable care and attention. They lived at 'Lilac Cottage', which Robert owned and which has registered title. Chris was paid a weekly wage but since 1990 this had never been increased and remained at £30 a week. Chris says that he paid the housekeeping expenses for both of them out of Robert's bank account, on which he was a signatory. They also went on holidays together, for which Robert paid. When they were on holiday, Robert often said to Chris: 'You are very good to me. When I am gone you will have a home of your own.' Chris says that he took this to mean that he would be left the house.

Robert has now died, and his will leaves all his property to his son, John. Chris says that, as far as he knows, John never had any contact with Robert. 'Lilac Cottage' is valued, at current prices, at £600,000.

Advise Chris on his chances of making a successful claim to 'Lilac Cottage', title to which is registered.

Answer plan

→ Explain the principle that there is no enforceable promise at common law and so we need to rely on estoppel.

→ Was there a representation?

→ Did Chris rely on it to his detriment? Would it be unconscionable for it to be withdrawn?

→ Possible award by the court.

→ Consider how Chris's rights could be protected.

Diagram plan

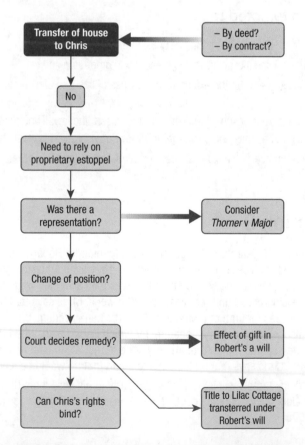

A printable version of this diagram plan is available from **www.pearsoned.co.uk/lawexpressqa**

Answer

[1] This kind of opening paragraph is essential. Never, in a problem question on estoppel, start with estoppel itself. Instead, explain that we need to use estoppel because one or more identified formalities have not been satisfied. Then, go on to estoppel. It is vital to identify that estoppel is an equitable principle, as we can then bring in the concept of unconscionability later and explain that the remedy is discretionary.

[2] You could, at this stage, list the elements of estoppel, but why? You will be mentioning them separately and analysing them as you go on, so avoid repetition when you could be bringing in new points and gaining extra marks.

[3] There is considerable analysis and discussion in this answer of the facts of the problem. This is essential in estoppel cases, as 'context is everything' – see *Thorner* v *Major*. However, you must tie your discussion into the basic principles.

[4] Use the word 'representation' and not, e.g. 'promise' in estoppel questions.

Under section 52(1) of the LPA 1925, a deed is required to convey a legal estate or interest in land and there is no evidence that Robert executed a deed during his lifetime conveying the house to Chris. Nor was there any contract, which in any event needs to satisfy the requirements of section 2 of the Law of Property (Miscellaneous Provisions) Act 1989. Therefore, in order to claim the house, Chris must rely on equity and, in this case, the doctrine of proprietary estoppel.[1]

The first element of an estoppel claim is to show that there was a representation, express or implied, by Robert to Chris that he would inherit the house.[2] Here, Robert often said to Chris: 'You are very good to me. When I am gone you will have a home of your own.' We are told that Chris took this to mean that Robert would leave him 'Lilac Cottage', but was it reasonable for Chris to think this?

The leading case is ***Thorner* v *Major*** [2009] UKHL 18, where D had worked at P's farm for no payment from 1976 onwards and, although no express representation had ever been made, D relied on various hints and remarks made by P over the years, which he claimed led him to believe that he was to inherit the farm. Also, in 1990, P had handed D a bonus notice relating to two policies on P's life, saying 'That's for my death duties'.

Lord Walker said in ***Thorner* v *Major*** that what is sufficient is 'hugely dependent on context' and here it was held that, as this was a family-type case and moreover between 'taciturn farming folk', the lack of an absolutely clear representation did not matter, as, in the context, it was clear that P intended D to have the farm. In this case, the context is[3] that Robert asked Chris to come and live with him as a housekeeper/companion and Chris now seems to have no home of his own. However, at that initial stage there was a kind of business arrangement and so no estoppel could arise. However, circumstances then changed and it seems that the relationship altered from the business arrangement when the weekly wage was never increased after 1990 and remained at £30 a week. Could it be argued that at that stage there was an implicit representation[4] by Robert that he would leave Chris his house and that this implicit representation only became explicit later when Robert said: 'You are very good to me. When I am gone you will have a home of your own.'?

[5] This is a classic example of exam technique. We cannot take this point further, so we simply assume that there is a sufficient representation so that we can go on and address the other issues. If we do not address them, we will lose marks.

[6] Note the two points: change of position, and also that it would be unconscionable for the representation to be withdrawn. Apply both to the question.

[7] It is vital to mention this – do not assume that if Chris wins on the estoppel issue, he will automatically receive what Robert represented to him that he would.

It is also significant that Robert said this when they were on holiday together: a holiday for which Robert paid. This could indicate that the relationship had become more than a business one by that time and that this gave rise to Robert's promise.

At this point, we must proceed on the basis that there was a sufficient representation for an estoppel.[5]

The next element of estoppel is for Chris to establish that he has changed his position in reliance on Robert's representation such that it would be unconscionable for Robert's promise of the house to be withdrawn.[6] There needs to be what Robert Walker LJ in *Gillett* v *Holt* [2001] Ch 210, CA called 'a sufficient casual link' between the representation and the change of position'

Any detrimental reliance would probably be after Robert made the representation by saying 'You are very good to me. When I am gone you will have a home of your own', unless there was an implicit representation before then. Chris continued to look after Robert at what was, by then, a very small weekly wage and he could argue that this amounted to detrimental reliance. The evidence that Chris paid the housekeeping expenses for both of them out of Robert's bank account, on which he was a signatory, and the fact that they went on holidays together is evidence that the relationship had changed, although this may not be detrimental reliance. We come back to Lord Walker's remarks in *Thorner* v *Major* about the importance of context and it is suggested that in the context of the changed nature of the relationship there was a representation by Robert that Chris certainly relied on to the extent of working at far lower wages then he would have received had this been a normal business arrangement.

If Chris succeeds in proving detrimental reliance, it is for the court to decide the remedy necessary to 'feed the estoppel'[7] and so Chris may not actually receive the house. In *Jennings* v *Rice* [2002] EWCA Civ 159, the owner of a house had represented to his gardener that he would be left his house, or possibly the entire estate, and the gardener had not been paid for his work after then. The house was valued at £435,000 and the whole estate at £1.3 million. An award of £200,000 was upheld, which was the cost of full-time nursing care.

[8] The law reports contain a continual flow of cases on estoppel. Be selective in the use you make of them as, in some cases, the matter is purely one of fact and not law. However, here we have a case that does contain a helpful explanation of a point and so a discussion of it will add to your marks.

In *Suggitt v Suggitt* [2012] EWCA Civ 1140, the Court of Appeal clarified the principle in *Jennings v Rice*.[8] It did not mean that there had to be a relationship of proportionality between the level of detriment and the relief awarded, but rather that if the expectations were extravagant or out of all proportion to the detriment suffered, the court should recognise that the claimant's equity should be satisfied in another, generally more limited way. Here, much will depend on the estimate made by the court of the difference between the wage actually received by Chris and what he would normally have expected, with a deduction for the value received by Chris of the housekeeping expenses paid by Robert together with the value of the holidays. The court will also need to assess when the detrimental reliance began, and in particular whether there was an earlier implicit representation. The court may hold that to expect a house valued at £600,000 would be out of proportion to the detriment suffered and award Chris only a monetary sum.

[9] Mention this point after the discussion on remedies, as if Chris was not awarded the house, this issue would not arise.

If Chris's claim to the house does succeed,[9] the leaving of the house by will to John will not affect Chris's claim (*Gillett v Holt*). Instead, John will take the house under the will but subject to the estoppel in favour of Chris.

[10] This is why you were told in the answer that title is registered! Mentioning this point will add to your marks, especially as it has recently been considered in another context by the Supreme Court.

[11] You can add to your marks by cross-referencing a land registration point.

Are Chris's rights protected under proprietary estoppel in the event of a sale by John?[10] Chris will have an equitable interest in it by virtue of estoppel and also under a trust if one is imposed. As he appears to be in actual occupation and title is registered, he may have an overriding interest under Schedule 3(2) to the Land Registration Act (LRA) 2002.[11] He might also claim that, under section 116 of the LRA 2002, his equity by estoppel can be protected by a notice on the register. In *Scott v Southern Pacific Mortgages Ltd* [2014] UKSC 52, the court held, in the context of land purchases, that the buyer had only a personal interest before completion of his purchase, which could not confer proprietary rights on the holder of the estoppel, and so section 116 did not apply. However, this may apply only in this particular context.

✓ Make your answer stand out

- Give an answer that combines a close analysis of the facts with an ability to relate those facts to the principles of proprietary estoppel.

- Check the possibility of a claim for unjust enrichment, as in *Cook* v *Thomas*.

- Look at the possibility of a remedial constructive trust, as suggested in *Thorner* v *Major*.

- Make reference to academic debate on what constitutes a representation in cases of estoppel. See, e.g. McFarlane, B. (2009) Apocalypse Averted: Proprietary Estoppel in the House of Lords. *Law Quarterly Review,* 125: 535.

! Don't be tempted to . . .

- Explain why we need to rely on estoppel at all.

- Spend too long on outlining the facts of cases and not enough on the principles.

- Mention estoppel cases in detail, which do not really relate to this question. *Inwards* v *Baker* [1965] 1 All ER 446, CA is a possible example – an excellent illustration of estoppel, but the facts do not help here.

- Fail to spot that we do not have enough information to decide whether there was a sufficient representation and come to too definite a conclusion on this point.

- Forget to mention the burden of proof.

📝 Question 4

'Proprietary estoppel should not become the penicillin of equity.' Dixon, M. (2009) Proprietary Estoppel: A Return to Principle. *Conv.* 260.

Do you agree?

Diagram plan

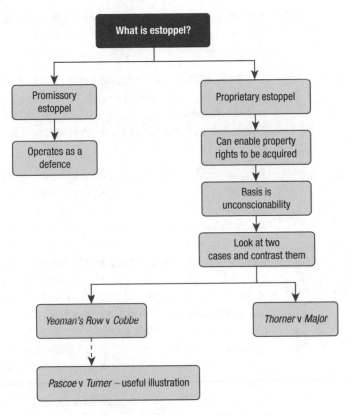

A printable version of this diagram plan is available from **www.pearsoned.co.uk/lawexpressqa**

Answer plan

→ Distinction between proprietary estoppel and promissory estoppel.

→ Estoppel based on unconscionability – Court of Appeal and House of Lords in *Yeoman's Row* v *Cobbe*.

→ Further example of unconscionability as the basis of estoppel: *Pascoe* v *Turner*.

→ Restriction on availability of proprietary estoppel to representations – comparison of Lord Scott's view in *Yeoman's Row* v *Cobbe* with the decision in *Thorner* v *Major*.

→ Proposed requirement that claimants must believe that they have been made an irrevocable promise.

Answer

The idea behind this quotation is that estoppel can be seen as a cure for many hardships that could result from a too-rigid application of principles of common law or statute law. Is this true?

This essay will argue that estoppel needs to steer a middle ground. It must not be so governed by its own principles that it is unable to undertake its main function nor so wide and general that it is impossible to see what that function is. In short, it should be penicillin but not a universal one.

There are distinct types of estoppel.[1] As *Hanbury & Martin: Modern Equity* (2015). London: Sweet & Maxwell. points out: 'Each has a separate origin and history' (p. 870). Promissory estoppel applies in contractual relationships and essentially operates as a defence to prevent a party from going back on a promise. Its best-known application was in ***Central London Property Trust v High Trees House Ltd*** [1947] KB 130, HC. This doctrine does not create a new cause of action; instead, it prevents a party going back on a representation, as in ***High Trees*** itself. Proprietary estoppel, by contrast, is a sword: it enables rights, especially property rights, to be acquired when none existed before. It involves a representation by one person (X) to another (Y), which X intends Y to rely on and where Y's actual reliance is reasonable in the circumstances. An objective test applies: thus, the question is whether a promise by X can reasonably be understood as a commitment by X to Y. If so, then X will be estopped from going back on the representation and asserting her strict legal rights.

Provided that the above elements are present, the basis of the doctrine can be seen as unconscionability: would it be unconscionable for X, when Y has relied on X's promise to his detriment, to then depart from that promise?[2]

This question was prompted by recent cases involving proprietary estoppel, not promissory estoppel, and so this essay will concentrate on this.[3]

The first issue is to ask whether proprietary estoppel should be available where conduct has been unconscionable, even though the essential elements of it are not present.

[1] Promissory estoppel and proprietary estoppel are so different that a definition covering them both would be too wide to be of use, especially in an essay like this. Better to say at once that there are two types, which then leads you on to discuss proprietary estoppel in detail – which is what this question is about.

[2] Your discussion of the issue raised in the question will be much clearer if you have started by stating what the essential elements of estoppel are.

[3] However, as we will see later, the mention of promissory estoppel is not wasted even though the question is primarily about proprietary estoppel.

In *Yeoman's Row Management Ltd v Cobbe* [2008] UKHL 55, an oral agreement between the company and Cobbe provided that a block of flats owned by the company would be demolished and Cobbe would apply for planning permission to erect houses in their place, with any excess of the proceeds over £24 million shared equally with the company. After planning permission had been obtained, the company went back on the oral agreement and demanded more money, as it now realised that the land was worth much more. Cobbe claimed that the company was estopped from going back on the agreement.

Lord Scott asked: what is the fact that the company is estopped from asserting? There was no question that the oral agreement was unenforceable and Cobbe did not claim a specific property right – merely a hope of entering a contract. He held that the Court of Appeal, which held in Cobbe's favour, had been influenced too much by the fact that it regarded the behaviour of the company as unconscionable, and in effect as penicillin, without requiring the essential elements of proprietary estoppel to be present. It is submitted that another case where estoppel acted too much as a general penicillin is *Pascoe v Turner* [1979] 1 WLR 431, CA.[4] The claimant and defendant had lived in the claimant's house. The defendant told the claimant that the house was hers and everything in it. In reliance on this, the claimant, to the defendant's knowledge, spent money on the house. She was given notice to quit by the claimant, but the court ordered the house to be conveyed to her although it was clear that her acts of reliance were only on the basis that she had a licence to live there for life.

[4] This case is outside the current debate but adds another angle to it. Mention of it ought to add to your marks.

However, although the courts should require that a proprietary estoppel claim satisfies the criteria set out above, there is also a danger of the courts going too far the other way and setting out criteria which would mean that proprietary estoppel would no longer apply to promises of future intentions such as promises to leave by will.[5]

[5] This is a crucial paragraph that links the first part of the answer to the second. You are showing that you are actually engaging with the question and writing a balanced answer that looks at two points of view – the type of paragraph that really adds to your marks!

In *Yeoman's Row Management Ltd v Cobbe*, Lord Scott considered that proprietary estoppel should be restricted to representations of specific facts or mixed law and fact by X, which stood in the way of a right claimed by Y.[6] This seemed to mean that proprietary estoppel was no different to promissory estoppel: it only applied as a defence to an action where those specific representations had been gone back on, and not to enable an independent right to be asserted. In cases of promises to leave by will, Lord Scott would use the remedial constructive trust.

[6] This is an essential point: the view of Lord Scott needs to be carefully stated.

[7] This is important: if Lord Scott's analysis was adopted then it would mean that not only promises to leave on death would be outside the scope of estoppel but others too. *Dillwyn* v *Llewelyn* is a good case to mention, as it has always been regarded as a classic estoppel case and it would seem startling if this type of case were no longer to be decided under estoppel.

The problem is that proprietary estoppel has always applied to representations of what will happen and not just to specific present facts as where there is a representation to someone that they will acquire property on the death of the representor, as in ***Gillett v Holt*** [2001] Ch 210, CA, and in cases such as ***Dillwyn v Llewelyn*** (1862)[7] 4 De GF & J 517, HC, where a father's encouragement to his son to build a house on the father's land meant that, on the father's death, the land built on was ordered to be conveyed to the son.

However, in ***Thorner v Major*** [2009] UKHL18, the majority did not accept that estoppel should be confined to representations of present fact. D had worked at P's farm for no payment from 1976 onwards, and, by the 1980s, hoped that he might inherit the farm.

No express representation had ever been made, but D relied on various hints and remarks made by P over the years. The House of Lords held that these amounted to an estoppel.

[8] This rounds off the answer, as it mentions a slightly different point from that made by Lord Scott. It shows that you have really looked at what the judges actually said in these cases, and will add to your marks.

Furthermore, the idea of Lord Walker in ***Yeoman's Row Management Ltd v Cobbe*** that the claimant must believe that they have been made an irrevocable promise was not accepted.[8] This would inevitably have meant that promises to leave by will would not be covered by promissory estoppel, as a will can be revoked. However, in ***Thorner v Major*** it was held that the question is whether a party has reasonably relied on an assurance by the other as to that person's conduct.

In conclusion, estoppel should be a penicillin that applies in as wide a variety of situations as possible, but that applies only if certain criteria are met.

✓ Make your answer stand out

- Discuss the remedial constructive trust.
- Make clear the extent to which promissory estoppel has moved on from the *Central London Property Trust* v *High Trees House* decision.
- Further point made by Lord Scott — the need for certainty of subject matter as to the subject of the representation.

- Academic literature – in addition to the article mentioned in the question, look at Sloan, B. (2009) Estop Me If You Think You've Heard It. *CLJ,* 68(3): 518, which is a concise summary.
- Cases following *Thorner* v *Major,* e.g. *Cook* v *Thomas* [2010] EWCA Civ 227, can be mentioned to show how the principle in *Thorner* v *Major* has been applied.

! Don't be tempted to . . .

- Just describe estoppel.
- Go into the question without distinguishing between proprietary and promissory estoppel.
- Just reel off cases on estoppel without looking at the underlying issues.
- Miss the point that there are two distinct issues raised by the discussion of *Yeoman's Row* v *Cobbe* and *Thorner* v *Major.*

Question 5

'At a high level of generality, there is much common ground between the doctrines of proprietary estoppel and the constructive trust.' (Robert Walker LJ in *Yaxley* v *Gotts and Another* [2000] Ch 162, CA).

Evaluate this statement especially in the light of recent case law on the relationship between constructive trusts and proprietary estoppel.

Answer plan

→ Explore what the quotation means and identify exactly what types of constructive trust are relevant to this discussion.

→ Look at the development of the common intention constructive trust and show how, although at one time it seemed to converge with proprietary estoppel, this is no longer so.

→ Explain the difference between the two concepts in the areas of remedies and the implications of the fact that a constructive trust is a substantive institution but proprietary estoppel is not.

→ Mention the similarity between the remedial constructive trust and proprietary estoppel.

→ Consider the problems caused by constructive trusts being specifically exempt from formal requirements in contracts for the sale of land, but those arising from proprietary estoppel are not.

→ End by a brief summing up with reference to the quotation in the question.

Diagram plan

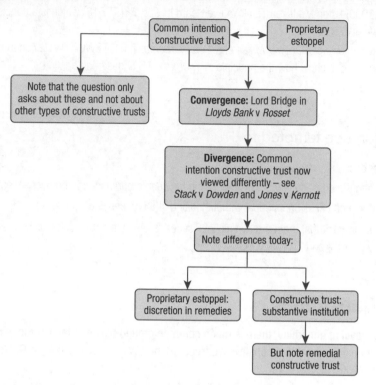

A printable version of this diagram plan is available from **www.pearsoned.co.uk/lawexpressqa**

Answer

In this quotation, Robert Walker LJ went on to say that both proprietary estoppel and constructive trusts are 'concerned with equity's intervention to provide relief against unconscionable conduct, whether as between neighbouring landowners, or vendor and purchaser, or relatives who make informal arrangements for sharing a home, or a fiduciary and the beneficiary or client to whom he owes a fiduciary obligation'.

[1] It is vital to clear the ground here and make it clear what type of trust Robert Walker LJ was referring to. Also, as this is a Land Law exam, you are clearly not expected to deal with areas, such as fiduciaries, that belong to equity.

This seems very wide, but in fact he was concerned with apparent similarities between proprietary estopppel and the common intention constructive trust[1] and he recognised this by saying that 'there are large areas where the two concepts do not overlap', giving one example of where a fiduciary derives an improper advantage from his client. Here, we are clearly in the realm of constructive trusts and not proprietary estoppel.

[2] In order to achieve a high mark, you need to sketch the development of the law.

At one time, there seemed to be a similarity between the common intention constructive trust and proprietary estoppel.[2] In **Lloyds Bank v Rosset** [1991] AC 107, HL, Lord Bridge referred to the need to find some 'agreement, arrangement or understanding reached between them (i.e. the parties) that the property is to be shared beneficially'. Once this was established, he said that the party must: 'show that he or she has acted to his or her detriment or significantly altered his or her position in reliance on the agreement in order to give rise to a constructive trust or a proprietary estoppel'. Thus, not only did Lord Bridge appear to merge the two concepts at the end of his speech, but this requirement of detrimental reliance on an agreement looks very much like the requirement in proprietary estoppel of detrimental reliance on a representation.

[3] This is really adding depth to your answer and you are showing that you have researched the development of this area of law.

If, however, there was a convergence between the two doctrines at one time, in more recent years they have grown apart,[3] as Lord Walker, as he then became, recognised in **Stack v Dowden** [2007] UKHL 17. He said that: 'Proprietary estoppel typically consists of asserting an equitable claim against the conscience of the "true" owner . . . It is to be satisfied by the minimum award necessary to do justice . . . which may sometimes lead to no more than a monetary award. A "common intention" constructive trust, by contrast, is identifying the true beneficial owner or owners, and the size of their beneficial interests.'

[4] Focus on this one word: 'imputed'. This gives you the key to the change in the law.

One reason is that the nature of the common intention constructive trust has changed from Lord Bridge's emphasis in **Lloyds Bank v Rosset** on the need to find the intentions of the parties as evidenced by some sort of agreement to the idea of 'imputing' an intention to the parties,[4] as seen in **Stack v Dowden** and **Jones v Kernott** [2011] UKSC 53, and indeed going further, because as Lord Wilson said: 'Where equity is driven to impute the common intention, how can it do so other than by a search for the result which the court itself considers fair?' By contrast, proprietary estoppel involves a representation by one person (X) to another (Y), which X intends Y to rely on and where Y's actual reliance is reasonable in the circumstances.

[5] This type of sentence is really excellent for earning you those extra marks; it shows how the argument is now moving on, as it needs to, and it gives your view of this topic.

[6] This is one type of case where we do need to give the facts to show what the court awarded.

[7] This is a vital point and must be mentioned.

[8] You do not need to go into details of the remedial constructive trust, but you must mention it to make this answer complete.

In fact, there are other fundamental differences between these concepts and it is suggested that it is desirable that they have now moved apart again, as any convergence would blur these differences.[5]

In a successful claim based on proprietary estoppel, the court has a discretion as to what remedy to award in order to 'feed the estoppel', and as Lord Walker said above in **Stack v Dowden**, is 'satisfied by the minimum award necessary to do justice'. This may lead to the promisee receiving less than he had expected. In **Jennings v Rice** [2002] EWCA Civ 159,[6] a gardener (X) who claimed that he had worked for nothing on the strength of a promise that he would be left his employer's (Y's) house, claimed either Y's whole estate (value: £1,285,000) or the value of the house (£435,000). He was awarded £200,000, as a larger sum would have been out of all proportion to what X might have charged for his services. By contrast, where there is a common intention constructive trust, which is typically based on contributions made to the acquisitions made to the family home, although there is some discretion as to how these contributions are to be measured, especially when they are not exclusively financial (see **Stack v Dowden** and **Jones v Kernott**), when they have been assessed the court has no discretion but to award the party whatever beneficial interest in the property is proportionate to those contributions.

Another fundamental distinction is that an institutional constructive trust as a substantive institution pre-dates any court order and the court simply declares that there is a trust in existence. By contrast, a proprietary estoppel exists from the date of the court order.[7] Moreover, although generalisations are dangerous, a constructive trust, and indeed all trusts, is fundamentally different in nature from proprietary estoppel in that the idea behind a trust is that titles (legal and equitable) are split, but in proprietary estoppel, as Matthews, P. (2009) The Words Which Are Not There: A Partial History of the Constructive Trust in C. Mitchell (ed.), *Constructive and Resulting Trusts*. Oxford: Hart Publishing points out, either the representee is left with the interest that he thought he had (i.e. a life interest in the bungalow in **Inwards v Baker** [1965] 1 All ER 446, CA) or the representor is prevented from asserting the interest that he thought he had.

There is less of a distinction between proprietary estoppel and the remedial constructive trust,[8] as this, like proprietary estoppel, comes into existence from the date of the court order. However, there remains some doubt as to whether the remedial constructive trust exists as such in English law, as it was rejected in *Halifax Building Society* v *Thomas* [1996] Ch 217, CA and *Re Polly Peck International Plc (No. 2)* [1998] 3 All ER 812, CA, although Lord Scott in *Thorner* v *Major* [2009] UKHL 18 did recognise the possibility of its use.

[9] This is an interesting final point that an examiner may not have been expecting, but which is relevant and will bring you those extra marks. However, do not let it take over this essay!

Problems have arisen where an agreement does not comply with section 2(1) of the Law of Property (Miscellaneous Provisions) Act 1989,[9] which provides that contracts for the sale or other disposition of an interest in land made on or after 27 September 1989 must be in writing, contain all the agreed terms agreed by the parties, and be signed by them all, although, by section 2(5), this does not apply to resulting, implied or constructive trusts. Thus, where the agreement does not satisfy the above provisions, it may be rescued by holding that the facts amount to a constructive trust even though, on the facts, it looks like estoppel. This is what happened in *Yaxley* v *Gotts and Another* itself. Similarly, in *Herbert* v *Doyle* [2010] EWCA Civ 1095 what looked like an estoppel case was forced into the constructive trust model to enable it to be upheld when it was not in writing.

[10] If you mention *Herbert* v *Doyle* then you must mention this case too.

However, this artificiality was ended by *Whittaker* v *Kinnear* [2011] EWHC 1479 (QB)10,[10] which held that proprietary estoppel in a case involving the sale of land *had* survived the enactment of section 2 of the Law of Property (Miscellaneous Provisions) Act 1989.

In conclusion, although the concepts of proprietary estoppel and the common intention constructive trust may at one time have seemed about to coincide, this is no longer so.

✓ Make your answer stand out

- Develop the point that rights arising under a constructive trust have retrospective effect, but that those under proprietary estoppel do not, and consider the effect of section 116 of the LRA 2002.
- There is a wealth of academic discussion on this area; look, in particular, at Matthews (2009) and at Bright, S. and McFarlane, B. (2005) Proprietary Estoppel and Property Rights. *CLJ,* 64(2): 449, and use the ideas here.
- Explore the idea that, at a deeper level, the two concepts do converge, as both are designed to relieve against unconscionable conduct.
- Question the decision in *Whittaker* v *Kinnear*.

! Don't be tempted to . . .

■ Just summarise proprietary estoppel and constructive trusts.

■ Overload your answer with cases – this is an answer about fundamental concepts.

■ Fail to distinguish between institutional and remedial constructive trusts.

■ Spend too much time on one area – this is a topic where you need to move reasonably quickly through the different points.

■ Ignore what the judges actually said in the cases.

■ Fail to mention any academic articles.

@ Try it yourself

Now take a look at the question below and attempt to answer it. You can check your response against the answer guidance available on the companion website (**www.pearsoned.co.uk/lawexpressqa**).

Critically consider the attempts in *Errington* v *Errington* [1952] 1 All ER 149 and *Binions* v *Evans* [1972] Ch 359, CA, to argue that a contractual licence should in some circumstances constitute a proprietary interest in land, and assess whether they still represent the law to any extent.

www.pearsoned.co.uk/lawexpressqa

Go online to access more revision support, including additional essay and problem questions with diagram plans, and you be the marker questions, and to download all diagrams from the book.

Leases

How this topic may come up in exams

You will need to check your syllabus to see the extent to which the detail of the law on leases is examined. Problem questions are likely, which can be challenging but, equally, give a lot of scope to earn extra marks.

An essay or problem question may ask you about the distinction between a lease and a licence (see also Chapter 5) and there is an old standard essay question on the distinction between legal and equitable leases. Another area for a problem question is the creation of legal and equitable leases: this may be linked to other areas and requires knowledge of material in Chapter 2.

■ Before you begin

It's a good idea to consider the following key themes of leases before tackling a question on this topic.

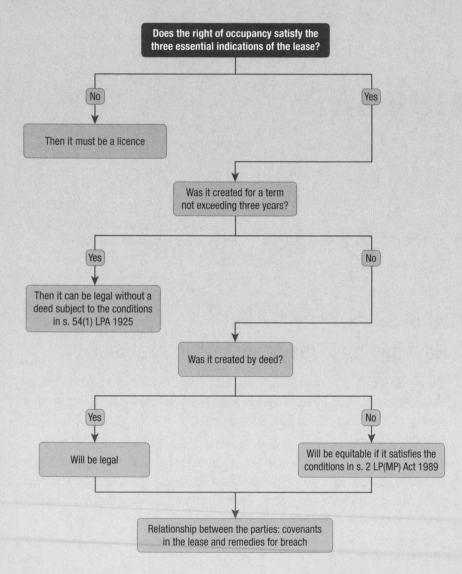

Does the right of occupancy satisfy the three essential indications of the lease?

No → Then it must be a licence

Yes → Was it created for a term not exceeding three years?

Yes → Then it can be legal without a deed subject to the conditions in s. 54(1) LPA 1925

No → Was it created by deed?

Yes → Will be legal

No → Will be equitable if it satisfies the conditions in s. 2 LP(MP) Act 1989

→ Relationship between the parties: covenants in the lease and remedies for breach

A printable version of this diagram is available from **www.pearsoned.co.uk/lawexpressqa**

❓ Question 1

Earlier this year, Bert purchased 1 High Street Downstairs from Vera. The freehold title to the property is registered at HM Land Registry. The property is divided into a flat and living accommodation for the owner upstairs.

When Bert purchased the property, the flat was already occupied by Joan under a document signed by Joan and Vera, headed 'Residential Property Occupation Licence'. This allows her to occupy the flat for four years for a payment of £250 a month. The agreement includes clauses declaring that it is not intended to create a lease and provides that Joan can be required to leave the flat and move to other premises provided by the landlord at any time.

The agreement also provides that the landlord agrees to do all of Joan's laundry and retains a key, so that he/she can enter the flat to collect and return the laundry. At the date of the sale of the freehold to Bert, Joan was away visiting her daughter in Germany.

Bert wishes to evict Joan so that he can turn the flat into an office. Ignoring any question of security of tenure, advise Bert as to whether the agreement with Joan is binding on him and whether he is entitled to take steps to evict Joan.

Answer plan

→ Explain the distinction between a lease and a licence.

→ Analyse the question of whether a licence can bind third parties in relation to this question.

→ Identify and explain the three criteria for indicating the existence of a lease.

→ Apply the facts of the problem to these criteria.

→ Consider the position if it should be a lease. Is it legal by deed, equitable or a legal periodic tenancy, and how does this affect the question of whether the lease binds third parties?

Diagram plan

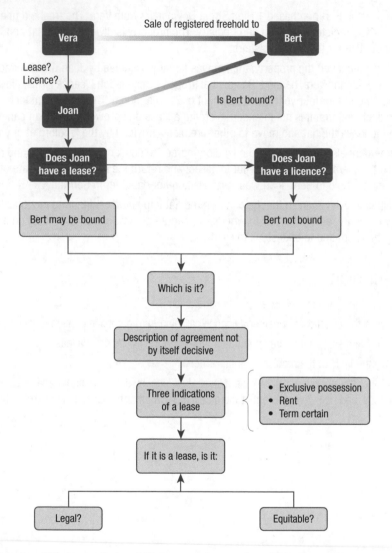

A printable version of this diagram plan is available from **www.pearsoned.co.uk/lawexpressqa**

Answer

[1] Note the wording: we have not decided, assuming that it is a lease, whether it actually does bind a third party. We must just say at this point that it is capable of doing so.

[2] There is an earlier authority (*Thomas* v *Sorrell* (1673) Vaugh 330), but especially as this is a problem question, we need only one.

[3] The average student would simply say that a licence does not bind third parties, but the good student would mention the one possible type of case where a licence might do so.

[4] This point is often missed by students, so a mention of it will certainly improve your marks!

[5] A vital word: these are not absolute rules and, in particular, if there is no requirement to pay rent this will not necessarily mean that there is no lease.

The question is whether Joan holds a lease or a licence. If she holds a lease, she has a proprietary right in the land which is capable[1] of binding a third party such as Bert. A licence does not, in general, create a proprietary right. In ***Street* v *Mountford*** [1985] 2 All ER 289, HL,[2] Lord Templeman said: 'A licence does not create an estate in the land to which it relates but only makes an act lawful which would otherwise be unlawful.' In ***King* v *David Allen & Sons Billposting Ltd*** [1916] 2 AC 54, HL, a licence to place advertisements on the wall of a cinema did not bind a third party. So, unless Joan can show that her licence arose through proprietary estoppel,[3] it would not bind Bert. All that she could argue is that she is entitled to reasonable packing-up time[4] and so does not become a trespasser at once. (See Lord MacDermott in ***Winter Garden Theatre (London) Ltd* v *Millennium Productions Ltd*** [1948] AC 173, HL.) Thus, if Bert tries to eject Joan without giving her any time to remove her property and, possibly, make alternative arrangements for their storage, Joan will have a claim against Bert in tort, for example, for assault if Bert tries to forcibly eject her.

The document is called a 'Residential Property Occupation Licence', but the use of the word 'licence' is not decisive. However, this does not mean that the description given by the parties to the agreement should be ignored. In ***Antoniades* v *Villiers*** [1990] 1 AC 417, CA, Bingham LJ said:

> A cat does not become a dog because the parties have agreed to call it a dog. But in deciding if it is a cat or a dog the parties' agreement that it is a dog may not be entirely irrelevant.

So, if other evidence points to a licence, the word 'licence' in the agreement could be taken into consideration.

The three indications[5] of a lease were stated by Lord Templeman in ***Street* v *Mountford*** as an intention to grant exclusive possession, for a fixed term, in consideration of periodical payments (rent). In ***Bruton* v *London and Quadrant Housing Trust Ltd*** [2000] 1 AC 406, HL, Lord Hoffmann indicated that the first two are essential, but referred to 'usually' the payment of rent. In this case, there are periodical payments of £250 a month. Although the agreement is for

LEASES

a fixed term of four years, Joan can be required to leave the flat and move to other premises provided by the landlord, and this appears to mean that it is not for a certain term and so cannot be a lease. We cannot be sure.

This leaves the question of exclusive possession.

It always adds to marks if you can mention, if only briefly as here, any underlying principle behind a point of law.

The rationale[6] of requiring exclusive possession for a lease is that, without it, the tenant would not be able to use the premises for the purposes of the letting (*Odey v Barber* [2008] Ch 175, Ch D). The agreement provides that the landlord can require her to move to other premises at any time. The question is, in the words of Oliver LJ in *AG Securities v Vaughan* [1990] 1 AC 417, HL, is this 'a sham . . . designed to conceal the true nature of the transaction'? On the evidence, it is impossible to say.

Although the landlord retains a key, this does not prevent there being a lease (*Aslan v Murphy* [1990] 1 WLR 766, CA). In that case, Donaldson MR emphasised that one must look at why the landlord retains a set of keys. In this case, it is to allow Vera to collect and return Joan's laundry and, once again, we must ask whether this actually happened. If not, it may be just a sham. We cannot say whether Joan has a licence or a lease.[7]

[7] Do not be afraid to say that you do not have enough information to come to a definite conclusion. You then gain marks by exploring both possibilities.

If Joan does not have a lease and only a licence, then, as stated above, it will not bind Bert; but if it is a lease, it is capable[8] of doing so. This depends on whether the lease is legal or equitable. As the lease is for four years, it must be created by deed in order to be legal (s. 52(1) of the LPA 1925), as the exception in section 54 of the LPA 1925, allowing the creation of legal leases without a deed, applies only to leases for a term not exceeding three years. The question uses the word 'document' and not 'deed' and, by section 2 of the Law of Property (Miscellaneous Provisions) Act 1989, the document must describe itself as a deed. If it is not in a deed, it may be an equitable lease under the principle in *Walsh v Lonsdale* (1882) 21 Ch D 9, HC. Section 2 of the Law of Property (Miscellaneous Provisions) Act 1989 provides that any contract for the sale or disposition of an interest in land, which includes an equitable lease, must be in writing, signed by the parties and contain all the terms. Although we know that the agreement is in writing and that it was signed by both parties, we do not know whether it contains all the terms[9] and so we cannot be certain whether it is a valid equitable lease. If it is, it will

[8] The word 'capable' is important, as you will lose marks if you say at this point that the lease will bind Bert. This is the point that we have to investigate.

[9] There will not be time in an exam to set out all the terms of the agreement and so remember that you will not be able to come to a definite conclusion.

118

[10] A good point for extra marks: you show the examiner that you know the distinction between a first and a subsequent registration.

[11] You should always watch for this in this type of question. First, ask whether the lease could be validly created by deed and so legal, then whether it could be a valid equitable lease, and, if you cannot come to a definite conclusion on this, ask whether it could be a valid periodic tenancy. If, however, rent has not actually been paid at regular periodic intervals, it cannot be a periodic tenancy.

[12] Do remember that it is three years here. Students often forget.

bind Bert if it is registered as an estate contract. If not, as Joan is in actual occupation at the time of the sale to Bert, she may have an overriding interest under Schedule 3, Paragraph 2 to the LRA 2002, which applies as this is a subsequent registration.[10] The fact that, at the time of the sale, Joan was away in Germany does not deprive her of her overriding interest, as temporary absence does not deprive one of occupation (*Chhokar v Chhokar* [1984] FLR 313, HC). However, under Schedule 3, Paragraph 2 to the LRA 2002, an occupier may lose an overriding interest if their occupation was not obvious on a reasonably careful inspection of the land at the time of the disposition to them or if they did not disclose their interest when it would have been reasonable to do so. If either of these applies, Bert will not be bound by Joan's interest.

Even if Joan does not have a valid equitable lease, she may have a legal periodical tenancy based[11] not on her agreement but on the regular payment of rent. As she pays rent monthly, she can have a periodic monthly tenancy which – as it is for a term not exceeding three years[12] – does not require writing. Moreover, as it is a legal lease for less than seven years, under Schedule 3, Paragraph 1 to the LRA 2002, it counts as an overriding interest by which Bert is bound.

✓ Make your answer stand out

- Refer to the speech of Lord Hoffmann in *Bruton* v *London and Quadrant Housing Trust Ltd* on what he suggested was a distinction between a lease as a contractual relationship and the notion of a lease conferring a proprietary interest in land.

- Read Bright, S. (2000) Leases, Exclusive Possession and Estates. *Law Quarterly Review*, 116: 7 on this issue.

- Mention the previous view on the relevance of the intentions of the parties in *Marchant* v *Charters* [1977] 1 WLR 1181, CA.

- Discuss the position if there is only a licence in some detail: students often rush to the conclusion that there is a lease.

- Read and refer to Wallace, H. (1990) The Legacy of *Street* v *Mountford*. *Northern Ireland Legal Quarterly*, 41: 143, who argues against an undue emphasis on exclusive possession in deciding whether there is a lease.

> **!** **Don't be tempted to . . .**
>
> - Just say that because the agreement says that it is a licence, it is a licence.
> - Come to a definite conclusion that the agreement is a lease or a licence.
> - Leave out any discussion of Joan's position if it turns out that she has only a licence.
> - Say that there is an equitable lease – we cannot know this.
> - Leave out discussion of overriding interests.

Question 2

'On balance, therefore, while it would be a mistake to regard *Bruton* as authority for the destruction of one of the most fundamental distinctions in property law – that is, the distinction between proprietary leases and personal licences – its use to create a "contract of tenancy" between the parties where they have some of the attributes of landlord and tenant cannot be discounted.' (Dixon, 2014a, p. 227)

Critically examine this statement.

Answer plan

→ Explain what the question is about: the nature of a lease.

→ Explain the facts of *Bruton* v *London and Quadrant Housing Trust* in relation to this issue.

→ Analyse the views of the Court of Appeal in *Bruton* v *London and Quadrant Housing Trust*.

→ Analyse the views of the House of Lords in *Bruton* v *London and Quadrant Housing Trust*, especially those of Lord Hoffmann.

→ Explore the practical consequences of the recognition of a new species of 'contractual tenancy' by looking at subsequent cases.

Diagram plan

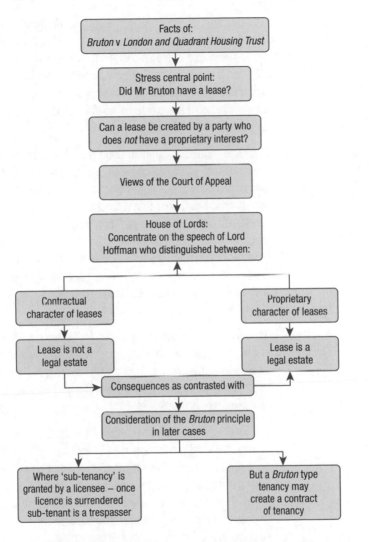

Facts of:
Bruton v London and Quadrant Housing Trust

Stress central point:
Did Mr Bruton have a lease?

Can a lease be created by a party who
does *not* have a proprietary interest?

Views of the Court of Appeal

House of Lords:
Concentrate on the speech of Lord
Hoffman who distinguished between:

Contractual
character of leases

Proprietary
character of leases

Lease is not a
legal estate

Lease is a
legal estate

Consequences as contrasted with

Consideration of the *Bruton* principle
in later cases

Where 'sub-tenancy' is
granted by a licensee – once
licence is surrendered
sub-tenant is a trespasser

But a *Bruton* type
tenancy may
create a contract
of tenancy

A printable version of this diagram plan is available from **www.pearsoned.co.uk/lawexpressqa**

Answer

The decision of the House of Lords in **Bruton v London and Quadrant Housing Trust Ltd** [2000] 1 AC 406, HL, raised questions about the nature of leases,[1] with which this question is concerned. We shall first look at the **Bruton v London and Quadrant Housing Trust Ltd** decision and then at its application in later cases to assess whether indeed it has created a 'contract of tenancy', as the quotation suggests.

The facts were[2] that Lambeth Council granted London and Quadrant Housing Trust (LQHT) a licence to use a number of its properties to provide temporary housing pending redevelopment. The Trust agreed with the local authority that it would not give security of tenure to any tenant without the local authority's consent and that no occupier would acquire security of tenure while in the property. The Trust then gave Mr Bruton the right to occupy one of the properties, a flat, 'on a weekly licence'. In fact, the planned development was abandoned and, by the time the case reached the House of Lords, Mr Bruton had been living in the flat for 10 years.

The essential point was simple: did Mr Bruton have a lease, as he claimed? The case was not concerned with security of tenure but with whether the Trust was subject to the repairing obligations imposed upon landlords by the Landlord and Tenant Act 1985, section 11, which applies only to 'leases'.[3]

The issue was that if a lease creates a proprietary interest in the land by way of a legal estate, a lease cannot be created by a party who does not themselves have a proprietary interest, and the Housing Trust did not, as it had only a licence.[4] Millett LJ, in the Court of Appeal,[5] pointed to the link with the fundamental requirement for a tenancy that there must be exclusive possession: 'If the grantor has no power to exclude the true owner from possession, he has no power to grant a legal right to exclusive possession and his grant cannot take effect as a tenancy.' So, as the Trust did not have exclusive possession, it could not give the right of exclusive possession to Mr Bruton.

The House of Lords disagreed. Lord Hoffmann distinguished between the contractual and the proprietary character of leases by saying that 'the term "lease" or "tenancy" describes a relationship between two parties who are designated landlord and tenant. It is not concerned with the question of whether the agreement creates an estate or other proprietary interest which may be binding upon third parties'. The agreement between the parties comes first, and not the proprietary interest. Thus, as, on the facts, the criteria for a lease laid down in **Street v Mountford** [1985] 2 All ER 289, HL, were satisfied and there was a lease.

If Lord Hoffmann's analysis is accepted, what are its consequences? The essence of his reasoning is that where the intermediate party which has granted a lease does not have a lease itself, this may not prevent it granting a lease to another party although this lease will not be proprietary.

Thus, there will be two categories: leases which are legal estates, and leases which are not legal estates.[6] Looking at it from the other direction, contractual rights of occupation could fall into one of three categories:

(a) proprietary leases giving an estate in land and enforceable against all third parties;

(b) contractual leases, which do not confer an estate in land but do confer exclusive possession;

(c) contractual licences, which do not confer either an estate in land or exclusive possession.[7]

This may in turn lead to some contractual licences[8] in category (c) being assimilated into category (b).

However, as a contractual lease does not give a proprietary interest, it seems that:

(a) The formality requirements set out in the Law of Property Act 1925,[9] sections 52 and 54, and the Law of Property (Miscellaneous Provisions) Act 1989, section 2, will not apply as they apply only to interests in land, and so contractual leases can be created informally.

(b) A contractual lease cannot be registrable under the LRA 2002 or count as an overriding interest under Schedules 1 and 3.

(c) Presumably, a contractual tenancy cannot be assigned by the tenant or the landlord,[10] for the ability to transfer leases flows

[6] This is the point that you need to bring out in this answer. You can then develop it and earn extra marks by discussing the possible consequences of such a distinction.

[7] This is a complex area and so it is vital to set out the different possibilities clearly, as here.

[8] You could, at this point, mention the status of contractual licences, but, at least, you must be clear that, as a general rule, they do not bind third parties.

[9] There is no need to mention these in detail: the point is that we do not know whether they will apply.

[10] You should resist the temptation to set out the rules on assignment of leases here, as we are just concerned with whether, in principle, a contractual licence can be treated in the same way as a lease.

from their proprietary status (see **Linden Gardens Trust Ltd v Lenesta Sludge Disposals Ltd** [1994] 1 AC 85, HL) and a contractual tenancy does not have this status.

(d)   However, as with contractual licences, there will be the right to recover possession from a trespasser and equitable remedies may be available, so that the lease may be enforceable against the grantor by specific performance or injunction (as in **Verrall v Great Yarmouth BC** [1981] QB 202, HC).

(e)   What of the rule that a lease must be created for a term certain? Will this apply to contractual leases?

The reasoning of the House of Lords in **Bruton v London and Quadrant Housing Trust** has had a mixed reception. In **Kay v Lambeth LBC** [2006] UKHL 10 and **Islington LBC v Green** [2005] EWCA Civ 56 the actual reasoning in **Bruton v London and Quadrant Housing Trust** was adopted, but, on the facts, it was held that there was only a contractual arrangement. The essential facts of both cases were that[11] the council (A) had granted a licence to (B) that it later surrendered to A. Did this affect the **Bruton**-type tenancy that B had granted to C? Under normal landlord and tenant law it would not, because, as Lord Scott explained: 'the subtenancy is a derivative interest created by the intermediate landlord out of the interest created by the head landlord' and so C would now hold directly from A. But precisely because there was no intermediate landlord but only a licensee, they had no interest out of which an interest for C could be created. Thus, C was a mere trespasser.

The contractual character of the **Bruton**-type tenancy can be seen in[12] **Wilkinson v Kerdene Ltd** [2013] EWCA Civ 44, where an owner of land sold it to his son but then entered into a tenancy agreement with a cricket club. The court held that, although it would not bind third parties, it did create a 'contract of tenancy' between the actual parties. The significance of this was that, later, the club paid rent to the actual owner and this was held to create a tenancy the terms of which were set out in the original agreement with the non-owner. Thus, in this limited respect, the **Bruton**-type tenancy had some legal effect.

Lord Hoffmann's attempt to create a new species of legal property right should be seen against the continuing concern over the lack of a proprietary status for certain types of contractual licences, especially residential ones.[13] Thus, the creation of a contractual

[11] We are earning extra marks by not just saying that the *Bruton* reasoning was not applied but showing the exact consequences of this.

[12] We are returning to the 'contract of tenancy' point mentioned in the question at the end.

[13] You will gain many marks if you show that you can think across the whole spectrum of property law in this conclusion.

tenancy might allow these licences to become contractual tenancies and so resolve a long-standing problem. However, before this happens, the practical problems of creating a new species of property right must be tackled first.

✓ Make your answer stand out

- Discuss the proprietary character of contractual licences.
- Demonstrate an ability to think across the spectrum of Land Law on the implications of the contractual tenancy.
- Read and refer to Bright, S. (2000) Leases, Exclusive Possession and Estates. *Law Quarterly Review*, 116: 7.
- Read and refer to Lower, M. (2010) The *Bruton* Tenancy. *Conv.* 74: 38.
- Read and refer to Roberts, N. (2012) The *Bruton* Tenancy: a Matter of Relativity. *Conv.* 76: 87, who gives yet another perspective.
- Mention the alternative argument in *Bruton v London and Quadrant Housing Trust* based on tenancy by estoppel: the Court of Appeal held that, as there was no purported grant of a tenancy, there could be no estoppel, but Lord Hoffmann, in the House of Lords, appeared to hold that the parties cannot deny that the lease is proprietorial in character – although this is not clear.

! Don't be tempted to . . .

- Spend too long on the facts of *Bruton* v *London and Quadrant Housing Trust*.
- Neglect the basics: here, the distinction between personal and proprietary rights.
- Fail to bring out the differences in approach between the Court of Appeal and the House of Lords.
- Miss explaining the detailed implications of this case across land law.
- Fail to set this idea of a contractual tenancy in a wider context.

📑 Question 3

In *Mexfield Housing Co-operative Ltd* v *Berrisford*, Lord Neuberger said that: 'There is no apparent practical justification for holding that an agreement for a term of uncertain duration cannot give rise to a tenancy.'

Critically consider the rationale for this rule and its application in recent case law.

Answer plan

→ State precisely what the rule means.

→ Explain the historical rationale for the rule, and refer to the 1925 property legislation.

→ Look at the decisions in both *Prudential Assurance Co. Ltd* v *London Residuary Body* and *Mexfield Housing Co-operative Ltd* v *Berrisford*.

→ Then look at the decision in *Southward Housing Co-operative v Walker*.

→ Critically examine the present-day reasons for the existence of this rule.

→ Examine the possibility of changes in this rule.

Diagram plan

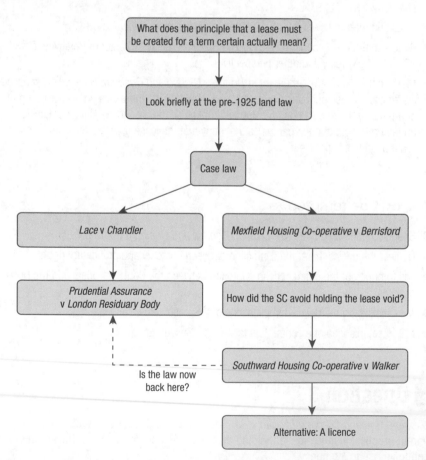

Answer

Lord Neuberger was referring to the fundamental principle that, to be valid, a lease must be created for a term that is certain. Thus, the start date, the duration and the end date of the lease[1] must be ascertainable at the commencement of the lease. It is, in fact, possible for the parties to agree that the lease will commence on a future uncertain event, such as when the property becomes vacant (**Brilliant v Michaels** [1945] 1 All ER 121, Ch D), but, once that event has happened, the lease must commence.

The rule received detailed consideration in **Mexfield Housing Co-operative Ltd v Berrisford** [2011] UKSC 52, where the principle was reaffirmed, albeit with reluctance, but, before we look at that decision, we need to examine the rationale and background for this rule.[2]

Its origin is to be found in the pre-1925 property legislation.[3] As Lord Neuberger put it in **Mexfield Housing Co-operative Ltd v Berrisford**: 'There is much authority to support the proposition that, before the 1925 Act came into force, an agreement for an uncertain term was treated as a tenancy for the life of the tenant, determinable before the tenant's death according to its terms.' However, the principle that where the term was uncertain a lease for life was created seems to have been forgotten in the cases following the 1925 legislation.

The operation of the rule can be seen in **Lace v Chantler** [1944][4] KB 368, CA, where a lease of a house for the duration of the war was held void. Many leases had been granted for the duration of the 1939–45 war and, following this case, Parliament passed the Validation of War-Time Leases Act 1944 to validate them.

In **Prudential Assurance Co. Ltd v London Residuary Body** [1992] 2 AC 386, HL, a local authority purported to lease land until it was required for road widening. It was held that the lease was void, but the tenant did have a periodic yearly tenancy by virtue of annual payment of rent. The House of Lords reached this decision with reluctance, Lord Browne-Wilkinson calling the outcome 'bizarre'.

In **Mexfield Housing Co-operative Ltd v Berrisford**, the claimant agreed to let a property to the defendant from month

[1] An average answer would just say that the term must be certain, but, in a good answer, you need to amplify this, as shown.

[2] You could, at this point, plunge into a detailed account of the facts of *Mexfield Housing Co-operative* v *Berrisford*. Better to leave that for later and first earn those extra marks by showing evidence of research and setting the principle in its context.

[3] This paragraph shows attention to research detail and that you have an appreciation of the relevance of the 1925 legislation.

[4] It is usually better to mention the earlier cases and then lead up to the latest one.

to month for a weekly rent. By clause 5, the defendant could end the agreement by giving one month's notice and, by clause 6, the claimant could end the agreement only if, for example, the rent was in arrears for a certain time. The Supreme Court held that this was not a monthly periodic tenancy because of clauses 5 and 6.[5] It would have been void as being of uncertain duration, but the court held that it took effect as a lease for life and so was saved by the operation of section 149(6) of the LPA 1925, which converted leases for lives into leases for 90 years. Thus, the court upheld the 'term certain' rule but managed to avoid its application in this case.

[5] This is important, as we shall see that, in other cases, the lease was saved by being regarded as a periodic tenancy.

If a court was unable to apply the reasoning in **Mexfield Housing Co-operative Ltd v Berrisford** to validate a lease, would that mean that there was no lease at all and so the 'tenant' was not a tenant at all but a mere licensee with no security of tenure?[6] If, as in the **Prudential Assurance** case, the tenant was already paying rent, there could be a tenancy, provided that the tenant has exclusive possession. The tenant can be considered a tenant at will.[7] The exact nature of tenancies at will has never been clear, but there is no doubt that the tenant does not obtain an estate in the land and the tenancy can be ended at any time by the landlord. If so, then, if the tenant pays rent, this will probably convert the tenancy into a periodic tenancy,[8] as it will be clear that the parties intended a lease. Thus, as it will be a tenancy for a period not exceeding three years, by section 54(2) of the LPA 1925, it can be valid even if not in writing.

[6] A good answer will start to ask questions such as this. In practice, it would be no good just telling a client that their lease did not satisfy the 'term certain' rule. The obvious question would be: 'Yes – so . . . ?'. Make sure that you always answer it!

[7] When you introduce a term such as this, make sure that you explain it.

[8] There is an argument that periodic tenancies fall foul of the 'term certain' rule, as they are leases of uncertain duration determinable by notice, but, in the _Prudential Assurance_ case, Lord Templeman said that such leases are saved from being uncertain as each party can determine the lease at the end of the period of the tenancy.

[9] This is where your hard work in keeping up to date pays off!

The effect of **Mexfield Housing Co-operative Ltd v Berrisford** has been considerably limited by **Southward Housing Co-operative v Walker** [2015] EWHC 1615 (Ch).[9] The tenancy agreement, which was of uncertain duration, stated that the landlord would only end it with a notice to quit on specified grounds, one of which was non-payment or persistent delay in payment of rent. This was the case here. The landlord therefore served a notice to quit but was met with the defence that, as the lease was not for a term certain, on the authority of **Mexfield**, it automatically turned the agreement into a 90-year lease. The significance was that if this were so, the lease could only be terminated earlier on the death of the defendants or by forfeiture, and there was no express forfeiture provision.

The court rejected this and emphasised the limited scope of **Mexfield**. It held that the question was one of intention: did the parties intend to create a lease for life? In **Mexfield**, they did; here, they did not. Thus, the uncertainty of the term of this agreement meant that it could not take effect as a lease; therefore it was a contractual licence and the licensors (i.e. the landlords under the 'lease') obtained possession.

This decision may be correct on the facts, but it has severely limited the impact of **Mexfield** and brought once more into focus the misgivings about the 'term certain' rule expressed by Lord Neuberger in the quotation in the question.

[10] Here, you earn those extra marks by showing familiarity with the actual reasoning in *Mexfield Housing Co-operative* v *Berrisford*.

The main reason that the Supreme Court in **Mexfield** did not change the law to allow leases with an uncertain term[10] was expressed by Lord Neuberger, who said that, 'it does appear that for many centuries it has been regarded as fundamental to the concept of a term of years that it had a certain duration when it was created'. Lord Neuberger referred to the not 'very attractive point' expressed by Lord Browne-Wilkinson in **Prudential Assurance Co. Ltd v London Residuary Body** that to change the law in this field 'might upset long established titles'. This is the root of the problem: if the law was changed by the courts, then it would affect not just future leases but present ones,[11] and this disturbance to existing property rights was felt not to be justified. This may not be an ideal reason for leaving the law as it is, but, of course, most leases are professionally drafted and the term certain rule is well known.

[11] Note that you are expressing your own views, based on the material you have presented. This is exactly what the examiner wants to see.

Thus, we have a rule that seems to have no clear rationale today, yet, when the courts attempted to mitigate its effect in **Mexfield Housing Co-operative Ltd v Berrisford**, it only produced further problems, as we saw in **Southward Housing Co-operative v Walker**. The way forward is not clear.

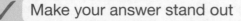

Make your answer stand out

- Show a grasp of the basic principles of the pre-1925 property legislation.
- Demonstrate that you have read the judgments in *Mexfield Housing Co-operative* v *Berrisford* and not just a summary of the facts.
- Note that the *Mexfield* solution will only work if there is a lease to an individual and not to a company.
- Show a clear understanding of land law principles – basic idea of a lease, distinction between leases and licences etc.
- Read and refer to Bright, S. (2012), who quotes the view of the Law Commission on this issue.
- Come to conclusions of your own, based on your analysis of what the courts have said.

! Don't be tempted to . . .

- Give lengthy accounts of the facts of the cases and fail to highlight the points of law.
- Just deal with the decision in *Mexfield Housing Co-operative* v *Berrisford* and not mention the other cases.
- Fail to look at the reasoning of the judges.
- Set out some quotations from the judgments, but fail to discuss them and to set out your own analysis.

📝 Question 4

A contract for a lease is not as effective in conferring rights against all persons as a lease.

To what extent do you agree that the above statement represents the law as it stands at present?

Diagram plan

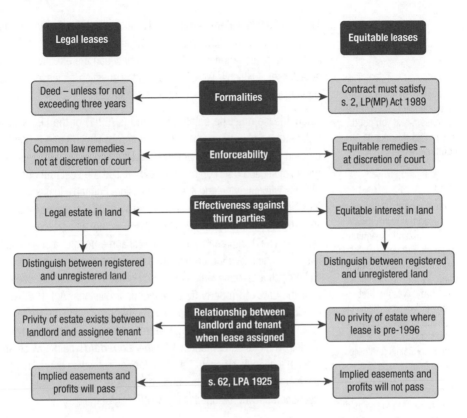

A printable version of this diagram plan is available from **www.pearsoned.co.uk/lawexpressqa**

Answer plan

→ Explain the formalities for the creation of legal and equitable leases.

→ Explain the availability of specific performance to enforce equitable leases.

→ Show how there are areas where rights are the same for both legal and equitable leases.

→ Explain the rules on the enforceability of legal and equitable leases against third parties.

→ Demonstrate the differences between legal and equitable leases: enforceability of covenants and application of section 62 of the LPA 1925.

Answer

I agree that this statement represents the present law. A contract for a lease is not as effective in all respects and against all persons as a lease. There are significant differences between the effectiveness of legal leases – which is what is meant in the question by 'leases' – and equitable leases, which are contracts for leases.[1]

A legal lease must be created by deed (s. 52(1) of the LPA 1925) unless it is for not less than three years, in which case it can be created without formalities provided that it complies with the requirements of section 54(1) of the LPA 1925: it is at the best rent obtainable, it is without a fine and it is in possession. Equitable leases can be created by agreement. The leading case on equitable leases today is[2] **Walsh v Lonsdale** (1882) 21 Ch D 9, HC, where an agreement for a lease was held enforceable. Here, an oral agreement for a seven-year lease was held binding on the grantor, on the principle that 'equity looks on that as done which ought to be done'.[3] Since then, section 2 of the Law of Property (Miscellaneous Provisions) Act 1989 has required all agreements for the sale or other disposition of an interest in land to be in writing, contain all terms agreed and be signed by the parties. The oral agreement in **Walsh v Lonsdale** would now create at most a periodic tenancy. Thus, the formal distinction between legal leases exceeding three years and equitable leases is reduced to the distinction between a deed and a written agreement.[4]

Thus, an equitable lease can, in principle, take effect as a lease against the landlord and be enforced against him whether it is made in law or in equity. However, an equitable lease is enforceable by equitable remedies, which are at the discretion of the court. So the court may, for example, refuse the grant of specific performance to enforce an equitable lease. In **Coatsworth v Johnson** (1886) 55 LJQB 220, HC, a tenant entered into possession under an agreement for a legal lease of farmland and so had an equitable lease. He claimed specific performance of the agreement for a lease, but this was refused as he was in breach of the covenant to farm with good husbandry. The equitable lease could not be enforced and he was held to be a mere tenant at will.

However, if an equitable lease is capable of being enforced by specific performance, then, as Jessel MR said in **Walsh v Lonsdale**,

---

[1] A point of clarification: the question refers to 'contracts for leases' and you need to say that this means an equitable lease.

[2] The reason that this answer has used the word 'today' is that the idea of an equitable lease did not begin with this case as students sometimes think. What was significant was that it was the first case on this topic since the passage of the Judicature Acts in 1873 which made equitable claims and defences available in all courts.

[3] Where, as here, you will need to refer to the facts of a case more than once in an answer, I suggest that you state the facts when you first mention the case.

[4] An examiner will expect you to show an understanding of where the difference between legal and equitable leases arises, but do not spend too long on this point!

'[the tenant] holds, therefore, under the same terms in equity as if a lease had been granted'. Thus, the rights and duties of the parties under the lease will be the same. Another point of similarity is that, by section 146(5)(a) of the LPA 1925, the provisions allowing a tenant to apply for relief from forfeiture apply to equitable leases and legal ones.[5]

[5] A point not often mentioned by students, so make sure that you do!

Nevertheless, as the question says, the equitable lease is not as effective against all persons[6] as a legal lease. An equitable lease creates only an equitable interest in land. When title to the land is unregistered, a legal lease is always binding on a purchaser of the freehold but an equitable lease is binding on a purchaser for money or money's worth from the landlord only if registered as an estate contract as a Class (iv) land charge (s. 4(6) of the Land Charges Act 1972). Where the title is registered, a legal lease for up to seven years is an overriding interest (Sched. 3, Para. 1 of the LRA 2002) and is binding on a purchaser without the need for registration. The fact that equitable leases are less effective than legal leases is shown by the situation where the holder of an equitable lease goes into possession and pays rent on a regular basis, such as monthly or yearly. They now have a legal periodic tenancy that can take effect as an overriding interest.[7] Leases for longer than seven years require substantive registration (s. 27(2)(b) of the LRA 2002). Equitable leases should be protected by a notice on the register as estate contacts, but, if the tenant is in actual occupation, he may be protected by Schedule 3, Paragraph 2 of the LRA 2002 as being a person who has an equitable interest in the land and who is in actual occupation. The overall picture is that it is far more likely that a tenant under an equitable lease will find that the lease is not binding on the purchaser of the freehold than the tenant under a legal lease will.

[6] The question, in effect, asks two things and this picks up one of them: the relative effectiveness of legal and equitable leases in connection with their enforceability against 'all persons', i.e. third parties.

[7] Here, you are making a direct contrast between equitable leases and legal leases in the form of periodic tenancies. This type of clear explanation always brings extra marks.

The fact that a lease is only equitable can affect the relationship between the landlord and tenant when the lease is assigned. If privity of estate[8] exists between parties to a lease, the covenants in that lease can be enforced between them. Where there is a legal lease, there is privity of estate between the landlord and any assignee tenant and between any tenant and any assignee of the freehold reversion. Thus, leasehold covenants can be enforced between new parties to a legal lease. Privity of estate does not exist between parties to equitable leases (*Purchase v Lichfield Brewery* [1915] 1 KB 184, KBD), although section 3(1) of the Landlord and Tenant

[8] This area is dealt with later in more detail, but here you do need to stress the term 'privity of estate', as this is the term on which this point hangs.

[9] It is vital to stress that the position is different if the lease was granted on or after 1 January 1996. Give only enough detail here to illustrate the distinction between legal and equitable leases.

(Covenants) Act 1995, which applies to leases granted on or after 1 January 1996,[9] provides that all landlord and tenant covenants, except those which are personal, are enforceable between successors in title of the original parties. Thus, this particular distinction between legal and equitable leases applies only to leases granted before 1 January 1996.

[10] You must show here just enough knowledge and understanding to illustrate this answer without going into too much detail.

[11] Students often forget that the rule also applies to profits.

[12] This is a separate point, as *Wright* v *Macadam* is, in effect, an extension of the principle in section 62.

[13] This is the extra detail that brings extra marks: by stating the statutory authority, you are lifting your answer to the level of a very good one.

Finally, the distinction between legal and equitable leases is important in connection with the implied grant of easements and profits under section 62 of the LPA 1925.[10] This provides that, on a conveyance of land, all rights appertaining to the land such as easements and profits[11] pass with the conveyance. As a result of *Wright* v *Macadam* [1949] 2 All ER 565, CA,[12] the conveyance may also elevate other rights to the status of easements, such as, in this case, rights of storage. However, an agreement for a lease is not a conveyance within the statutory definition of a conveyance (s. 205(1)(ii) of the LPA 1925)[13] and so an assignment of an equitable lease will not automatically carry with it the easements and profits that the assignor tenant will have enjoyed. Instead, the easements and profits will have to be spelt out in the assignment of the lease. Nor will it allow the creation of new easements or profits under the principle in *Wright* v *Macadam*.

[14] Note the reference back to the words of the question.

Therefore, it can be seen that, in all these ways, a contract for a lease is not as effective in all respects and against all persons as a legal lease.[14]

 Make your answer stand out

- Mention academic arguments, e.g. Gardner, S. (1987) Equity, Estate Contracts and the Judicature Acts: *Walsh* v *Lonsdale Revisited. Oxford Journal of Legal Studies*, 7(1): 60 on specific performance of equitable leases.
- Lord Browne-Wilkinson in *Tinsley* v *Milligan* [1994] AC 340 at 370–1 considered that, now that law and equity are fused, there 'is one single law of property made up of legal and equitable interests'. What are the implications of this for this question?
- Likelihood that legal leases for three years or more will be overriding interests to bring them into line with the rule that only legal leases for three years or more require a deed.

! Don't be tempted to . . .

- Go into detail about the types of lease – tenancies at will, leases for lives, etc.; just concentrate on looking at legal and equitable leases.
- Discuss leases and licences – irrelevant.
- Forget to check constantly that you are saying legal leases when you should and equitable leases when you should; it is all too easy to just say 'lease', in which case you will lose marks for inaccuracy.
- Forget that, throughout, you are actually comparing legal and equitable leases and not writing about each of them in turn.
- Give too much detail on section 62 of the LPA 1925: just enough to make your point in relation to the comparison between legal and equitable leases.

? Question 5

Earlier this year, Barbara bought the freehold of 13 Mill Lane, Downtown, from Eve. This has registered title and is divided into a downstairs office and an upstairs residential flat.

(a) The office is occupied by Fred under a 10-year lease contained in a deed, at a monthly rent of £400. This provides that Fred is to use the premises solely as an office. Barbara has discovered that Fred is using the office as a betting shop and that he has demolished a wall at the side to enable customers to park their cars at the back.

(b) The flat is occupied by Tom under a two-year oral lease, at a weekly rent of £350. Tom is complaining that he cannot sleep because of the constant revving-up of motorbikes by Fred, who is a motorbike enthusiast, and he feels that the flat should have had adequate soundproofing installed. As a result, Tom has withheld the rent for the last two weeks.

Ignoring any question of security of tenure, advise Barbara as to whether the agreements made by Eve with Fred and Tom are binding on her and whether she can take steps to evict them.

Answer plan

→ Consider whether the leases are legal or equitable.

→ Explain whether they bind Barbara.

→ Identify the covenants in the leases.

→ Analyse whether Barbara can sue on the covenants.

→ Explain the remedies of the landlord and relate them to the question.

Diagram plan

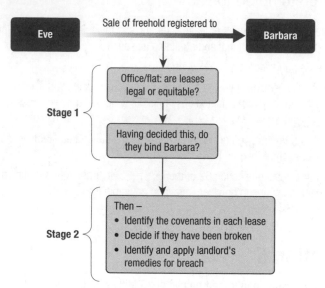

Sale of freehold registered to

Eve → **Barbara**

Stage 1
- Office/flat: are leases legal or equitable?
- Having decided this, do they bind Barbara?

Stage 2
- Then –
  - Identify the covenants in each lease
  - Decide if they have been broken
  - Identify and apply landlord's remedies for breach

A printable version of this diagram plan is available from **www.pearsoned.co.uk/lawexpressqa**

Answer

(a) The first question is whether Fred's lease is legal or equitable and, as we are told that it is contained in a deed, it is legal, as it complies with section 52(1) of the Law of Property Act (LPA) 1925, which requires a deed for the creation of a legal estate or interest in land. Title to the property appears to be already registered.[1] The lease to Fred is for 10 years, which, by section 27(2)(b) of the Land Registration Act (LRA) 2002, requires substantive registration to bind Barbara. We are not told whether it has been registered, but, if not, Fred may have a legal monthly periodic tenancy based on payment of rent monthly. If so, as this lease clearly does not exceed seven years, and as this is not a case of first registration, it falls within Schedule 3, Paragraph 1 to the LRA 2002, which provides that legal leases not exceeding seven years are overriding interests, and thus it will bind Barbara even though it is not registered.

[1] It is always worthwhile checking whether title is already registered or not and putting this in your answer. Make this a habit. This is relevant in this question because the rules on what is an overriding interest differ depending on whether it is a case of first or subsequent registration.

Fred is in breach of an express covenant in his lease to use the premises as an office, as he is using them as a betting shop. In addition, he has demolished a wall. This is in breach of an implied covenant often known as 'not to commit waste'. In **Warren v Keen** [1954] 1 QB 15, CA, Denning LJ said that 'the tenant must take proper care of the place' and that the tenant must not damage the property wilfully or negligently. Clearly, Fred is in breach of this.

The landlord, Barbara, may claim damages from Fred for breach of covenant and/or claim an injunction to restrain the breach. The injunction could be used to stop Fred using the premises as a betting shop. In addition, Barbara may claim to forfeit the lease, but she can do this only if the lease contains a forfeiture clause.[2] If there is, Barbara must serve a notice on Fred under section 146 of the LPA 1925, which:[3]

(i) specifies the breach;

(ii) requires it to be remedied if it is capable of remedy;

(iii) requires the tenant to pay compensation for the breach.

If the tenant fails to do (ii) and (iii) within a reasonable time, usually considered to be three months, the landlord may proceed to forfeit the lease.

The main issue is (ii), as, in some cases, the courts have held that breaches are incapable of some remedy, as where the breach has cast a stigma over the premises but this does not seem to be so here.

(b) Tom's lease is oral, but, as it is for two years, section 54 of the LPA 1925 applies, which provides that leases not exceeding three years can be valid even though not by deed or in writing, provided that three conditions set out in section 54(2) are satisfied.[4] These are that:

(i) The lease takes effect in possession. This means that the lease must not be granted in advance of taking possession. We do not know whether this is the case here.[5]

(ii) At the best rent. This means the best commercial rent. We are told that the rent is £350 a week. Is this the best rent?

(iii) Without a fine. A fine means a premium that is paid by the tenant, and there is no evidence that this was paid.

[2] You will lose marks if you do not state all the possible remedies that the landlord has, although you should look in more detail at forfeiture.

[3] Problem questions on leases normally expect you to discuss the landlord's remedy of forfeiture in detail. Do note that the procedure is different depending on whether the tenant's breach is of the covenant to pay rent or for other breach of covenant.

[4] Students often ignore these conditions and simply assume that section 54 applies as the lease does not exceed three years.

[5] The rule is strict: for section 54 to apply, the lease must take effect in possession. Exam questions do not always make it clear whether this is so.

137

We cannot tell, on the facts, whether the lease was valid. If it was, then, as this lease is for less than seven years, it will be an overriding interest, as in the case of Fred discussed earlier. However, if Tom has paid rent weekly, he will have a weekly periodic tenancy that, as in the case of Fred, will be an overriding interest.

[6] Do not assume that a covenant for quiet enjoyment means a covenant against excessive noise.

As the lease is oral, there can be no express terms, but Tom might claim that the revving-up of motorbikes by Fred is a breach of the implied covenant for quiet enjoyment. However, he will not succeed.[6] In *Southwark LBC v Mills* [2001] 1 AC 1, HL, tenants sued their landlords as the activities of their neighbours were clearly audible; and it was accepted that, although there was soundproofing, it fell short of modern standards. The House of Lords approved the statement of Kekewich J in *Jenkins v Jackson* (1888) 40 Ch D 71, Ch D that quiet in the covenant for quiet enjoyment 'does not mean undisturbed by noise' and instead means that the tenant's actual possession will not be disturbed by the lessor or those acting under him. Furthermore, the court declined to imply a covenant that a landlord must install adequate soundproofing. Lord Hoffmann pointed out that Parliament has dealt with the problems of substandard housing on numerous occasions, but declined to impose a covenant requiring adequate soundproofing, and so it was not for the courts to do this.

[7] Do not make the mistake of saying that Tom is entitled to withhold rent as he thinks that the landlord is in breach. Two wrongs do not make a right!

If Tom withholds the rent, he will be in breach of an implied covenant to pay rent and, even if the landlord was in breach of covenant, this would not justify a breach by Tom.[7]

The landlord's remedies for a breach of a covenant by the tenant to pay rent are to bring an action for arrears of rent and to claim forfeiture for non-payment of rent. If Barbara claims forfeiture, she must make a formal demand for rent, unless, as is usually the case, the lease provides that this need not be done. Under section 212 of the Common Law Procedure Act 1852, if the landlord sues for possession and the tenant, at any time before the trial, pays into court all arrears of rent and costs, all proceedings are stayed. Even if the tenant does not do this and judgment is given against him, he may apply for relief within six months after judgment, and the court may grant relief on terms of payment of rent and costs and any other terms that it deems appropriate.

✓ **Make your answer stand out**

- Refer to the Law Commission (1996) Landlord and Tenant: Responsibility for State and Condition of Property, No. 238. http://lawcommission.justice.gov.uk/docs/lc238_land lord_and_tenant_responsibility_for_stake_and_condition_of_property.pdf on which covenants should be implied on a letting of property, and especially Paragraph 11.16.

- Mention the Law Commission's proposals for reform of the law on forfeiture – see Law Commission (2004) Termination of Tenancies for Tenant Default, No. 174. http://lawcommission.justice.gov.uk/docs/cp174_Termination_of_Tenancies_Consultation.pdf.

- Give a clear account of remedies, avoiding too much detail but relating the answer specifically to this question.

! Don't be tempted to . . .

- Ignore the question of whether the leases are legal or equitable.
- Ignore the fact that title to the land is registered.
- Confuse the landlord's remedies for breach of covenant to pay rent with remedies for breaches of other covenants.
- Assume that 'quiet enjoyment' literally means quiet.

❓ Question 6

In 2012, by a legal lease that was properly executed, Teresa granted Maggie a lease of a shop for 10 years. The lease makes the tenant liable for repairs, but, although the shop was in disrepair when the lease was granted, Maggie has not made any repairs since taking it over. The lease also contains the following covenants:

(a) that the premises shall be used only as a high-class grocer;

(b) that the lease cannot be assigned without the landlord's consent;

(c) that, at the end of the lease, the tenant has the option to purchase the freehold;

(d) that the landlord may forfeit the lease in the event of a breach of covenant by the tenant.

In 2014, Teresa sold the freehold to Richard.

It is 2017 and Maggie wishes to assign the lease to Fred, but Richard objects on the ground that Fred runs a cut-price grocery shop elsewhere and he fears that Fred will run this shop in the same way.

Richard asks your advice on the following:

(a) What action should he take in respect of the breach of the repair covenant?

(b) Can he refuse a request by the tenant to purchase the freehold?

(c) Can he refuse consent to the proposed assignment of the lease, and, if he does give consent, are there any conditions that he can impose?

Answer plan

→ Identify that this is a legal lease and also that it is a post-1996 lease and explain why this is significant.

→ Explain the position when freehold reversion is sold.

→ Consider the liability to repair.

→ Assignment of lease.

→ Conditions that may be imposed.

Diagram plan

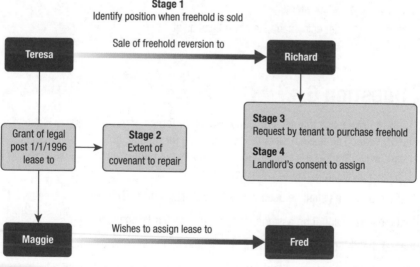

A printable version of this diagram plan is available from **www.pearsoned.co.uk/lawexpressqa**

Answer

[1] Always begin an answer to a problem question on covenants in leases with the two points in this paragraph.

The first points to note are that this is a legal lease and the date when it was granted.[1] Here, it was granted in 2010, which means that the lease is governed by the Landlord and Tenant (Covenants) Act 1995, which applies to all leases, both legal and equitable, granted on or after 1 January 1996.

[2] Make sure that you are clear who the parties are before you get to grips with the details of the question; otherwise you may get confused later.

The original landlord, Teresa, has sold the freehold reversion to -Richard.[2] Under section 3(1) of the Landlord and Tenant (Covenants) Act 1995 (LT(C)A), the benefit of all landlord and tenant covenants passes on a sale of the freehold reversion. By section 2(1) of the Act, the phrase 'landlord and tenant covenants' has a wider meaning than the 'touch and concern' test under the law applicable to pre-1996 leases and means that all covenants that affect the relationship of landlord and tenant pass, but not personal covenants. Clearly, here, all the covenants satisfy this test.

(a) Liability to repair the premises depends on the provisions in the lease. As Denning MR observed in **Warren v Keen** [1954] 1 QB 15, CA, 'Apart from express contract, a tenant owes no duty to a landlord to keep the premises in repair'. Here, the lease makes the tenant liable for repairs, but Maggie may object that they were in disrepair at the start of the lease and so she has no duty to make repairs. However, this argument will not succeed, as, in **Payne v Haine** (1847) 16 M & W 541, Exch, it was held that, even if premises are in disrepair at the start of the lease, the tenant must put them into repair at his own expense. The standard of repair is

[3] It will usually be impossible to tell from the question whether the standard has been broken, but always state this test.

that of the reasonably minded owner after making allowance for the locality, character and age of the premises[3] (**Proudfoot v Hart** (1890) 25 QBD 42, CA). If the lease is assigned to Fred, he will be liable on the covenant, as such a covenant is governed by section 3 of the LT(C)A 1995, which provides that, on an assignment of a lease, the burden of all landlord and tenant covenants will pass. The meaning of the phrase 'landlord and tenant covenants' was explained above and obviously includes a covenant to repair. As the lease contains a forfeiture clause if Fred does not make the repairs, Richard may bring forfeiture proceedings against him. Richard must, by section 146(1) of the LPA 1925, serve a notice specifying the breach, requiring it to be remedied and requiring the tenant to pay compensation.

[4] It is worth mentioning the pre-1996 law here in order to explain the post-1996 law.

(b) The question is whether the covenant giving the tenant the option to purchase the freehold binds Richard as a landlord and tenant covenant under section 3 of the LT(C)A 1995. Before the passage of this Act, the test in *Spencer's Case* (1582) 5 Co Rep 16a applied[4] to all leases and this was whether the covenant 'touched and concerned the land'. If it did, then subsequent parties were bound. In *Woodall v Clifton* [1905] 2 Ch 257, CA, it was held that this type of covenant did not 'touch and concern the land'. However, section 2(1) of the 1995 Act applies whether or not the covenant has reference to the subject-matter of the lease and it is submitted that this will bind Richard and he will not be able to refuse a request from a tenant to purchase the freehold.

[5] Always check what the lease says about assignment before you apply the statute.

(c) The proposed assignment of the lease is governed by both the terms of the lease and also by statute.[5] The lease provides that the lease cannot be assigned without the landlord's consent. Under the Landlord and Tenant Act 1927, section 19(1A) (added by section 22 of the LT(C)A 1995), the landlord and tenant of a non-residential lease, which this is, may agree in the lease what circumstances will justify the landlord in withholding consent. We are not told of any such circumstances, and so we will assume that there are none.[6]

[6] It will be the usual practice in an exam for there not to be any agreement between the landlord and the tenant setting out when consent can be withheld. This is so that you can discuss the general principles set out in the next paragraph.

Section 19(1) of the Landlord and Tenant Act 1927 provides that, in such a case, the landlord cannot withhold consent unreasonably. In *International Drilling Fluids Ltd v Louisville Investments Ltd* [1986] All ER 321, CA, it was held that the landlord is entitled to be protected from having the premises used or occupied in an undesirable way by an undesirable assignee, but consent to an assignment cannot be refused on grounds that have nothing to do with the relationship of landlord and tenant. So, a personal dislike would not be enough. In *Kened Ltd and Den Norske Bank Plc v Connie Investments Ltd* [1997] 1 EGLR 21, CA, Millett LJ said that the essential question is 'Has it been shown that no reasonable landlord would have withheld consent?'.[7] However, where the landlord reasonably believes that a proposed assignment would lead to a breach of covenant in the lease, this will be a valid reason for withholding consent. (See the House of Lords' decision in *Ashworth Frazer Ltd v Gloucester City Council* [2001] UKHL 59.) In this case, the permitted use is a high-class grocer and we do not know that Fred intends to use the shop in breach of this. However, if Richard

[7] Obviously, the examiner will not expect you to recall long quotations, but it will add to your marks if you recall straightforward ones such as these and apply them to the question.

can prove that he will use it as a cut-price grocer in the same way as he appears to run his other shop, he is entitled to refuse consent. He also needs to remember that section 1(3) of the Landlord and Tenant Act 1988 provides that, if the tenant asks for consent in writing, the landlord must give or refuse consent in writing and must do this in a reasonable time, and that, under section 1(6), it is for the landlord to prove that a refusal of consent was reasonable and that consent was given or withheld in a reasonable time.

Richard has also asked whether there are any conditions that he can impose if he does give consent to the assignment of the lease. Under section 5(2) of the LT(C)A 1995, the tenant, on assigning the lease, is released from the tenant covenants, but, by section 16, the landlord may, as a condition of giving consent to an assignment, require the tenant to enter into an authorised guarantee agreement.[8] This means that the assignor tenant (Maggie) guarantees that the assignee tenant (Fred) will perform the covenants, but this guarantee ends when the assignee tenant himself assigns the lease. At that point, Richard, or whoever is now the landlord, can require them to enter into a similar covenant. In view of the continuing liability for failure to repair the premises, it would clearly be wise for Richard to insist on Maggie entering into an authorised guarantee agreement.

[8] If an exam question asks you about conditions that the landlord may impose on an assignment, you should mention this point.

✓ Make your answer stand out

- Provide criticism of the old 'touch and concern' test for the running of covenants and how it was replaced by a wider test in the Landlord and Tenant (Covenants) Act 1995.
- Mention the Law Commission's proposals for reform of the law on forfeiture – see Law Commission (2004) Termination of Tenancies for Tenant Default, No. 174. http://lawcommission.justice.gov.uk/docs/cp174_Termination_of_Tenancies_Consultation.pdf.
- Clearly state the law on running of covenants where there is a freehold reversion.
- Look in detail at the House of Lords' decision in *Ashworth Frazer Ltd* v *Gloucester City Council* [2001] UKHL 59.
- Note recent decisions on authorised guarantee agreements, e.g. *EMI Group Ltd v O & H Q1 Ltd* [2016] EWHC 529 (Ch) HC.

! Don't be tempted to . . .

- Forget that the Landlord and Tenant (Covenants) Act 1995 applies here.
- Forget the different test for the running of covenants in the Landlord and Tenant (Covenants) Act 1995.
- Forget that, on an assignment of a post-1996 lease, the landlord can require the tenant to enter into an authorised guarantee agreement.

@ Try it yourself

Now take a look at the question below and attempt to answer it. You can check your response against the answer guidance available on the companion website (**www.pearsoned.co.uk/lawexpressqa**).

Jim is the freehold owner of 17 North Street, which consists of an office block. The leases of each tenant provide that the lease can be assigned with the consent of the landlord, but there is an express covenant against sub-letting and use for any purpose except that of an office.

Pam, who holds the lease of Office One, has sub-let it to Charles, who appears to be living there. Jim wishes to take action against Charles to stop the unauthorised use, and also against Pam to terminate the lease.

Advise Jim on whether he can do this and, if he can take steps to have Pam evicted, what procedure he should follow.

Richard, who holds the lease of Office Two, wishes to assign the lease to Amanda. However, Jim does not wish to consent to this, as Amanda had an unhappy relationship with Jim's son some years ago.

Advise Jim on whether he is entitled to refuse consent on this ground.

www.pearsoned.co.uk/lawexpressqa

Go online to access more revision support, including additional essay and problem questions with diagram plans, and you be the marker questions, and to download all diagrams from the book.

Covenants affecting freehold land

How this topic may come up in exams

Exam questions in this area are traditionally regarded as difficult by students, but the range of possible problem questions is considerably restricted and a clear plan for an answer carried through logically will pay tremendous dividends! Do not avoid this area, but think of it as a challenge, as examiners, knowing the complexities of the law here, will readily reward students who make a really sound attempt. The proposals of the Law Commission for reform of the law in this area have given us an obvious, and not too difficult, area for essays and a useful point to mention at the end of problems.

■ Before you begin

It's a good idea to consider the following key themes of covenants affecting freehold land before tackling a question on this topic.

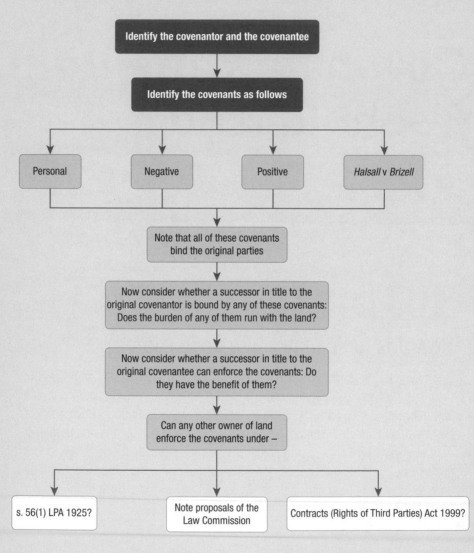

A printable version of this diagram is available from **www.pearsoned.co.uk/lawexpressqa**

🖎 Question 1

Steve is the registered proprietor of 155 High Street, a freehold property consisting of a shop and a vacant plot at the side. Title is registered. In 2012, Steve sold a plot to Bert. In his transfer, Bert covenanted as follows:

(a) not to carry on any trade, business or profession on the land;

(b) to maintain all fences on his land that border on land retained by Steve in good repair;

(c) not to keep any pets at any house built on the land.

Bert subsequently built a house on his plot, known as '155A High Street'.

Since then, Bert has sold his property to Richard, an accountant. Now Richard has started an accountancy business from the house, having obtained planning permission for the change of use, and he is refusing to repair a fence which blew down in a recent gale. He also keeps a pet alligator that lives at 155A High Street.

Advise Steve, who wishes to take action to enforce the covenants.

How, if at all, would your answer differ if the recommendations of the Law Commission (2011) Report, *Making Land Work: Easements, Covenants and Profits à Prendre* (LC 327) were implemented?

Answer plan

→ Identify the parties – Steve is the covenantee and Bert is the covenantor.

→ Note that the question requires you to consider the running of the burden of the covenants.

→ Go through the covenants and decide which are positive, which are negative and which are merely personal.

→ Decide whether Richard is liable on any of them in an action by Steve.

→ Identify and apply the remedies available against Richard.

→ Apply the proposals of the Law Commission in its report (LC 327) to the situations.

Diagram plan

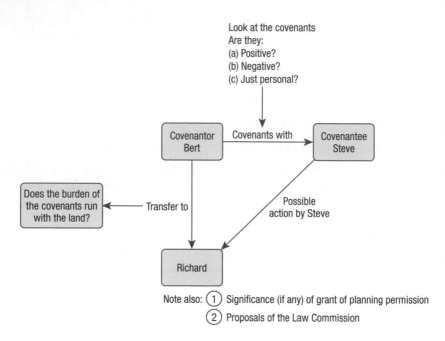

Look at the covenants
Are they:
(a) Positive?
(b) Negative?
(c) Just personal?

Covenantor
Bert

Covenants with

Covenantee
Steve

Does the burden of
the covenants run
with the land?

Transfer to

Possible
action by Steve

Richard

Note also: ① Significance (if any) of grant of planning permission
② Proposals of the Law Commission

A printable version of this diagram plan is available from **www.pearsoned.co.uk/lawexpressqa**

Answer

[1] Right at the start of a question on restrictive covenants, identify exactly who the parties to the covenant are.

In this question, Bert, the covenantor, has entered into a number of covenants with Steve, the covenantee.[1] Bert then sold the land, with the burden[2] of the covenant, to Richard. We are asked whether Steve can take action against Richard on the covenants.[3]

[2] Point out that the covenantor's land has the burden of the covenant.

[3] In this short paragraph, we have picked up a number of marks by clearly identifying the parties and the relevant terms. Questions on this area are not easy, but if you lay a solid foundation like this, you will gradually build up your marks.

Bert, as the original covenantor, remains liable on the covenants and so Steve can claim against him in the event of a breach by Richard.[4] This rule is not only one of common law but is also implied by section 79(1) of the Law of Property Act 1925 (LPA 1925), which provides that a covenant relating to any land of the covenantor shall be deemed to be made 'on behalf of himself and his successors in title'. However, the rule in section 79(1) will not apply if the covenant provides that the liability of the original covenantor is to cease when he or she sells the land. Here, we are not told whether this is so. It is the universal practice, when land is sold, for the covenantor to take an indemnity

[4] This is a straightforward
and easily remembered point
and should be placed near
the start of any answer to a
problem question.

covenant from the buyer so that, if the covenantor, Bert, is sued for a
breach committed by Richard, Richard will have to indemnify Bert for
any damages that he has to pay.

The common law rule on covenants was established in **Austerberry
v Oldham Corporation** (1885) 29 Ch D 750, CA, where it was held
that, at common law, covenants do not bind subsequent owners of
land, and this was followed in **Rhone v Stephens** [1994] 2 All ER 65,
HL. Thus, at common law, no action can be brought against Richard
for breach of any of the covenants. However, it was held in **Tulk v
Moxhay** (1848) 1 H & Tw 105, HC that, in equity, a covenant can
bind subsequent owners, on certain conditions. This rule was refined
in subsequent cases so that it only applied to negative covenants.
In **Haywood v Brunswick Permanent Benefit Building Society**
(1881) 8 QBD 403, CA, Brett LJ referred to covenants 'restricting the
use of the land' and this is a good working definition of a negative
covenant.[5] A rule of thumb is: does the covenant require the spending
of money? If so, it is positive.

[5] A good way of improving
your mark: an average
answer would simply refer to
'negative' covenants but this
answer goes one step further
and looks more closely at
what 'negative' means.

Here, covenant (a), not to carry on any trade, business or profession on the land, is clearly negative and in principle can bind
Richard under the principle in **Tulk v Moxhay**. Covenant (b), to
maintain all fences on Richard's land which border on land retained
by Steve, is clearly positive and so cannot be enforced under **Tulk
v Moxhay**.[6] The final covenant (c), not to keep pets at 155A High
Street, is subject to the rule that a covenant, in order to bind successors in title, must 'touch and concern' the land, and this means
that it must actually benefit the dominant land, in this case 155
High Street,[7] and not be merely personal. In **Re Gadd's Land
Transfer** [1966] Ch 56, Ch D, Buckley J referred to 'something
affecting either the value of the land or the method of its occupation or enjoyment', and it is submitted that a covenant, not to allow
pets on the land, does not come in this category and so will bind
only Bert and not Richard.

[6] Note that we have not said
'cannot be enforced' and left
it at that, as this covenant
may be enforceable under
other rules that it is better to
look at later.

[7] This is often missed: the
whole point of restrictive
covenants is that they are
interests in land which one
piece of land (the dominant
tenement) has over other
land (the servient tenement),
and so any covenant over
the servient land must confer
a benefit over the dominant
land, otherwise there is no
connection between them.

Given that covenant (a) is negative, it can then bind Richard, provided
that the following other conditions are satisfied[8]:

(a) The covenantee must own land for the benefit of which the covenant was entered into (**LCC v Allen** [1914] 3 KB 642, CA). Here,
Steve owns 155 High Street, which adjoins Richard's land.

[8] Do not assume that,
because the covenant is
negative, it is automatically
binding.

(b) The covenant must touch and concern the dominant land. It is clear that this covenant does satisfy the test mentioned above.

(c) It must be the common intention of the parties that the covenant shall run. Covenants made on or after 1 January 1926 are deemed to be made with subsequent parties (s. 79 of the LPA 1925).

(d) The assignee (i.e. Richard) must have notice of the covenant. As title to the land is registered, this means that the covenant must be protected by a notice on the register of that title (s. 29 of the LRA 2002). If it is not, the covenant will not bind a purchaser.

[9] This point often appears in a question on covenants (and also on easements and profits where the answer is the same).

Finally, the fact that Richard has obtained planning permission for the change of use to enable him to run a business from the house does not affect the validity of the restrictive covenant[9] (*Re Martin's Application* (1988) 57 P & CR 119 at 124).

[10] Here is where you get the extra marks: it is not the actual existence of planning permission that is directly relevant but the fact that it can be used as evidence to discharge the covenant.

However, Richard may apply to the Upper Tribunal to modify or discharge this covenant, under section 84 of the LPA 1925, and the fact that planning permission has been obtained may be a factor in persuading the Tribunal to grant the application.[10]

[11] Make it a rule always to end an answer to a question on covenants with the remedies that are appropriate.

The only covenant that is binding on Richard is covenant (a), as a negative covenant. If he refuses to discontinue his use of the house to carry on his accountancy practice, an action for damages may be brought and/or an injunction to restrain the continued use in the case of (a).[11]

[12] You could just quote the actual report, but it is better to set out the words of the draft Bill, as you can then apply them to the question.

The proposals of the Law Commission on this area were set out as clause 2(1) of a draft Bill[12] presented to Parliament in 2016 attached to the 2011 report on covenants. If they were implemented, the answers would be affected, as the Law Commission has proposed that, in future, all obligations expressed as covenants will take effect as land obligations and will be capable of binding the land, provided that:

1 The covenantor owns an estate in land.

2 The obligation is capable of being imposed under clause 1. Clause 1 refers to obligations for the benefit of an estate in land and that touches and concerns the land.

3 The benefit of the covenant touches and concerns land in which the covenantee has an estate.

4 The covenant is not expressed to be personal to either party.

[13] You may be tempted to say that clause 2(1)–(4) above applies, as it says that covenants will not bind as land obligations if they are expressed to be personal to either party. However, this will apply only where the covenant actually *says* that it is personal to the parties. In this case it is the *nature* of the covenant that makes it personal.

The effect would be that the distinction between positive and negative covenants would be abolished, and clause 1(3) provides that land obligations include both negative and positive obligations and so both would be capable of binding third parties. Thus, the answer on covenant (a) would be the same, as the covenant is binding under the present law, but whereas covenant (b) is not binding now, as it is positive, it would be binding under the Law Commission's Bill as a land obligation. However, in both cases, the benefit of the covenant would need to be protected by registration. However, covenant (c) is a personal covenant and would not pass the test set out above, as the benefit of the covenant would not touch and concern land in which the covenantee (Steve) has an estate.[13]

✔ Make your answer stand out

- Give a clear structure to your answer, first identifying the covenantor and covenantee, then identifying who has the benefit and who has the burden of the covenant.
- Read Cooke, E. (2009) To Restate or Not to Restate? Old Wine, New Wineskins, Old Covenants, New Ideas. *Conv.* 448. This article, written by the Law Commissioner responsible for property law, is essential reading for a good mark, as it gives her thinking on the Consultation Paper.
- Read also the article by Davis, C.J. (1998) The Principle of Benefit and Burden. *CLJ*, 57(3): 522, which reviews this whole area.
- Although a grant of planning permission does not discharge a restrictive covenant, the implementation of that permission may alter the standard of what constitutes reasonable use (see Morritt LJ in *Watson* v *Croft Promo-Sport Ltd* [2009] EWCA Civ 15). Although this will probably not be the case in this answer, it is a point worth mentioning.

! Don't be tempted to . . .

- Rush in and start an answer before you have clearly identified the parties and the relevant terms.
- Fail to distinguish clearly between the four different covenants – the law, as is usual in these questions, is different for each.
- Explain what a personal covenant is.

? Question 2

Ted owned a large property, Firtrees, which did not have registered title. In 1980, he built a house, Oak Lodge, in the grounds of Firtrees and sold it to Laura. In 1981, he built a second house, Pinetrees, in the grounds of Firtrees and sold it to Roger. In 1982, he built a third house, Birches, in the grounds of Firtrees and sold it to Mark here Ted retained some land.

In 1984, Roger sold Pinetrees to Babs.

In each case, the buyers from Ted entered into covenants that restricted their use of land but which imposed different restrictions in each case. In the case of Roger, the covenants that he entered into were:

(a) not to allow the hedges surrounding Pinetrees to grow to more than 6 metres in height;

(b) not to erect any building on Pinetrees that exceeds 10 metres in height.

Laura and Mark tell you that Babs has allowed the hedges to grow to at least 20 metres high and that she has told them that she is applying for planning permission to erect another storey on Pinetrees, which will take its height to 20 metres.

Advise Ted, Laura and Mark on what action can be taken and against whom.

Diagram plan

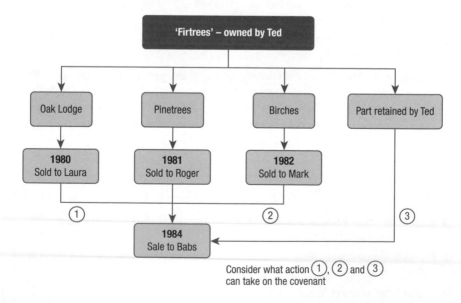

Answer plan

➜ Identify the parties – Laura, Roger and Mark are all covenantors and Ted is the covenantee.

➜ Note that the question requires you to consider the running of the burden of the covenants and also the benefit of it.

➜ Go through the covenants and decide which are positive and which are negative.

➜ Decide whether Babs is liable on any of them.

➜ Then consider separately whether Ted, Laura and Mark can take action against Babs.

➜ Finally, identify and apply the remedies available against Babs.

Answer

In this question, Laura, Roger and Mark have entered into covenants with Ted and so they are all covenantors. Ted is the covenantee. Roger then sold the land with the burden of the covenant to Babs. We are asked whether Ted, Laura and Mark can take action against Babs on the covenants.[1]

There are different considerations to be borne in mind when considering the position of Laura and Mark, but, before we look at whether they can sue, we need to decide whether there has been any breach of the covenants and, if so, who might be liable.[2]

Roger, as the original covenantor, remains liable on the covenants and is potentially liable in the event of a breach by Babs.[3] This rule is not only one of common law but is also implied by section 79(1) of the LPA 1925, unless the covenant provides that the liability of the original covenantor is to cease when he or she sells the land. Here, we are not told whether this is so. It is the universal practice, when land is sold, for the covenantor to take an indemnity covenant from the buyer, so that if the covenantor (Roger) is sued for a breach committed by Babs, Babs will have to indemnify Roger for any damages that he has to pay.

However, it is obviously better to claim against Babs, as, not only is she actually responsible for the breach, but also an injunction can be claimed against her, as well as damages, whereas only damages would be available against Roger.

The common-law rule on covenants was established in **Austerberry v Oldham Corporation** (1885) 29 Ch D 750, CA, where it was held that, at common law, covenants do not bind subsequent owners of

[1] Identify the parties and the relevant terms, making sure that you identify who has the benefit of the covenant and who has the burden. The party with the benefit will be the claimant and the party with the burden will be the defendant.

[2] This question clearly involves questions on the running of the burden of the covenant (i.e. can third parties be sued on the covenant?) and the running of the benefit of the covenant (i.e. can third parties sue for any breaches of the covenants?). First, deal with running of the burden as, if there turns out to be no one who *can be* sued (i.e. the burden does not run), there is no point in asking who *can* sue.

[3] This is a straightforward and easily remembered point and should be placed near the start of any answer to a problem question of this kind.

land, but in *Tulk v Moxhay* (1848) 1 H & Tw 105, HC, it was held that in equity a covenant can bind subsequent owners on certain conditions. This rule was refined in subsequent cases so that it only applied to negative covenants. In *Haywood v Brunswick Permanent Benefit Building Society* (1881) 8 QBD 403, CA, Brett LJ referred to covenants 'restricting the use of the land' and this is a good working definition of a negative covenant. A rule of thumb is: does the covenant require the spending of money? If so, it is positive. If it does not, it is negative. Covenant (a) is positive even though it is actually phrased in negative terms as Babs will have to take positive action to prevent the hedges growing more than 6 metres in height. Thus, it will not bind her and any action in respect of its breach will have to be taken against Roger. However, the covenant not to erect buildings that exceed more than 10 metres in height is negative and can bind Babs provided that the following other conditions are satisfied:

(a) The covenantee must own land for the benefit of which the covenant was entered into (*LCC v Allen* [1914] 3 KB 642, CA). Ted owns 'Firtrees'. There is, however, a question as to whether Laura and Mark are covenantees, but this will be considered later.[4]

(b) The covenant must touch and concern the dominant land. This means that the covenant must actually benefit the land, and it is clear that a covenant to keep buildings to a certain height will do so.

(c) It must be the common intention of the parties that the covenant shall run. Covenants made on or after 1 January 1926 are deemed to be made with subsequent parties (s. 79 of the LPA 1925).

(d) The assignee (i.e. Babs) must have notice of the covenant. As title to the land was unregistered at the time,[5] and as the covenant was entered into on or after 1 January 1926, it must be registered as a Class D(ii) land charge, otherwise it will not bind a purchaser.

Ted can take action against Roger, as they were the original parties to the covenant, and he can also take action against Babs. The question is then whether Laura and Mark can claim the benefit of the covenants.[6] One way would be through a building scheme where all parties

[4] 'Park' this for now, as, if you deal with it at this point, you will go completely off your present point, which is whether *anyone* can sue Babs.

[5] When you come to this point in your answer, do glance back at the question and check again whether title was registered or unregistered.

[6] Make this point follow on from the previous one: the original parties can, of course, sue but whether successors in title can sue will depend on whether the benefit has passed to them.

have entered into identical covenants and so create a kind of local law for a particular area. The conditions were laid down in **Elliston v Reacher** [1908] 2 Ch 374, but one element, that of mutuality, is lacking as each purchaser entered into different covenants[7] and this is a requirement (see **Emile Elias v Pine Groves** (1993) 66 P & CR 1).

Laura purchased Oak Lodge in 1980, before the sale of Pinetrees to Roger in 1981.[8] This is significant, as it means that Laura cannot claim that, when she bought Oak Lodge, the benefit of the covenant entered into by Roger was annexed to Oak Lodge, as at that time the covenants had not been imposed. Similarly, it cannot be argued that the benefit of the covenants imposed on Pinetrees had been assigned to Oak Lodge. Laura cannot claim that the provisions of section 1 of the Contracts (Rights of Third Parties) Act 1999 apply here, as the covenants were entered into before the Act came into force.[9] The only other possibility is the use of section 56(1) of the LPA 1925, which enables a party to 'take . . . the benefit of any condition, right of entry, covenant or agreement over or respecting land or other property, although he may not be named as a party to the conveyance or other instrument'.[10] This will apply only where Laura was able to be a party to the covenant and identifiable and in existence at the date of the covenant (**White v Bijou Mansions** [1937] Ch 610). We would need to see the exact words of the covenant to decide whether Laura was intended to be a party. If so, she can claim; if not, she cannot.

Mark is in a different position, as he bought Birches after the sale of Pinetrees to Roger. He may claim that the benefit of Roger's covenant has been expressly assigned to the Birches, or he may claim that the benefit of the covenant has been expressly annexed to his land, as in **Rogers v Hosegood** [1900] 2 Ch 388, CA,[11] but, again, we would need to see the exact words of the conveyance to Mark.[12]

The final possibility, and the one most likely to be used by Mark, is to claim that the benefit of the covenant has passed to him by implied annexation under the principle in **Federated Homes v Mill Lodge Properties Ltd** [1980] 1 All ER 371, CA.

If Babs is successfully sued, the remedy sought[13] would probably be an injunction to restrain her from going ahead with the building.

[7] This point often arises in a question, and you should watch for it.

[8] Watch for the scenario in this question where land with the burden of the covenant is sold after one piece of land (Oak Lodge, here) and before the sale of another piece of land (Birches). The answer, as we see here, will be different in each case.

[9] Watch for this point! If you do not, you could waste time, and thus marks, on an explanation of the Act.

[10] Where you get a person in Laura's position, you need to think of two points: first, the Contracts (Rights of Third Parties) Act 1999 and then section 56(l) of the LPA. Here, the 1999 Act does not apply, so we have had to turn to section 56(1).

[11] See that there are two possibilities: assignment or express annexation. We do not know whether they will apply, so the examiner will just expect you to mention them.

[12] Note how this question does not close off these possibilities, as the examiner is hoping that you will earn marks by looking at them all.

[13] Never forget to mention remedies!

✓ Make your answer stand out

- Clear distinction in your answer between the questions of who has the burden of the covenants and who has the benefit. It is absolutely crucial to get this right at the start.
- Distinguish between when section 56(1) of the LPA 1925 applies and when section 1 of the Contracts (Rights of Third Parties) Act 1999 applies.
- Read Stevens, R. (2004) The Contracts (Rights of Third Parties) Act 1999. *Law Quarterly Review*, 120: 292, who argues that this Act does not, in fact, have a very wide application.
- Read the judgment of Neuberger J in *Amsprop Trading Ltd* v *Harris Distribution Ltd* [1997] 1 WLR 1025, Ch D, on the circumstances in which section 56(1) of the LPA 1925 can apply.

! Don't be tempted to . . .

- Assume that Ted, Laura and Mark all have the same rights to enforce the covenant. If they had, you would not have been asked to advise them separately.
- Although the more difficult parts of the question deal with enforceability of covenants, remember to deal with who can be liable first – i.e. has the burden passed?
- Apply only section 1 of the Contracts (Rights of Third Parties) Act 1999 or section 56(1) of the LPA 1925. Both need to be considered.

❓ Question 3

John owns an industrial estate that has registered title. The land has previously been subject to flooding and John has installed an expensive drainage scheme that should prevent flooding in future, but there will be a continuing cost from keeping the drains in repair. He has also built a road serving all of the estate.

He wishes to sell individual units on the estate, while retaining two for himself, and to:

(a) Oblige each owner of a unit to contribute to the cost of the upkeep of the estate road and the drains.

(b) Prevent each unit owner from using the land sold to him in such a way that further flooding is caused.

In addition, John wishes to impose extra covenants on particular areas of land sold.

John also wishes to be able to take action himself on the covenants in the event of a breach, and he also wishes anyone who acquires his land in the future to be able to do so.

Advise John on how he can achieve these objectives.

Answer plan

→ Identify who is to be able to enforce the covenants and who the covenants are to be enforced against.

→ Explain the ways in which the benefit of the covenants can pass in equity.

→ Distinguish the passing of the benefit of the covenant at common law from that in equity.

→ Passing of the burden of the covenants – distinguish between covenants (a) and (b).

Diagram plan

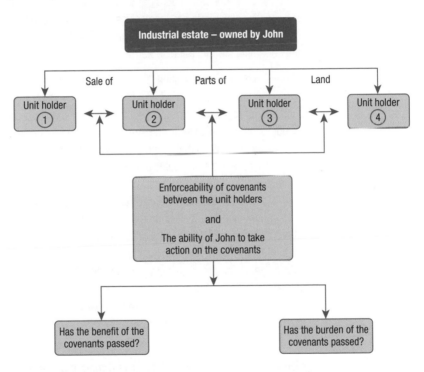

A printable version of this diagram plan is available from **www.pearsoned.co.uk/lawexpressqa**

Answer

This question is concerned with how John can make certain covenants that he intends to impose on sales of land binding on the buyers and also how to enable each buyer to sue any other buyer who is in breach of them. In addition, he wishes to be able to enforce them.

Each person who buys a unit and enters into these covenants will be the covenantor and John, as the person with whom they enter the covenants, will be the covenantee.[1] There is no problem with John taking action against any owner of a unit who breaches the covenant, as they are both parties to it. However, problems could arise in cases when one unit owner wishes to sue any other owner, as John intends, on the grounds that they have breached covenants (a) and/or (b).

Suppose that one owner (X) claims to sue another owner (Y), then X who sues will be a third party to the original covenant made between John and Y.[2] In general, a third party cannot sue on a covenant, but, as restrictive covenants are themselves interests in the land itself, it is possible in some cases for third parties to sue and our objective must be to enable this to be so here.[3]

Where X in our example wishes to sue Y, X must show that the benefit of the covenant has passed to him. One clear way in which this can be done is by the existence of a building scheme that enables a common vendor, John in this case, to transfer the benefit of any covenant to every buyer of a unit so that a kind of 'local law' is created whereby all the parties have the same rights and obligations under the covenants and may enforce them against each other in equity. The requirements were laid down in ***Elliston v Reacher*** [1908] 2 Ch 374, Ch D, but there cannot be a building scheme where different buyers are under different obligations (***White v Bijou Mansions*** [1937] Ch 610, Ch D). We are told that, here, extra covenants are to be imposed on different units of land.[4] The practical answer is to impose the same covenants mentioned in the question on all the buyers, thus creating a building scheme, and then quite separately require particular buyers to enter into separate covenants as appropriate.

Another possibility is expressly to annex the benefit of the covenants to each unit of land when it is sold. Thus, in ***Rogers v Hosegood*** [1900] 2 Ch 388, CA, the benefit of a covenant was held to be expressly annexed to land where the covenant's wording was that 'the covenant may enure to the benefit of the vendors, their successors and assigns and others claiming under them to all or any of their lands adjoining'. Compare these words with those in ***Renals v Cowlishaw***[5] (1878) 9 Ch D 125, Ch D, where the covenant had been made with the vendors, 'their heirs, executors, administrators and assigns'. The crucial difference was that in ***Rogers v Hosegood*** the covenant mentioned the actual land to be benefited, but in **Renals v Cowlishaw** it did not. The message is clear: John can achieve his object by expressly annexing the benefit of the covenants by using similar language to that in **Rogers v Hosegood**.

[6] Assignment of the benefit of covenants is now less important in view of the decision in *Federated Homes v Mill Lodge Properties*, which made implied annexation much easier. However, as we are advising a client in general, it must be mentioned.

There seems to be no problem with all units benefitting from both the road and the drainage scheme. Even so, for the avoidance of doubt, the covenants should state that they apply to 'each and every part of the land', as held in **Marquess of Zetland v Driver** [1939] Ch 1, CA.

Even if this is not done, it may be possible to argue that the benefit of the covenants has been annexed to the lands sold by implied annexation, under the decision in **Federated Homes v Mill Lodge Properties Ltd** [1980] 1 All ER 371, CA. This held that implied annexation is provided for by section 78(1) LPA 1925 which says that, 'A covenant relating to the land of the covenantee shall be deemed to be made with the covenantee and his successors in title.' In **Federated Homes v Mill Lodge Properties Ltd** itself the covenant said that it related to 'land of the covenantee' and in this case that will be the land owned by John. So it is essential that the covenant makes this clear.

[7] It is easy to get completely lost here, so just remember this: if you get a question where Y is the original covenantee and has sold the land with the benefit of the covenant to X, X can sue on it provided that he or she is suing the original covenantor – the person who entered into the covenant with Y. However, the common-law rule will not enable X to sue anyone who has subsequently acquired the land. To do this, X must use the rules in equity. See the next note.

Another possibility is that, instead of annexing the benefits of the covenants to the land sold, the benefit could be assigned.[6] This method was used, for example, in **Roake v Chadha** [1984] 1 WLR 40, Ch D, but it does depend on the benefit of the covenant being expressly assigned each time the land is sold. Express annexation is more straightforward.

[8] This is very important and so do remember it, otherwise you could go completely astray in the exam and lose lots of marks! If a person wishes to claim that the burden of the covenant runs in equity under the rule in *Tulk v Moxhay*, they must show that the benefit has passed to them in equity under the three rules mentioned above: by the existence of a building scheme, by annexation or by assignment.

Anyone who buys John's own land from him in future will be a successor in title and will be able to sue any unit owner who has bought their land from John and is in breach of the covenants. This is because, at common law, the benefit of a covenant can run to enable the successor in title of the original covenantee to sue the original covenantor.[7] (See **The Prior's Case** (1368) YB 42 Edw 3 and, for a modern illustration, **Smith and Snipes Hall Farm v River Douglas Catchment Board** [1949] 2 KB 500.) However, the common-law rule will not enable a successor in title to John to claim that the benefit has passed to them to enable them to claim against successors in title to the original covenantor.[8] In order to do this, they must prove that the benefit has passed to them in equity and this can be done on proof that the benefit of the covenant has been annexed to them or has been assigned to them, or that there is a building scheme, all of which have been discussed above.

[9] The question asks you about action being taken on the covenants, but, to make the answer complete, you do need to mention briefly who can actually be sued, which is what this final section does.

In addition, we must decide whether the burden has passed to successors in title of the original covenantors.[9] Although this is not directly raised by the question, we must mention this point to make the answer complete. Covenant (a) is positive and so is only binding on the original covenantor but may be binding on successors in title, under the principle in *Halsall v Brizell* [1957] 1 All ER 371, Ch D HC that a person who takes the benefit of a deed of covenant must also share its burden, so that, as a particular owner benefits by observance of the covenant by other owners to keep the drains in repair, so he must do likewise.

This principle was applied in *Elwood v Goodman and others* [2013] EWCA Civ 1103, CA, where it was held that a positive covenant, such as one under the *Halsall v Brizell* principle, was not capable of creating an estate or interest in registered land and so it did not require to be registered for it to bind successors in title of the original covenantor.

The principle in *Halsall v Brizell* could apply in (b) also, but, if covenant (b) is negative, under the rule in *Tulk v Moxhay* (1848) 1 H & TW 105, HC, it will, in principle, bind subsequent parties anyway. In this case, though, it must be registered against the burdened land.

✓ Make your answer stand out

- Approach the question from the right angle: it is not asking you (as questions often do) to decide on the validity of existing covenants but to address the more practical issue of how covenants can be made binding on buyers of land and how to enable each buyer to sue any other buyer who is in breach of them.
- Deal with the issues of benefit and burden separately.
- Distinguish between the positions at common law and in equity.
- Read *Crest Nicholson Residential (South) Ltd* v *McAllister* [2004] 1 WLR 2409, CA, which considered the decision in *Federated Homes* v *Mill Lodge Properties*. Chadwick LJ held that statutory annexation under section 78(1) of the LPA 1925 could occur only if the covenant, or conveyances in which the covenant was contained, identified the land to be benefited either specifically or by implication. By contrast, if you look at the wording in *Rogers* v *Hosegood* (see the answer above), where annexation was express, the actual land was not precisely identified. The result is that the rules seem tighter for implied annexation.

■ Research *Cosmichome Ltd* v *Southampton City Council* [2013] EWHC 1378(Ch) on the position where a covenant is expressed to be for the benefit and protection of so much of the seller's adjoining or adjacent land.

■ Research *Wilkinson* v *Kerdene Ltd* [2013] EWCA Civ 44 on the application of the *Halsall* v *Brizell* principle.

! Don't be tempted to . . .

■ Fail to set out the different issues right at the start.

■ Distinguish between the different ways in which the benefit can run.

■ Leave out one of the two methods of annexation.

■ Confuse running of the benefit of the covenants in equity and at common law.

■ Leave out a mention of when the burden can pass and distinguish between the different covenants.

🖎 Question 4

Critically consider the proposition that the present law on freehold covenants is unnecessarily complex and evaluate the proposals contained in the Law Commission (2011) Report, *Making Land Work: Easements, Covenants and Profits à Prendre* (LC 327) for reform in this area.

Diagram plan

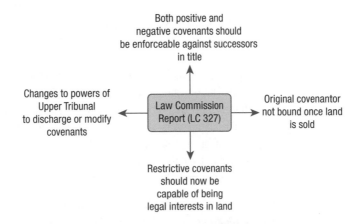

A printable version of this diagram plan is available from **www.pearsoned.co.uk/lawexpressqa**

Answer plan

→ Identify the main problems and give a brief historical background.

→ Explain the rule that positive covenants do not run with the land – and how this has caused problems – and then look in detail at how the Law Commission intends to deal with it.

→ Explore other areas, especially the proposals on the running of the benefit of covenants.

→ Mention the proposal of the Law Commission that covenants will be legal interests.

→ Conclusion – do restrictive covenants play any useful purpose in the law anyway?

Answer

[1] You should see from the question that you are asked two things and not one, and so you need to make this clear in your introduction. This will at once impress your examiner and earn you extra marks. You could, of course, take the opposite view – that the proposals will not achieve their desired result – but there is general agreement that at least their implementation will improve the law.

[2] It often helps to 'anchor' your answer on a general point like this if you can give the facts of a case.

The present law on freehold covenants is unnecessarily complex and I consider that the proposals of the Law Commission Report (2011) LC 327 will go a long way towards both clarifying and modernising the law.[1]

There is no problem where the original covenantee wishes to claim against the original covenantor, but problems certainly exist in two cases:

(a) where it is sought to make a successor in title to the original covenantor liable on the basis that the burden of the covenant has passed to them;

(b) where a successor in title to the original covenantee wishes to sue on the basis that the benefit of the covenants has passed to them.

The problem in (a) is that, whereas the burden of the covenant may pass to a successor in title if the covenant is negative, it will not if it is positive. The difficulties that this rule can give rise to can be seen in **Rhone v Stephens** [1994] 2 All ER 65, HL,[2] where the owner of a building, having divided it into two dwellings, sold one part, a cottage, and retained the other, the house. On the sale of the cottage, he covenanted to maintain the roof that projected over the cottage. In fact, the roof leaked and damaged the cottage. The present owners of the cottage, to whom the benefit of the covenant had been expressly assigned, sued the successors in title of the original covenantor, but it was held that, as the covenant was positive, there could be no liability. If, for example, the covenant had been negative, such as not to run a business on the land, then there would have been liability.

In fact, although the case that is the fountain head of the law here, **Tulk v Moxhay** (1848) 1 H & TW 105, HC, actually concerned a negative covenant, the court did not distinguish between positive and negative covenants, and this development only came later in – for example, ***Haywood v Brunswick Permanent Benefit Building Society*** (1881) 8 QBD 403, CA.

[3] This is the main issue raised by the question, and you need to spend most of your answer on it.

[4] You should at least identify the ways in which positive covenants can be made to run in order to give a complete picture. If you have time, you could explain how and why they are not satisfactory (e.g. the problems in identifying when the principle in *Halsall* v *Brizell* applies), but do not let this get you off the main point of the Law Commission's proposals.

[5] If you have time, you could say more on this, but the essential point is that it can apply as an alternative to leasehold. In fact, you could do some research and show that the take-up of commonhold has been very small.

[6] This was the main conclusion, and so you should make this one of the central points of your answer.

[7] This is one of those essential connecting sentences that really add to your marks. Many students will write about only the positive covenants, but there is much more to the Report than this.

The failure of positive covenants to bind successors in title was described by the Law Commission (2008) Consultation Paper, Easements, Covenants and Profits 'a Prendre. No. 86. http://lawcommission. justice.gov.uk/docs/cp186_Easements_Covenants_and_Profits_a_ Prendre_Consultation.pdf (Para. 7.39) as the 'greatest and clearest deficiency' in the law.[3] The Report that followed the Consultation Paper outlines (in Paras. 5.23–5.26) the ways in which positive covenants can be made to run with the land, such as long leases, a right of entry annexed to an estate rentcharge, indemnity covenants and the 'benefit and burden' principle in ***Halsall v Brizell*** [1957][4] 3 All ER 371, Ch D, but the Report concludes, rightly, that none of them is satisfactory as 'they can all be made to work but only indirectly, with unnecessary cost and risk' (Para. 5.27).

The Report did not consider that the 'commonhold' method, which was introduced by Part 1 of the Commonhold and Leasehold Reform Act 2002, was a solution,[5] as it pointed out at Paragraph 5.17 that it applied where developers of freehold land wished to establish schemes of mutually enforceable covenants and is 'designed for truly interdependent developments such as flats, or business units that share facilities and physical structure'.

Thus, the Law Commission has proposed that the law on positive covenants should be reformed (Para. 5.63) and that they should be enforceable against successors in title as negative covenants are.[6]

However, this then brings with it the question of who can enforce those covenants, especially as the law, by permitting the enforcement of covenants against successors in title, will be making the operation of covenants more burdensome.[7] To meet this point, obligations are carefully defined (Para. 6.38) and consist of:

- a promise not to do something on the covenantor's land (these are the old negative covenants);
- a promise to do something on one's own land or on a boundary structure;
- a promise to make a reciprocal payment.

There is also a requirement that the benefit of the promise touches and concerns the land of the covenantee, and that the promise is not expressed to be personal. This would exclude, as now, personal covenants.

The Commission had noted in the Consultation Paper (Para. 7.37) that the present rules as to the running of benefit and burden of restrictive covenants are a significant defect in the law because of their complexity. However, its Report points out (Para. 6.45) that not all consultees agreed, and 'we accept that practitioners have learnt to live with the rules and to operate them efficiently'. Thus they will remain.[8]

[8] This is an important point: do not confine your answer to the proposed change in the law on positive covenants.

Underlying these changes is a more fundamental one. Restrictive covenants have always been equitable interests in land and the Report points out that 'These are generically different from easements and profits, because they cannot exist as legal interests in land'. It points out (Para. 5.4) that the fundamental idea of a covenant is that it is a contractual right, and not a property right.[9] This contractual status is reflected in the fact that contractual liability between the original parties to a covenant persists despite changes in the ownership of the land; when the land is sold, the original covenantor remains liable. Nevertheless, restrictive covenants have a hybrid status in that they can be made to bind a purchaser of land if they take effect as equitable interests.

[9] It is vital that you are clear on this, as this point underlies much of the present law, e.g. the fact that the covenantor remains liable on the covenant after he/she has parted with the land.

[10] This is an important change that the examiner will expect you to mention.

The Commission proposes that all of this should be swept away and restrictive covenants should now be legal interests created by deed and added to the list of legal interests set out in section 1(2)(a) of the LPA 1925.[10] In addition, they should be capable of being created only where title to the land is registered (Para. 8.38).

Moreover, clause 2(2) of the draft Bill attached to the Report of the Law Commission specifically provides that promises in the form of restrictive covenants (e.g. not to build on land etc.) will take effect as land obligations and not covenants, although the word 'covenant' can still be used. They will run with the benefited land, and bind successors in title to the burdened land, because they are interests in land, but they will not bind the original covenantor. This means that the taking out of indemnity covenants so that the original covenantor will be indemnified against future breaches will not be necessary.

The Law Commission recommends that land obligations should be able to exist in equity, where, for example, the obligation was not created by deed but is in a written agreement that complies with the Law of Property (Miscellaneous Provisions) Act 1989 or is not registered. However, the Law Commission (Para. 6.52) feels that there should be very few that remain equitable, as, generally, land obligations will be contained in transfers of land and will become legal upon registration, in the same way as easements.

[11] Most students ignore this point, but the jurisdiction under section 84 is important in practice.

Finally, the powers for the Upper Tribunal to exercise its jurisdiction under section 84 of the LPA 1925 to discharge or modify covenants will be clarified and made more transparent.[11]

Overall, it is submitted that these proposals will bring clarity to an area where this has long been lacking. A draft bill implementing these proposals was introduced in 2016.

✓ Make your answer stand out

- Look at how the law on restrictive covenants has developed in other jurisdictions – the Law Commission Report has many references, so follow one or two up!
- Read Cooke, E. (2009) To Restate or Not to Restate? Old Wine, New Wineskins, Old Covenants, New Ideas. *Conv.* 448, a very readable article explaining the Law Commission's proposals in depth. Note, though, that it is commenting on the consultation paper and not the final report.
- Look at Simpson, A.W.B. (1986) *A History of the Land Law*. Oxford: Oxford University Press, especially at pp. 256–60: this will give you some excellent background material on how and why the law of restrictive covenants developed.
- Do some research on how the jurisdiction of the Upper Tribunal (formerly the Lands Tribunal) exercises its jurisdiction under section 84 of the LPA 1925. How might this change, and what will its effects be?

! Don't be tempted to . . .

- Just say what the law on restrictive covenants is: a merely descriptive answer to what is a specific question will earn you a very bad mark!
- Overlook one area at the expense of another: deal with problems in the law, but not the Law Commission's proposals or vice versa.
- Do set the scene – do not plunge into an answer without first making sure that you have explained what the problems are.

Question 5

Critically consider the law on when a person who is not a party to a restrictive covenant can sue on that covenant.

Answer plan

→ Show where this point fits into the law on covenants.

→ Explain how section 56(1) of the LPA 1925 enables a third party to sue, and mention what problems there are in the interpretation of this.

→ Reinforce this by distinguishing between two contrasting cases.

→ Now evaluate the effect of section 1 of the Contracts (Rights of Third Parties) Act 1999, indicating the problems in the interpretation of this.

→ Round off the answer by evaluating how the proposals in the Law Commission Report would change the law.

Diagram plan

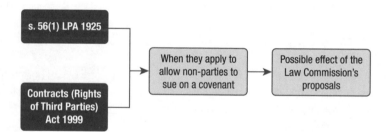

A printable version of this diagram plan is available from **www.pearsoned.co.uk/lawexpressqa**

[1] The word 'making' of the covenant is important and shows the examiner that you know exactly what you are talking about. When the covenant is made, successors in title of both the original covenantor and covenantee will be third parties, but this is dealt with by the rules on the running of the benefit and burden of the covenant. A draft bill implementing these proposals was introduced in 2016.

Answer

This question concerns the position of those who are third parties to the making of a covenant[1] and whether they can claim under it. For example, suppose that Ned covenants with John not to use Greenacres for business purposes, but also enters into the same covenants with 'the owners of land adjacent to the land conveyed'. Amy is the

[2] It really does help, especially in a complex area such as this, to set the scene with an example, but do remember to refer to it as you go on.

[3] Here, we are stating a very basic point, but one that puts the question in its context of privity.

[4] This should be the next point.

owner of land adjoining and she wishes to enforce the covenant against Ned, who has broken the covenant.[2]

The simple answer is that, as Amy is a third party to the covenant, under the doctrine of privity of contract, she cannot claim any rights under it nor be under any obligations under it.[3] This rule applied to deeds as well as contracts. However, Amy may be able to sue using section 56(1) of the Law of Property Act (LPA) 1925,[4] which provides that: 'A person may take . . . the benefit of any condition, right of entry, covenant or agreement over or respecting land or other property, although he may not be named as a party to the conveyance or other instrument.'

[5] Now you start to earn some extra marks, as you are showing that you are aware of problems with this area.

The effect of this has never been entirely clear.[5] In **Beswick v Beswick** [1966] Ch 538, CA, Denning MR gave it such a wide interpretation as to completely abolish the doctrine of privity of contract. The majority of the House of Lords ([1968] AC 58) held that section 56 was inapplicable, but this case did not concern real property – rather, a promise to pay money. The probability is then that section 56 allows a person in some circumstances to take the benefit of a covenant to which they are not a party, but not in all cases, so that they cannot claim simply by saying that it was made for their benefit. What are these cases?

[6] This shows the advantage of our example at the start, as it helps to make this point clear.

The main point is that it must have been possible for that person to have been a party. Thus, in our example, the fact that the covenant was also made with 'the owners of land adjacent to the land conveyed' indicates that it was possible for Amy to have been a party.[6] Suppose that, instead, the covenant was expressed to be made with anyone who might at any future date become an owner of any land adjoining? That person would not come within section 56(1) and could not enforce the covenant because it would not necessarily have been possible for them to have been a party. This is often expressed by saying that the third party must have been in existence and identifiable when the covenant was made.

[7] Looking at a pair of cases and contrasting them is always an excellent way of adding depth to your answer and adding to your marks.

This can be seen by looking at two contrasting cases.[7] In **Re Ecclesiastical Commissioners Conveyance** [1936] Ch 430, Ch D, a covenant was entered into with the covenantor to observe certain restrictive covenants, but, in addition, the covenantor covenanted to observe the same covenants with the owners of land 'adjoining or adjacent to' the land with the benefit of the covenant. It was held that this covenant was enforceable by those who, at the date of the conveyance of his land to the covenantor, did in fact own adjoining or adjacent land. The point was that they were the present owners of the land and, as such, they were in existence and identifiable when the covenant was made.

In **White v Bijou Mansions** [1937] Ch 610 Ch D, X had bought land that was part of an estate and he covenanted to use the land for residential purposes only. Moreover, the covenantee agreed that any future conveyance of any part of the estate would contain a similar covenant. The question was whether a person who had bought land on the estate later and entered into a similar covenant could be sued by X. It was held that he could not; the crucial difference from that case and **Re Ecclesiastical Commissioners Conveyance** was that, here, the covenant was sought to be enforced against a future owner of land who may have been in existence when the first covenant was made but was not identifiable.[8]

Neuberger J in **Amsprop Trading Ltd v Harris Distribution Ltd** [1997] 1 WLR 1025, Ch D put it this way: 'The true aim of section 56 seems to be not to allow a third party to sue on a contract merely because it is for his benefit; the contract must purport to be made with him', i.e. does the covenantor actually promise the covenantee that owners of adjacent land will benefit?

Under the Contracts (Rights of Third Parties) Act 1999,[9] section 1, a person who is not a party to a contract can take the benefit of a contractual term that purports to confer a benefit on him. Although this Act covers the whole of the law of contract, not just this area, here this Act and section 56(1) of the LPA 1925 overlap.

How far does section 1 apply to enforcement of contracts by non-parties? It is arguable that the Act applies only to contracts and not to deeds. Even if it applies to deeds, provided that the original covenant is valid, it will permit the enforcement of covenants in wider circumstances than in the past. However, the essential condition is that the covenant purports to confer a benefit on the third party, and this will have to be by express words. Provided that this is so, the third party may enforce it and it will not be necessary for the third party to have been in existence at the date of the covenant. Thus it is suggested that the decision in **White v Bijou Mansions** would have been different had this Act been in force at the time. In our example at the start of this answer, the phrase 'the owners of land adjacent to the

[8] If you do use pairs of cases and contrast them, do make sure that you bring out the essential differences between them.

[9] There are two main areas to consider in this answer: the first was section 56 (1) of the LPA 1925, but the examiner will also expect a discussion of section 1 of the Contracts (Rights of Third Parties) Act 1999. The point to get across is that they *appear* to cover the same ground and allow a third party to claim the benefit of a covenant, but there are differences of detail. It is when you indicate these differences that you start to really earn high marks.

land conveyed' could then include not just present owners, as under section 56(1) but also future owners.

It cannot be denied that this area of the law is complex and, in conclusion, it is worth noting that clause 3(1) of the draft Bill attached to the Law Commission (2011) Report, Making Land Work: Easements, Covenants and Profits à Prendre (LC 327). http://lawcommission. justice.gov.uk/docs/lc327_easements_report.pdf provides that the benefit of a covenant should pass to any person who is a successor in title of the original owner of the benefited estate or any part of it or who has an estate derived out of the benefited estate or any part of it.[10] This would, it is suggested, have the same effect as section 1 of the Contracts (Rights of Third Parties) Act 1999, but the language would be that of property law and not contract law. Presumably the 1999 Act would run alongside this provision, which itself might lead to confusion. There is yet more work to be done on this area of law.

[10] This is a really excellent way to round off an answer. You are seen to be up to date and you are also showing very clearly how the proposals in the Law Commission's Report would affect the present law.

✓ Make your answer stand out

- Look in detail at the debate on what was decided in *Beswick* v *Beswick*: read the judgments of both the majority and the minority.
- Read the note on *Re Ecclesiastical Commissioners Conveyance* at (1937) *Conveyancer* 74 and that on *White* v *Bijou Mansions* in (1938) *Conveyancer*, 2: 260.
- Read in detail exactly what the Contracts (Rights of Third Parties) Act 1999 says. A good place to start is MacMillan, C. (2000) A Birthday Present for Lord Denning: The Contracts (Rights of Third Parties) Act 1999. *Modern Law Review*, 63(5): 721.
- Refer to the words of the draft Bill attached to the Law Commission's report rather than to its recommendations: this will gain marks as, if the draft Bill becomes law, it is these words that will matter.

! Don't be tempted to . . .

- Stray away from the precise issue: this is not a general question on covenants but concerns only the rights of third parties to enforce them.
- Mention only one area: remember that there are two areas of law that can apply in this situation.
- Forget to mention the proposals in the Law Commission Report.

@ **Try it yourself**

Now take a look at the question below and attempt to answer it. You can check your response against the answer guidance available on the companion website (**www.pearsoned.co.uk/lawexpressqa**).

> John owned a large property, Southbourne. He built a house, Westbourne Lodge, in the grounds of Southbourne and sold it to Liz.
>
> The following year, he built a second house, Eastbourne, in the grounds of Southbourne and sold it to Tony, who entered into the following covenants
>
> a. Not to allow the hedges surrounding Eastbourne to grow to more than 6 metres in height.
>
> b. Not to allow pets to dwell on the premises.
>
> c. To pay one-third of the costs of maintaining the private drainage system that services all three properties.
>
> d. Not to make any alterations to Eastbourne without the consent of the owners of land now or formerly forming part of Southbourne.
>
> The next year, John sold Southbourne to Lucy and, in the same year Tony sold Eastbourne to Kate. Lucy and Liz tell you that Kate has allowed the hedges to grow to at least 20 metres high, she has a pet alligator that dwells at the property, and she is proposing to erect a conservatory at the back of Eastbourne although she has not sought the required consents. Kate is also refusing to pay the costs of maintaining the sewers.
>
> Advise Lucy and Liz on what action can be taken and against whom.

www.pearsoned.co.uk/lawexpressqa

Go online to access more revision support, including additional essay and problem questions with diagram plans, and you be the marker questions, and to download all diagrams from the book.

Easements and profits

8

How this topic may come up in exams

Problem questions on easements and profits tend to revolve around their character-istics and the methods of their creation, together with prescription. Within this area there are two topics that need careful thought: whether there can be an easement of exclusive use, including car parking, and the creation of easements by implication. Both are also likely subjects for essays, as there have been recent cases on them and the law is not entirely settled. As with covenants, the proposals of the Law Commission for reform of the law in this area have given us an obvious topic too.

■ Before you begin

It's a good idea to consider the following key themes of easements and profits before
tackling a question on this topic.

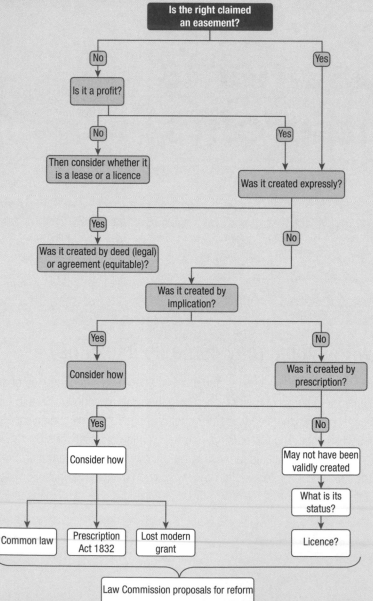

A printable version of this diagram is available from **www.pearsoned.co.uk/lawexpressqa**

❓ Question 1

In 2016, John bought 21 Elms Avenue, which is part of 'Elms Estate', a development of detached houses adjoining a golf course. When the estate was developed in 2010, a written agreement was made between Bunkers Plc, the owners of the golf course, and all the owners of the houses on the estate, granting the owners the right to:

(a) Use both the golf course and all the other leisure facilities in it, including a swimming pool.

(b) Use the hard standing at the entrance to the golf course to park cars and other vehicles.

In 2017, Bunkers Plc wrote to John and all the other estate owners, stating that it was no longer profitable for them to allow use of these facilities free of charge and that, in future, there would be a charge for using them.

John asks you for advice on whether Bunkers Plc are entitled to impose this charge.

Diagram plan

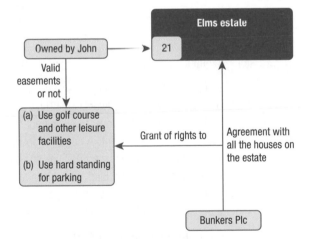

A printable version of this diagram plan is available from **www.pearsoned.co.uk/lawexpressqa**

Answer plan

→ Are the alleged rights capable of existing as easements?

→ In particular, is the right to enjoy leisure facilities capable of being granted by deed?

→ Can a right of car parking be an easement?

→ Are they legal easements/profits created by deed?

→ Are they equitable easements/profits created by written agreement?

→ Can they be enforced against Bunkers Plc?

Answer

In this case, we have two possible easements: the right to use the swimming pool and other facilities, and the right to use the hard standing to park cars.

[1] It is vital that you address this issue in all problem questions on easements and profits, although it may be that the answer is obvious, in which case you need only to mention the topic briefly.

The first question is whether the alleged rights are capable of existing as easements.[1] In **Re Ellenborough Park** [1955] 3 All ER 667, CA, it was held that, to be valid as an easement, the right must have the following characteristics although these are guidelines rather than requirements as in a statute.[2]

[2] It is worth making this point because, as we shall see in other questions in this chapter, the law of easements needs to develop with the times and its development should not be confined by rigid criteria.

(a) There must be a dominant and a servient tenement.

(b) The right must benefit the dominant land.

(c) The dominant and servient tenements must not be both owned and occupied by the same person.

(d) The right must be capable of being granted by deed.

[3] We could have gone directly to the cases, but, instead, we have added to our marks by first setting the issue in a wider context by linking it to fundamental points.

The significance of the right being capable of being granted by deed is that, to do so, it must be clearly defined.[3] Thus, a right to just wander anywhere that a person liked over the dominant tenement (DT) would be unlikely to be an easement. A negative easement exists where the owner of the servient tenement (ST) has no actual obligations but is restricted in the use of the land, and this is the case here. If new negative easements are created, this imposes further restrictions on the right of the owner of the ST to use his property.

However, in **Re Ellenborough Park** itself, the court accepted an easement of recreational use that gave the owners of certain houses in a square the right to use the park in the middle of the square. The owners were sufficiently defined, and so was the right.

This was applied in **Regency Villas Title Ltd v Diamond Resorts (Europe) Ltd** [2015] EWHC 3564 (Ch), where there was a claim to use the sporting and leisure facilities on the 'adjoining estate'. The court, looking at the characteristics of an easement, held that there were dominant and servient tenements; that the right did benefit the

[4] In any question on whether a right can exist as an easement, always look at whether it does satisfy all these characteristics, even where, as here, it is clear that the main issue concerns only one of them. In that case, just mention the others briefly.

[5] Once you have decided that the right is an easement, you must always follow on with this point.

[6] It is also possible to have easements that are legal created by implication, under the rule in *Wheeldon v Burrows* (1879) 12 Ch D 31, CA, so, if you had just said that 'to be legal an easement must be created by deed', that would not give a complete and accurate picture and you would lose marks.

[7] This is a common examination point.

[8] As in the previous scenario, here too we are setting the issue in a wider context.

dominant land as it was not just a right of recreation; and that the dominant and servient tenements were owned and occupied by different people.[4]

The main issue was the fourth characteristic: was the right capable of being granted by deed? The court held that it was. Purle J observed that: 'There is nothing vague or of excessive width in the present rights'. It is suggested that the same applies here: given that recreational rights can, in principle, be easements on the authority of *Re Ellenborough Park*, the rights to use 'both the golf course and all the other leisure facilities in it including a swimming pool' are very similar to those in the *Regency Villas* case and so John can claim an easement.

The next question is whether the easement was validly created.[5] We are told that, when the estate was developed in 2010, a written agreement was made. If an expressly created[6] easement or profit is to be legal, then, by section 52 of the Law of Property Act 1925 (LPA 1925), it must be created by deed. If it is a deed, by section 27 of the LRA 2002, it must be registered, and if it is then it will bind Bunkers Plc.

It is not clear whether this is so, as the question refers only to an 'agreement'.[7] If it is not in a deed, the agreement must satisfy section 2 of the Law of Property (Miscellaneous Provisions) Act 1989. This provides that a contract for the sale or other disposition of land (which includes an equitable easement) must be in writing, contain all the agreed terms and be signed by each party. Again, we cannot be sure whether this is the case as, in particular, we do not know whether the agreement contained all the terms. If it is a valid equitable easement, it must be protected by a notice to bind Bunkers Plc (s. 29 of the LRA 2002).

The claim to use the hard standing at the entrance to the golf course to park cars and other vehicles needs to be considered in the context of the rule that an easement cannot amount to a claim to exclusive use of the land – often known as the 'ouster' principle.[8] In *Copeland v Greenhalf* [1952] 1 All ER 809, Ch D, the claimant owned land on which the defendant had stored and repaired vehicles for 50 years. He claimed an easement by prescription. It was held that this was a claim to beneficial use of the land and so could not be an easement. Upjohn J described it as 'virtually a claim to possession of the servient tenement'. In **Batchelor v Marlow** [2001] EWCA Civ 1051, A claimed a right to park up to six cars between 9.30am and 6pm on land owned by B. A claimed an easement, as B still had 120 hours a week to use the land as he wished. The court applied the ouster principle and held that B had no reasonable use for the land for parking, as he could not park on it when parking spaces were most needed, and so the claim failed. As the court put it: 'His right (i.e. the right of the dominant owner) is curtailed altogether for intermittent periods during the week.'

[9] This extra detail that really boosts your marks. You are showing how the law has gradually evolved.

However, the law seems to be changing as, in **Moncrieff v Jamieson** [2007] UKHL 42,[9] Lord Scott, in the House of Lords, proposed the test of whether the servient owner 'retains possession and, subject to the reasonable exercise of the right in question, control of the servient land'.

It is suggested that as, in this case, Bunkers Plc has only granted parking rights over an area of hard standing at the entrance to the golf course to park cars and other vehicles, this may amount to an easement as the area seems small. In **R Square Properties Ltd v Nissan Motors (GB) Ltd** (LTL 14 March 2014), an easement was claimed of an exclusive right to use 80 parking spaces on land, and it was held that this was a valid easement as the owner of the DT had not lost reasonable use of the land by virtue of exclusive right of the owner of the ST to park, since it retained reasonable use of the land for other purposes. The question will then come down to one of fact: to what extent does the right to parking enjoyed by owners of 'Elms Estate' interfere with the reasonable use of their land by Bunkers Plc?[10]

[10] This is one of those fact-sensitive cases that often occur in exams, and so you will not lose marks by failing to give a definite answer. In fact, it is the definite answer that would be wrong!

[11] A final point not to omit!

If there is a valid easement, the rules on whether it was properly created, stated above, will apply here also.[11]

✓ **Make your answer stand out**

■ Mention that the Law Commission (2011) Report, Making Land Work: Easements, Covenants and Profits à Prendre (LC 327). http://lawcommission.justice.gov.uk/docs/lc327_easements_report.pdf has proposed the abolition of the ouster principle, and see also clause 24 of its draft Bill now the Law of Property Bill 2016.

- Note the comparison made in the Law Commission Report (2011) LC 327, between exclusive possession in the law of leases and the ouster principle in the law of easements (see 3.193–3.204).
- When discussing the right of car parking, look carefully at the use made by the courts of the principles that the owner of the DT must retain 'possession' of the land, that he/she must retain 'reasonable use' of the land and that he/she must retain 'control' of the land. Is there any significance in this?

! Don't be tempted to . . .

- Spend too long on asking whether the rights claimed satisfy the characteristics of easements laid down in *Ellenborough Park*.
- Miss the significance of the words 'agreement in writing'.
- Come to a very definite conclusion, especially on the car parking claim.
- Fail to set the cases in the context of fundamental principles.

❓ Question 2

John has owned Red Farm for a number of years, together with Blackacre which adjoins it. In 2017, he sold Red Farm to Mike but retained Blackacre. When John transferred Red Farm to Mike, the transfer did not mention any easements or other rights.

Mike asks your advice on the following:

(a) Fred, who owns nearby Green Farm, claims that he has the right to graze his cattle on a field that is part of Red Farm, as the owners of Green Farm have done this 'for centuries'. However, Mike knows that, during the outbreak of foot and mouth disease in 2001, Fred's herd was destroyed and so he could not have exercised this right then, although Fred does now have a herd.

(b) The only direct access from the road to Red Farm is on a track that is unsuitable for motor vehicles. Mike knows that John always used another route across Blackacre to reach Red Farm, and Mike wishes to know whether he has now acquired the right to use it.

(c) Sam has had a licence, granted annually for the last 30 years, to use a path across a field on Red Farm. Sam has now written to Mike, saying that as he has had the licence for so long it is now 'his for good'.

Answer plan

→ Consider whether there is a claim to a profit by prescription.

→ What about an easement of necessity?

→ Consider the law on acquisition of easements by implication under *Wheeldon* v *Burrows* and whether this could be applicable here.

→ Similarly, consider the possible relevance of a claim to an easement by implication under section 62 of the LPA 1925.

→ Claim to a right of way: conditions for a claim to an easement by prescription.

Diagram plan

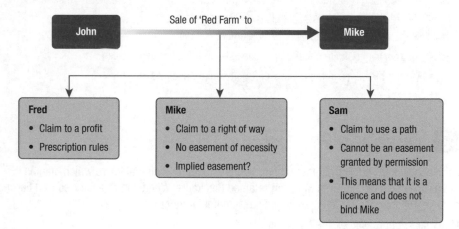

A printable version of this diagram plan is available from **www.pearsoned.co.uk/lawexpressqa**

Answer

(a) Fred's claim is to a profit as grazing is taking something from the land. It is obviously not based on any written evidence and so the profit cannot be either an express legal profit or an equitable profit. He claims that the owners of Green Farm have grazed cattle on Red Farm 'for centuries',[1] and this must be a claim arising by prescription. Under section 2 of the Prescription Act 1832, a claim to a profit by prescription requires 30 years' continuous use, but where the easement was exercised with the oral agreement of the servient owner, it is 60 years.[2] There is no

[1] Language like this must mean a possible claim by long use (prescription).

[2] Do make a note of these two periods.

evidence of any oral permission, so the period is 30 years, but, by section 4 of the Prescription Act 1832, the period must be 'next before' the action and this is obviously not the case here, as there was an interruption in 2001.[3] The next possibility is a claim to prescription at common law, which requires use since 'time immemorial', which technically means since 1189. In practice, use since 1189 will be presumed, provided that the profit has been exercised for as long as anyone can remember and could have been exercised in 1189.[4] Use since 1189 will depend on proving that the farms were in different ownership since 1189, as otherwise there could not be a dominant and a servient tenement, and it is very unlikely that it will be possible to do this.

[3] This is a familiar point in exam questions. The effect is that there cannot be a successful claim under the Prescription Act 1832, and so you then need to consider other possibilities.

[4] The message is not to get worried about the actual date of 1189.

The final hope is to use the doctrine of the lost modern grant[5] which involves the court making two assumptions: that there was originally a grant of the right and that it has now been lost. In **Dalton v Angus** (1881) 6 App Cas 740, HL, it was held that a grant will be assumed if there has been 20 years' continuous use and that the grantor was not legally incompetent to make the grant. There is 20 years' use, and the rule in section 4 of the Prescription Act 1832 requiring that the period must be next before action does not apply here. The grantor would be the owner of Red Farm and there is no evidence that they were not competent to make the grant. Thus it seems likely that Fred will have a valid claim to a profit by prescription. The Law Commission (2011) Report, Making Land Work: Easements, Covenants and Profits 'a Prendre (LC 327). http://lawcommission.justice.gov.uk/docs/lc327_easements_report.pdf[6] proposed that the present rules law on acquisition of easements by prescription should be abolished and replaced by one single method of acquisition by prescription with a proposed period of 20 years (Para. 3.123).

[5] This will usually be the last possibility you examine.

[6] This reference will increase your marks, as, although a detailed knowledge of the Law Commission's proposals is not required (so resist the temptation to describe them in detail), good students do keep up to date!

(b)   This is a claim to a right of way, which can, of course, exist as a valid easement. The problem is that there is no evidence that it has been expressly created, either by deed, which would make it legal, or in writing, which would make it equitable.

Nor can Mike claim an easement of necessity, as there is an alternative route to his land. If there had been no alternative access, Mike's claim might have succeeded, and the fact that he needs access in order to use motor vehicles would not prevent a claim, as an easement allows access for any purpose that is essential to maintain the enjoyment of the land.

However, Mike will have a claim to an easement under the rule in **Wheeldon v Burrows** (1879) 12 Ch D 31, CA, which provides that, on a grant of land, the grantee (e.g. the buyer) will acquire, by implication, all easements which are continuous and apparent and have been and are at the time of the grant used by the grantor for the benefit of the land. This rule applies where land has one owner who then sells off part, and the effect is that if, before the sale, the owner enjoyed a quasi-easement over part of his land, that will become an actual easement by implied grant on the sale. Here, part of John's land[7] (Red Farm) enjoyed a quasi-easement over other land that he owned (Blackacre), and so when Mike bought Red Farm this quasi-easement could become[8] an actual easement. The next question is whether the exercise of the right of way was continuous and apparent.[9] There is no need for the road to be a made road, so as long as it is apparent, as in **Hansford v Jago** [1921] 1 Ch 322, where a strip of land marked with rough tracks was within the rule in **Wheeldon v Burrows**. The use is obviously continuous, as we are told that John always used this route to reach Red Farm. Thus, Mike can claim an easement, which, as it is implied into the grant to him by John of Red Farm, will be a legal easement.

In addition, Mike may be able to claim an implied easement under the operation of section 62 of the LPA 1925,[10] which provides that a conveyance of the land shall be deemed to convey and shall operate to convey with the land all privileges, easements, etc. appertaining or reputed to appertain to the land at the time of the conveyance.

The traditional view was that there were two requirements for section 62(1) to apply:

(a) There is diversity of occupation, i.e. each piece of land is occupied by different people (**Sovmots Investments Ltd v Environment Secretary** [1977] 2 All ER 385, HL).

(b) The easement is continuous and apparent.

However, in **P & S Platt Ltd v Crouch** [2003] EWCA Civ 1110, it was held that, provided that the easement was continuous and

---

[7] A small point, but an important one: it is not John personally who enjoys the easement. Instead, his *land* enjoys it.

[8] You should say 'could', not 'would', as we have not yet established whether the conditions for this rule to apply have been satisfied.

[9] When you have decided that *Wheeldon* v *Burrows* could apply, you should then move on to this next point.

[10] This is exactly the kind of thinking that lifts an answer from an average 2.2 to a good 2.1.

apparent, there was no need for diversity of occupation, and this was approved by the Court of Appeal in **Alford v Hannaford** [2011] EWCA Civ 1099.

[11] Note how we have used this case to make an extra point and add to our marks, but note also below how, because we do not know all the facts, we have had to leave our answer on this point open.

In this case, there is no diversity of occupation, as, prior to the sale to Mike in 2015, John owned both Red Farm and Blackacre, but if the decision in **P & S Platt Ltd v Crouch** is correct, section 62 will still apply, provided[11] that the easement of a right of way was continuous and apparent; and here, we do not know whether the actual route that John took satisfied these requirements. It is worth mentioning that the Law Commission Report (2011) LC 327 has proposed (Para. 3.64) that easements should no longer be capable of creation by implication under section 62 of the LPA 1925, although section 62 itself would remain.

[12] The facts of this case were actually more complex than in the problem, but a good answer would recognise that there is no need to go into detail. What is important is to recognise that the essential point of the case is the same as the facts of the problem.

(c) Sam will not have a claim to an easement here, as, although he has exercised the right of way for 30 years, which would satisfy the prescription period of 20 years under section 2 of the Prescription Act 1832, provided that it was continuous, he is exercising it under a licence. One of the conditions for claiming an easement by prescription is that the use shall not be by permission, and here it is. In addition, licences are not binding on third parties (**King v David Allen** [1916] 2 AC 54, HL) and so a licence granted by a predecessor in title will not bind Mike. In **London Tara Hotel Ltd v Kensington Close Hotel Ltd** [2011] EWCA Civ 1356, a claim to an easement also failed, as use was by licence.[12]

✓ Make your answer stand out

- Clear explanation of the different methods of prescription in (a).
- Recognition in (b) that the situation could involve the application of section 62 of the LPA 1925 as well as *Wheeldon* v *Burrows*.
- Reference to the Law Commission Report (2011) LC 327. Look both at the proposals it contains and at its account of the law. Law Commission consultation papers and reports set out the law remarkably clearly and can add to your knowledge – and your marks.
- Read and refer to Bridge, S. (2009) Prescriptive Easements: Capacity to Grant. *CLJ*, 68(1): 40.

> **!** **Don't be tempted to . . .**
>
> - Forget in (a) to investigate all three methods of prescription.
> - Spend too long on deciding whether the rights are actually easements and profits: they obviously are, except in (c).
> - In (b), miss that, although you need to mention easements of necessity, in fact this does not apply and so you need to investigate other areas.
> - Just mention the actual rule in *Wheeldon* v *Burrows*, but also mention the conditions for it to apply.

📝 Question 3

Consider the situations where easements may be created in the absence of an express grant together with proposals for reform in this area.

Answer plan

→ Start by looking at easements of necessity.

→ Move on to easements implied by common intention and by estoppel.

→ Explain acquisition of easements under *Wheeldon* v *Burrows* in more detail.

→ Equally explain how section 62 of the LPA 1925 can enable an easement to be acquired.

→ Conclude by evaluating the effect of the Law Commission proposals in this area.

Diagram plan

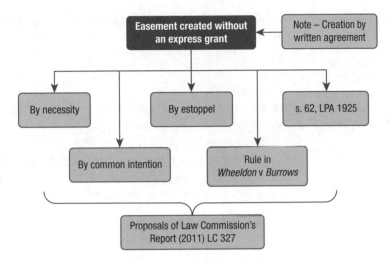

A printable version of this diagram plan is available from **www.pearsoned.co.uk/lawexpressqa**

Answer

This question deals with the way in which easements can be created in the absence of an express grant. Where there is an express grant, a legal easement is created, but here we are looking at ways in which, despite the absence of a grant, easements can be created by some form of implication. Easements can also be created by written agreement, in which case they are equitable,[1] but here we are dealing only with creation of easements by implication. They all have the common feature that, although created by implication, the easement is then implied into the grant and so technically these end up as express easements.

[1] This question is clearly about implied easements, as the reference to 'the absence of an express grant' shows. However, it could theoretically also involve equitable easements, as these are created in the absence of an express grant, and so best to make it clear at the start that you will not be dealing with them.

The methods of creation will first be examined, and then proposals for reform in what is a complex area.

The first example is easements by necessity, e.g. access to land-locked land. A good case is **Adealon International Proprietary Ltd v Merton LBC** [2007] EWCA Civ 362, where land only had access to a road to the north over land owned by another, and access to a road to the south could only be obtained by a grant of planning permission.

The court held that an easement of necessity would not be granted, as there was a realistic possibility of access to the land in future.

[2] An average answer would simply say that this case is an example of an easement by estoppel, but a good answer would identify that the exact *ratio* is somewhat obscure and that a possible explanation is an easement by estoppel.

A possible example of an easement by estoppel[2] is ***Ives Investments Ltd v High*** [1967] 2 QB 379, CA, where the defendant agreed with the claimant's predecessor in title that foundations of the claimant's flats might remain on the defendant's land. In return, the defendant, whose access to his house was affected by the building of the flats, could gain access to his garage by crossing the claimant's land. Although the decision was partly on the 'benefit and burden' principle in ***Halsall v Brizell*** [1957] Ch 169, Ch D, it could also be argued that the right of access is an example of an easement by estoppel arising through expense by the defendant in resurfacing the access road in reliance on the promise that he would have the right of access.

In ***Wheeldon v Burrows*** (1879) 12 Ch D 31, CA, it was held that an easement can be acquired by implied grant. The principle is that, on a grant of land, the grantee (e.g. the buyer) will acquire, by implication, all easements that:

(a) are continuous and apparent;

(b) have been, and are at the time of the grant, used by the grantor for the benefit of the land.

[3] Always use an example when you need to convey exactly what a somewhat complex point really means. If you do, it will make sure that the examiner understands the points you are making.

As an example, suppose that John owns Blackacre and Whiteacre, but then sells Whiteacre to Sue. Access to the main road from Whiteacre is along a path that crosses Blackacre. Sue will acquire an implied easement of a right of way across Blackacre under this rule.[3] The effect of the rule in ***Wheeldon v Burrows*** is that what was a quasi-easement before the sale, as of course a person cannot have an easement over land that they own, becomes an actual easement on sale.

The final method of creation of easements by implication is under section 62 of the Law of Property Act 1925 (LPA 1925), which provides that a conveyance of the land shall be deemed to convey and shall operate to convey with the land all privileges, easements, rights appertaining or reputed to appertain to the land at the time of conveyance. This provision is not itself controversial: it merely provides that, on a conveyance of land, certain rights that it has (e.g. easements and profits) are automatically also conveyed. What is controversial is the use that has been made of it to create easements where none seemed to exist before.[4] In **Wright v Macadam** [1949] 2 All ER 565, CA, the defendant let a flat to the claimant and gave her permission (i.e. a licence) to store coal in it. He later granted her a new tenancy. It was held that the grant of the tenancy was a conveyance under section 62(1) and, as a right to store coal was a right capable of being granted by law, the grant of the new tenancy had the effect of converting what was a licence into an easement.

[4] Often, students are confused and imagine that the principle in *Wright* v *Macadam* represents the main use of section 62. This is not so: explain how section 62 of the LPA 1925 works first, as we have done here, and then mention this case.

In **Sovmots Investments Ltd v Environment Secretary** [1977] 2 All ER 385, HL, it was considered that 'diversity of occupation' is needed for section 62 to apply, i.e. it is necessary for each piece of land to be occupied by different people. This was doubted in **P & S Platt Ltd v Crouch** [2003] EWCA Civ 1110, where it was held that, provided that use of the easement was continuous and apparent, diversity of occupation was not needed. Here, an easement was implied under section 62 even though the land had been owned by the same person.[5] If this principle is accepted, the scope of **Wheeldon v Burrows** would be greatly reduced, but **P & S Platt Ltd v Crouch** is open to the serious objection that rights cannot be apparent if they are exercised by an owner over his or her own land as there is no need for a right as such to be able to do this.

[5] There is no space to give the actual decision in *P & S Platt* v *Crouch*, so confine yourself to the principle.

If an easement by implication is established, as it is implied in the actual grant of the easement, it will be legal[6] – unless the easement was implied in a written agreement, in which case it will be equitable.

[6] There are many consequences from the fact that easements acquired by implication are legal, so make a habit of pointing this out.

The law on the acquisition of easements by implication is complex and, in particular, the relationship between **Wheeldon v Burrows** and section 62 of the LPA 1925 is unclear. For example, it cannot be right that a claim to an implied easement can succeed under section 62 of the LPA 1925 but not under **Wheeldon v Burrows**.

The Law Commission asked whether the law on acquisition of easements by implication should be recast into statutory form. It regards section 62 as a 'trap for the unwary', as the parties may not know how it works, or even that it will apply, and so they will not take it into account when negotiating the transfer. Moreover, there are uncertainties over its precise scope and its relationship with **Wheeldon v Burrows**, as mentioned above.

⁷ As always, reference to relevant Law Commission reports and consultation papers is the kind of detail that lifts your answer from the average to the good or very good!

⁸ It would be excellent to include all five factors, but, as here, you may not have time. So show the examiner that you know how many there are, and select some significant factors to mention.

The Law Commission (2011) Report, Making Land Work: Easements, Covenants and Profits à Prendre (LC 327). http://lawcommission. justice.gov.uk/docs/lc327_easements_report.pdf proposed that easements should no longer be capable of creation by implication under section 62(1) of the LPA 1925.[7] Section 62 itself would remain, but the **Wright v Macadam** principle that was engrafted onto it would not. It recommended that the methods of creation of easements by necessity, common intention and under **Wheeldon v Burrows** should be abolished and replaced by a single statutory principle that easements will be implied where they are necessary for the reasonable use of the land (Para. 3.45), bearing in mind five factors,[8] e.g. the use of the land at the time of the grant; and the potential interference caused to the servient land by the use of the easement or inconvenience to the servient owner. Profits could not be created in this way.

Although some areas of the law on acquisition of easements by implication perform a useful function, such as easements by necessity, others should be restricted in scope or abolished.

✓ Make your answer stand out

- Discussion of the decision in *P & S Platt* v *Crouch*.
- Further explanation of the Law Commission Report (2011) LC 327.
- Contrast *Wheeldon* v *Burrows* with section 62 of the LPA 1925.
- Mention the views of Mummery LJ in the Court of Appeal in *Adealon International Proprietary Ltd* v *Merton LBC*, who observed that the principle of an easement of necessity was not a free-standing rule of public policy but one of implication in all the circumstances. What counted against the claimant was that he had owned the land to the north and could have stipulated for an easement over that land when he sold it.

! Don't be tempted to . . .

- Avoid the section at the end on proposals for reform.
- Make sure that you contrast *Wheeldon* v *Burrows* with section 62 of the LPA 1925 and do not just describe them in a mechanical way.
- Omit to mention all the ways in which easements can be created by implication.

📐 Question 4

Critically consider the place of the ouster principle in the law of easements, especially in the light of claims to an easement of car parking and the proposals in the Law Commission (2011) Report, *Making Land Work: Easements, Covenants and Profits à Prendre* (LC 327).

Diagram plan

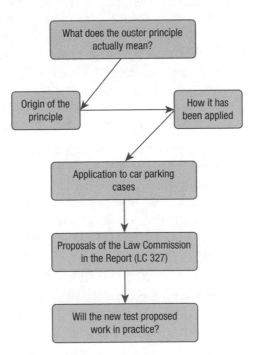

A printable version of this diagram plan is available from **www.pearsoned.co.uk/lawexpressqa**

Answer plan

→ Explain what the idea of an ouster clause is in relation to easements.

→ Outline the history of ouster clauses.

→ Analyse their application to claimed easements of car parking.

→ Consider the problems that exist in ascertaining exactly what the present law is.

→ Consideration of the proposals of the Law Commission.

Answer

The principle that an easement cannot give the grantee exclusive use of the servient land (known as the ouster principle) is based on the need to distinguish easements from freehold and leasehold estates in land, which give the holder the right to exclusive possession, as distinct from use, of the land. A lesser right such as an easement cannot therefore allow the holder the right to, in effect, treat the land as his own, but only to exercise certain rights over it, such as a right of way. It is also important to distinguish an easement from a licence, which, although not an estate in land, nevertheless gives the licensee rights over the whole land which is licensed.[1] The Law Commission, in its report, was clear that a grant of exclusive possession of land could not be an easement, although, of course, it could be a lease or licence. The problem is with ouster clauses, which can give exclusive use.

[1] You should mention licences separately, although they do not, of course, give an interest in land. This is because, in many cases, such as rights of storage, if a right cannot be an easement, it will have to take effect as a licence.

This origin of the ouster principle is probably the decision in *Dyce* v *Hay* (1852) 1 Macq 305, HL, and its application is seen in *Copeland* v *Greenhalf* [1952] 1 All ER 809, Ch D, where the claimant owned land on which the defendant had stored and repaired vehicles for 50 years. He claimed an easement by prescription. It was held that this was a claim to beneficial use of the land and so could not be an easement. Upjohn J described it as 'virtually a claim to possession of the servient tenement if necessary to the exclusion of the owner'.

[2] This is the theme of the essay and so needs to be mentioned clearly near the start.

However, the exact extent of the ouster principle is uncertain and it has not always been consistently applied by the courts.[2] In *Attorney General for Southern Nigeria* v *John Holt & Co Ltd* [1915] AC 599, PC, a right to store materials and other goods on the servient land was held to be an easement, and in *Wright* v *McAdam* [1949] 2 All ER 556, CA, the claim to storage of coal in a shed appeared to be a claim to an exclusive right to store, although the claim proceeded on the basis of an implied easement under section 62 of the Law of Property Act 1925 (LPA 1925). The ouster principle was not applied in *Miller* v *Emcer Products Ltd* [1956] Ch 304, CA[3] to a claim to the use of a lavatory, as the court made the sensible point that all easements involve the exclusion of the dominant owner to some degree, as, when a right of way over a path is exercised, at that moment no one else can literally occupy that part of the path.

[3] An answer on areas where the principles in the case law have not been consistent does need a clear review of the cases, where you recognise that it is not possible to find a consistent theme in the judgments.

In *London and Blenheim Estates Ltd* v *Ladbrooke Retail Parks Ltd* [1994] 1 WLR 31, CA, Judge Baker proposed a test of

⁴ It is obviously impossible to recall long quotes, but try to keep short and sharp ones like this in mind.

degree: 'A small coal shed is one thing. The exclusive use of a large part of the alleged servient tenement is another.'[4]

The question is now the extent to which these principles have been applied in car parking cases. The existence of an easement of car parking was recognised for the first time in **Newman v Jones** (1982) (unreported), Ch D, where Megarry VC said: 'I feel no hesitation in holding that a right for a landowner to park a car anywhere in a defined area is capable of existing as an easement.' What, though, is the position where a right to park in a defined space is claimed? In **London and Blenheim Estates Ltd v Ladbrooke Retail Parks Ltd**, the right was to park cars on any available space in the car park and, although the claim failed on other grounds, it was held that this was capable of being an easement.

⁵ This is the leading modern English authority on car parking and must be mentioned in an answer on car parking and ouster clauses.

In **Batchelor v Marlow** [2001] EWCA Civ 1051,[5] A claimed a right to park up to six cars between 9.30am and 6pm on land owned by B. A claimed an easement, as B still had 120 hours a week to use the land as he wished. The court applied the ouster principle and held that B had no reasonable use for the land for parking, as he could not park on it when parking spaces were most needed, and so the claim failed. As the court put it: 'His right (i.e. the right of the dominant owner) is curtailed altogether for intermittent periods during the week.' One issue was whether there should be a different test where the right was claimed by express grant from where it was claimed by prescription.[6] There is some merit in this, as, obviously, there would then be a stricter test where prescription was claimed, as, where there was an express grant, the owner of the servient tenement (ST) would have expressly agreed to it. However, the Court of Appeal disagreed.

⁶ This is an example of the extra research detail that improves your marks.

⁷ Do emphasise that this is a Scottish decision, as Scottish law in this area is slightly different.

⁸ It is always difficult to state the *ratio* of a case where there have been a number of judgments (or speeches in this case) that say slightly different things. This is why I have been tentative and said that his view 'probably' represents that of the majority.

In **Moncrieff v Jamieson** [2007] UKHL 42, the House of Lords held that Scottish law[7] recognised that there could be a servitude (an easement) of parking. Here, the property, when sold, had no direct vehicular access and so the seller granted the buyer the right of access across his land and a right to park to unload. The issue was whether there was an extra right to park for longer periods. It was held that an easement would be implied, but there was a difference of view over the test to be applied. The view of Lord Scott probably represents that of the majority,[8] and he said that it was sufficient if the owner of the ST retained possession and control of the land. In effect, the ouster point is sidestepped.

[9] If you can find a quote that can give you a neat conclusion, then this is ideal!

Haley, M. (2008) Easements, Exclusionary Use and Exclusive Principles: The Right to Park. Conv. 72: 244[9] suggests that the law should recognise that, in appropriate circumstances, there can be a right to park, provided that the claimant is not asserting permanent and exclusive rights in relation to the entirety of the ST, and this may be as far we can get towards a general principle.

The Law Commission Report (2011) LC 327 has proposed the abolition of the ouster principle, and clause 24 of its proposed draft Bill states that 'Use of land is not prevented from being of a kind which may be the subject of an easement by reason only of the fact that it prevents the person in possession of the land from making any reasonable use of it'. However, if the easement grants exclusive possession, it will not be valid. The effect of these proposals would be, as the Law Commission recognises, to reverse the decisions in **Copeland v Greenhalf** and **Batchelor v Marlow**. However, the Commission feels that it is important to bring more certainty to the area of easements of car parking, especially in view of the practical importance of this right. It points out that recent Land Registry data suggest that over 7,500 exclusive rights to park were created in 2009–10.[10]

[10] You can easily find this kind of research detail in documents such as Law Commission reports. If used in the right place, it can really add value to your answer.

The problem is going to be drawing a distinction in practice between an easement that attempts to give exclusive possession, which will not be valid, and one that stops short of exclusive possession, even if it deprives the owner of all reasonable use of the land, which will be valid. Will this lead to too many fine distinctions being drawn?

✓ Make your answer stand out

- Show a clear understanding of the basic principles of the law on leases and licences as well as easements.
- Research *Wright* v *Macadam* – note that there 'appeared' to be an exclusive right of storage.
- Refer and research articles on car parking and ouster clauses, such as Hill-Smith, A. (2007) Rights of Parking and the Ouster Principle after *Batchelor* v *Marlow*. *Conv.* 71: 223–34. Junior, G. (2008) Warning – Parking Problems Ahead (*Moncrieff* v *Jamieson* Applied). *Scots Law Times*, 1: 1–2; and Haley (2008).
- Investigate the reasons for and against having different tests for an easement of car parking, depending on whether the claim is based on express grant or prescription.

Question 5

Consider the proposition that the categories of easements are never closed, especially in the light of the remarks in the Supreme Court in *Coventry (t/a RDC Promotions)* v *Lawrence* [2014] UKSC 13 and other modern cases involving the possible creation of new easements.

Answer plan

→ Consider briefly what the question is about.

→ Make the distinction between positive and negative easements clear.

→ Problems with negative easements and possible solutions.

→ Application of the law to car parking.

→ Conclusion – will the law recognise new easements?

Diagram plan

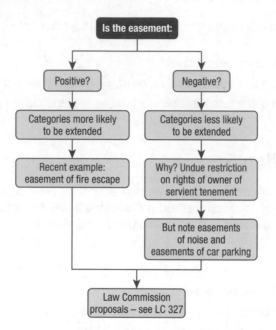

```
                    ┌─────────────────────┐
                    │  Is the easement:   │
                    └─────────────────────┘
                             │
              ┌──────────────┴──────────────┐
              ▼                              ▼
      ┌──────────────┐              ┌──────────────┐
      │  Positive?   │              │  Negative?   │
      └──────────────┘              └──────────────┘
              │                              │
              ▼                              ▼
   ┌──────────────────────┐      ┌──────────────────────┐
   │ Categories more likely│      │ Categories less likely│
   │   to be extended      │      │   to be extended      │
   └──────────────────────┘      └──────────────────────┘
              │                              │
              ▼                              ▼
   ┌──────────────────────┐      ┌──────────────────────┐
   │  Recent example:      │      │ Why? Undue restriction│
   │ easement of fire escape│     │  on rights of owner of│
   └──────────────────────┘      │   servient tenement   │
              │                   └──────────────────────┘
              │                              │
              │                              ▼
              │                   ┌──────────────────────┐
              │                   │  But note easements   │
              │                   │    of noise and       │
              │                   │ easements of car parking│
              │                   └──────────────────────┘
              │                              │
              └──────────────┬───────────────┘
                             ▼
                    ┌──────────────────────┐
                    │  Law Commission       │
                    │ proposals – see LC 327│
                    └──────────────────────┘
```

A printable version of this diagram plan is available from **www.pearsoned.co.uk/lawexpressqa**

Answer

[1] As this answer progresses, we will come to areas where there is some doubt about what the law is. This is why it is important to begin by explaining where the law *is* settled.

In general, the categories of easements are well known and well settled. Familiar examples are rights of way, light and support and a right to have a fence maintained by a joint owner.[1] The question is whether these categories are closed or whether new categories can be created.

[2] Although we obviously need to discuss the case mentioned in the question, it is often best to set it in context first, and this is what we are doing here.

We must first distinguish between negative and positive easements.[2] A negative easement exists where the owner of the servient tenement (ST) has no actual obligations but is restricted in the use of the land. Thus, a right to light restricts a neighbour from building on her land. There is a reluctance to extend the categories of negative easements to include, for example, the right not to have television reception interfered with.[3] In **Phipps v Pears** [1964] 2 All ER 35, CA, for example, there was a claim to an easement to protection of one house from rain and frost by another house. This would mean that the other house

[3] A simple example helps to make the idea clear.

could not be demolished. The claim was rejected. The problem is that if new negative easements are created, this imposes further restrictions on the right of the owner of the ST to use his property. As Denning MR put it in **Phipps v Pears**, 'if we were to stop a man pulling down his house, we would put a brake on desirable improvement'. In **Hunter v Canary Wharf Ltd** [1997] AC 655, HL, Lord Hope said that as negative easements 'represent an anomaly in the law because they restrict the owner's freedom, the law takes care not to extend them beyond the categories which are well known to the law'.

[4] As much of this discussion concerns negative easements, you need to be clear on the distinction between negative and positive easements.

On the other hand, the categories of positive easements, which involve a landowner going onto or making use of something in or on a neighbour's land,[4] are more likely to be extended. Examples of well-recognised positive easements are rights of way and storage of goods, and in **Magrath v Parkside Hotels Ltd** [2011] EWHC 143 (Ch), it was held that there is nothing wrong in principle with an easement of fire escape where the owner of the ST would have to permit the owner of the dominant tenement (DT) to escape across his land. The right would be exercised only rarely and unexpectedly, and this met the argument that, as it was not a claim to a defined route across the ST's land but a general right to flee, it was too ill defined and uncertain to be an easement.

In fact, the courts have recognised new categories of negative easements, although this recognition has often been tentative. Thus, in **Coventry (t/a RDC Promotions) v Lawrence** [2014] UKSC 13 the issue was whether there can be an easement to create noise. The issue was noise from a stadium during speedway and stock car racing. The claimants complained to the local council, which issued noise abatement orders, but the claimants argued that they had been ineffective and so claimed an injunction to restrain a nuisance.

The claimants succeeded but the justices of the Supreme Court held that, in principle, there could be an easement to create a noise even though this would clearly be a negative easement. Thus, Lord Neuberger concluded that 'the right to carry on an activity which results in noise, or the right to emit a noise, which would otherwise cause an actionable nuisance is capable of being an easement'. However, it is vital to note that these remarks were strictly *obiter* and that no actual easement to create a noise was recognised.

[5] As this report proposes such major changes in the law of easements, you will be expected to mention what these are and will lose marks if you do not.

The Law Commission (2011) Report, Making Land Work: Easements, Covenants and Profits à Prendre (LC 327). http://lawcommission.justice.gov.uk/docs/lc327_easements_report.pdf[5] recommended that, in future, attempts to create negative easements expressly will give rise to land obligations if the requirements of clause 1 of the draft Bill are met, but existing negative easements will remain. The reason is that the rights capable of being created by a land obligation would be much greater than those covered by the present restrictive covenants, and in particular it would be possible for a positive covenant to take effect as a land obligation. For example, it might be possible to create a positive obligation of the kind that was claimed in *Phipps v Pears* (above) but that would take effect as a land obligation.

The other area where there is the question of a new easement being recognised is car parking rights. It seems clear that there can be an easement of car parking, as was recognised in *Newman v Jones* (1982) (unreported), where Megarry VC said that 'I feel no hesitation in holding that a right for a landowner to park a car anywhere in a defined area is capable of existing as an easement'.

[6] This is a crucial sentence, as it links the question of car parking easements with a general issue on the law of easements.

The question is not whether there is such an easement, but how the exercise of it affects the principle that an easement must not give the owner of the DT exclusive use of the ST.[6] This accords with the general reluctance of the courts to recognise new categories of easements on this ground. Thus, in *Batchelor v Marlow* [2001] EWCA Civ 1051, a claimed right to park up to six cars between 9.30am and 6pm failed, as it prevented the ST from using this land when he most needed to.

[7] It is important to emphasise that this is a Scottish decision, as the law in Scotland differs from English law and any decisions on Scottish law are of only persuasive authority in England.

In *Moncrieff v Jamieson* [2007] UKHL 42, the House of Lords held that Scottish law[7] recognised that there could be a servitude (an easement) of parking. Here, the property, when sold, had no direct vehicular access and so the seller granted the buyer the right of access across his land and a right to park to unload. The issue was whether there was an extra right to park for longer periods. It was held that a servitude would be implied, but there was a difference of view over the test to be applied. The view of Lord Scott, which probably represents that of the majority, was that it was sufficient if the owner of the ST retained possession and control of the land. In effect, the ouster point is sidestepped.

The Law Commission Report (2011) LC 327 recommends in its draft Bill (clause 24) that use of land 'should not prevented from being of a kind which may be the subject of an easement by reason only of the fact that it prevents the person in possession of the land from making any reasonable use of it'. This would have the effect of reversing the effect of **Batchelor v Marlow** (see Paras 3.188–3.205).

[8] You do need a conclusion that tries to propose some ideas on what the law should be.

The law does still have the capacity to recognise new easements, and although some have been positive, such as easements of car parking and a right of fire escape,[8] others have been negative, such as the right to stop a noise. It is surely right that new easements can be created to take account of new uses of land such as the use of land to park cars for stock car racing. It is, however, vital to recall the point made by Lord Hope in **Hunter v Canary Wharf Ltd** that easements, by their nature, restrict the freedom of an owner of land and to maintain a balance between the rights of the owner and those of his neighbours.

✓ Make your answer stand out

■ Point out possible alternative remedies where the court has refused to recognise an easement: in a *Phipps* v *Pears* situation, for instance, there could today be a possible action in negligence.

■ See Dixon, M. (2014b) Editorial: Reaching Up for the Box in the Attic. *Conv.* 78: 165, discussing *Coventry (t/a RDC Promotions)* v *Lawrence*.

■ See Dawson, I. and Dunn, A. (1998) Negative Easements – A Crumb of Analysis. *Legal Studies*, 18: 510.

■ See the Law Commission Report (2011) LC 327.

■ See the Scottish Law Commission (1998) *Real Burdens*. Discussion Paper No. 106. www.scotlawcom.gov.uk/index.php/download_file/view/94/127/.

■ Mention *Regency Villas Title Ltd* v *Diamond Resorts (Europe) Ltd* [2015] EWHC 3564 (Ch). HC Is this an example of a new easement or the development of an old principle?

! Don't be tempted to . . .

- Begin with a long account of the characteristics of easements as laid down in *Re Ellenborough Park* [1955] 3 All ER 667.
- Give a descriptive account of the law on what can be an easement.
- Confuse what a negative and a positive easement are – make your terms clear.

@ Try it yourself

Now take a look at the question below and attempt to answer it. You can check your response against the answer guidance available on the companion website (**www.pearsoned.co.uk/lawexpressqa**).

'The law on acquisition of easements and profits by prescription is both muddled and out of date.' Comment critically on this statement and evaluate the impact of proposed reforms in this area.

www.pearsoned.co.uk/lawexpressqa

Go online to access more revision support, including additional essay and problem questions with diagram plans, and you be the marker questions, and to download all diagrams from the book.

Mortgages

9

How this topic may come up in exams

Problem questions on the terms of a mortgage are generally considered good prospects to obtain marks, although you need to remember that the law is not always clear cut and you may well not be able to come to a definite conclusion. In addition, you can expect problems on priority of mortgages, which can be more difficult, and applications by the mortgagee for a sale. There is also a possibility of a question with an angle on undue influence.

Essays can focus on mortgage conditions and on the law on remedies of the mortgagee.

All in all, this is not a difficult area – with the possible exception of priorities – and so is a 'must' for revision!

◼ Before you begin

It's a good idea to consider the following key themes of mortgages before tackling a question on this topic.

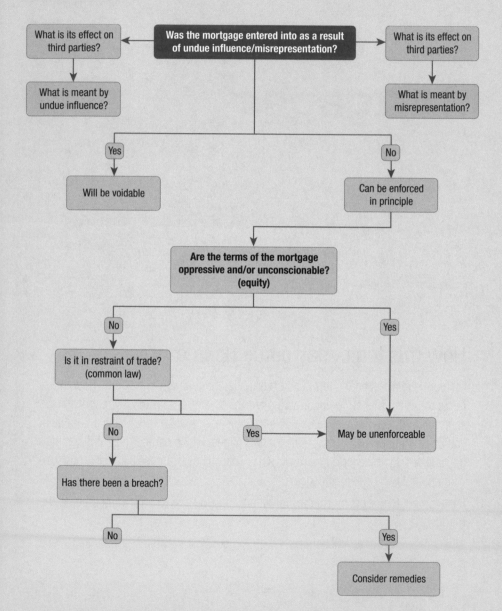

🖊 Question 1

Critically consider the extent to which equity can intervene in the law of mortgages to guard against unconscionable conduct on the part of the mortgagee.

Answer plan

→ Set the scene by looking at the historical basis of equitable intervention.

→ Explain how the principle of an equity of redemption developed into the principle that there must be no clog on the equity of redemption.

→ Explain how the principle that there must be no clog on the equity of redemption applies in two types of situation.

→ Assess the extent, if any, to which this principle is still valid in today's world.

→ Explain other ways in which equity has intervened and may do so in future.

→ Conclude by coming back to the idea of unconscionability

Diagram plan

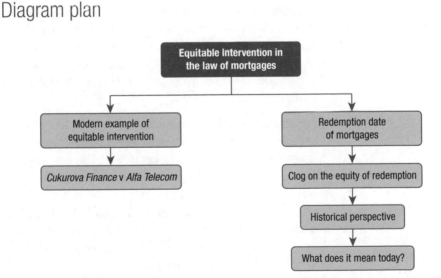

A printable version of this diagram plan is available from **www.pearsoned.co.uk/lawexpressqa**

Answer

[1] You do need to mention equity in general at the start, and to set the scene as to what the nature of equity is. It is impossible to understand how the present law of mortgages works without understanding the crucial part played by equity in its development.

[2] Stress the changing character of mortgages over the years.

[3] In any essay on mortgages, it is important that you make this clear.

[4] Equitable doctrines are often very old and it will add to your marks if you are able to go back to the source of them and trace their development.

Equity[1] has played a significant part in developing the law on mortgages. Mortgages were traditionally entered into when someone needed a loan as they were in debt, and so they might be persuaded into entering a mortgage on onerous terms. Thus, equity aimed to protect them and proceeded on the basis that the terms of the mortgage were likely to be dictated by the mortgagee.

Today,[2] mortgages are usually made because a person wishes to buy or lease a house rather than because he is in debt and is desperate for a loan on virtually any terms. However, it is still true that the terms of the mortgage are dictated by the mortgagee, as lenders usually require borrowers to enter into mortgages on standard terms and there is no room for individual negotiation.

As the question states, equity intervenes to guard against unconscionable conduct, which sets a high bar to anyone seeking equitable relief. In **Knightsbridge Estates v Byrne** [1939] Ch 441 (HC), Greene MR put it: 'But equity does not reform commercial transactions because they are unreasonable.[3] It is concerned to see two things – one that the essential requirements of a mortgage transaction are observed, and the other that oppressive or unconscionable terms are not enforced.'

Equity first intervened where the common law insisted that, if the mortgagor did not redeem on the date fixed for redemption, the right to redeem the mortgage would be lost for ever. This was especially significant when the mortgagee obtained the legal estate in the mortgaged property and so, if the mortgagee failed to redeem, by even a few hours, he would lose his property. Equity first allowed the mortgagor to redeem after the redemption date where there were special circumstances, such as a delayed payment by mistake.[4] By the date of **Emmanuel College v Evans** [1625] 1 Ch. Rep.18, HC, equity granted relief against forfeiture of the land routinely, and today the equitable right of redemption is part of the law of mortgages even though now the mortgagee no longer gets the legal title to the mortgaged property but only a charge over it.

As soon as equity had recognised the right of the equity of redemption, it went further to ensure that the actual right of redemption was not hindered by any provisions in the mortgage deed.[5] This became the rule that there 'must not be any clog on the equity of redemption'. In **Jennings v Ward** (1705) 2 Vern 520, CA, Trevor MR said that 'a man shall not have interest for his money on a mortgage, and a collateral advantage besides for the loan of it'. Thus, when the mortgage is repaid, there shall be no 'clog' on it. This evolved into a fundamental equitable principle expressed by Lord Davey in **Noakes & Co. Ltd v Rice** [1902] AC 24, HL: 'Once a mortgage, always a mortgage.' So if there are any terms in the mortgage that prevent this happening, these are known as clogs on the equity of redemption, and, historically, equity viewed these as objectionable. One example is where the mortgagor is obliged to buy goods from the mortgagee or sell them to him for a period that continues after the mortgage has ended.

However, the doctrine that there must be no clog on the equity of redemption has long gone as an absolute principle, and in a celebrated passage in **Krelinger v New Patagonia Meat and Cold Storage Co. Ltd** [1914] AC 25, HL, Lord Mersey described the doctrine as an 'unruly dog, which, if not securely chained to its kennel, is apt to wander into places where it ought not to be'. This is because, in many cases, the parties were businesses who were bargaining on equal terms and so equitable intervention was not needed. This linked with the growing emphasis in general on freedom of contracts.

In **Krelinger** itself, a firm of woolbrokers lent money on a mortgage that could be repaid at any time in the next five years. The mortgagor also agreed to give the mortgagee first refusal on all their sheepskins and to pay commission on any sold to a third party. This agreement was to last for the full five years. This collateral agreement was upheld on the basis that the agreement to give first refusal was, in fact, a separate agreement[6] from the mortgage and so was not a clog on the right to redeem.

Another application of the 'clog' principle is that the mortgagor should be able actually to redeem the mortgaged property when the mortgage ends, and this has been held to conflict with a stipulation that the mortgagee has the right to purchase the mortgaged property when the term of the mortgage ends.[7] In **Samuel Jarrah Timber v Wood Paving Corporation Ltd** [1904] AC 323, HL, the House of Lords applied this principle with reluctance, so that an option to purchase was held void. Lord Halsbury LC regretted that what he

6 This is the vital point about Krelinger v New Patagonia Meat and Cold Storage.

7 In an essay on the equity of redemption, do remember that it affects various ways in which the law has developed.

called a 'perfectly fair bargain' to purchase the property was void as it was linked to a mortgage. The consequences of this rule were avoided in *Reeve* **v** *Lisle* [1902] AC 461, HL, where the option to purchase was contained in a separate agreement but the doctrine was applied, with reluctance, by the Court of Appeal in *Jones* **v** *Morgan* [2002] 1 ELGR 125. In this case, Philips MR was blunt: 'the doctrine of the clog on the equity of redemption . . . is an appendix to our law which no longer serves any useful purpose'.

[8] In essay questions, always try to end with some positive ideas of your own, based on your research on how the law should develop.

It is suggested that, although this doctrine has outlived its usefulness, its abolition should not mean the end of equity's jurisdiction in the area of mortgages. Instead, renewed emphasis should be placed on the fundamental principle of equity[8] that there must be no unfair or unconscionable collateral advantage for the mortgagee, as illustrated, for example, by *Cityland and Property (Holdings) Ltd* **v** *Dabrah* [1968] Ch 166, Ch D.

[9] This is an example of a complex case where, if you try to unravel the facts, it will take you off at a tangent, as they concerned a specific area. Instead, use the quotations from the judges.

A possible modern example of the intervention of equity is *Cukurova Finance International Ltd & Anor* **v** *Alfa Telecom Turkey Ltd* [2009] UKPC 20,[9] where Lord Mance suggested that 'equity can and should respond by a special order as to interest or costs in exceptional situations where the mortgagee has by words or conduct rejected, made impossible or delayed repayment of the mortgage debt'. This seems to pave the way for equity to have a wide discretion to intervene to grant relief from forfeiture, going beyond cases of unconscionable conduct. However, Lord Neuberger dissented, saying that this would lead to too much uncertainty in the law.

[10] This is an example of where you need to just mention a point, but with no detail.

Finally, the doctrine of undue influence is also an example of equitable intervention in this area[10] but it is not based on the same principles as apply to equitable intervention in the law of mortgages, and, in any event, undue influence is not confined to mortgages.

One could say, in conclusion, that, although the original purpose of equity to guard against unconscionable conduct by the mortgagee is still valid, the circumstances in which this type of conduct can arise have changed.

✓ **Make your answer stand out**

■ Read and refer to the Law Commission Report (1991) 'Transfer of Land: Land Mortgages' No. 204, which recommended the abolition of the equitable jurisdiction dealing with clogs on the equity of redemption. Even though it is somewhat dated, it is still valuable.

■ Read and refer to Thompson, M.P. (2001) Do We Really Need Clogs? *Conv.* 502. This will add depth to your answer on this aspect.

■ Read and refer to the essay by Burns F. 'Clogs on the Equity of Redemption: a story of changing equitable intervention' (2012). It is full of ideas and is very readable.

■ Read *Warnborough Ltd* v *Garmite Ltd* [2003] EWCA Civ 1544 – interesting remarks by Jonathan Parker LJ on the clog on the equity of redemption.

! **Don't be tempted to. . .**

■ Just go through the cases without explaining that they are examples of equitable intervention.

■ Omit to give your essay a structure by building your account of the cases round the two separate areas where the 'clog' principle has been applied.

■ Fail to point out that the cases themselves show inconsistencies in approach, and show how this is so.

■ Fail to adopt a critical approach.

■ Give too much detail on undue influence.

❓ Question 2

In 2005, Frank purchased a 21-year legal lease of a petrol station. He mortgaged the premises to Wells Co., a petrol company, in order to finance the purchase. The mortgage deed included the following covenants by Frank:

(a) Only to sell petrol and oil supplied by Wells Co. for a period of 30 years from the commencement of the mortgage.

(b) To pay the principal and interest over a period of 20 years and, if he wishes to redeem the mortgage before the expiration of 20 years, to pay a sum equal to five years' interest to Wells Co.

Frank has now been approached by Drills Ltd, another petrol company, that is keen to buy the lease from Frank and, pending the purchase, to supply him with petrol and oil. Advise Frank on whether, and to what extent, the above covenants are binding.

Answer plan

→ Explanation of fundamental equitable principles: idea of a clog on the equity of redemption and that equity will intervene only if the terms of the mortgage are oppressive.

→ Application of these principles to situation (a): changing attitude of the courts. Is the collateral agreement enforceable?

→ Possibility of doctrine of restraint of trade applying here?

→ Application of these principles to situation (b): equity's attitude to penalties on early redemption.

Diagram plan

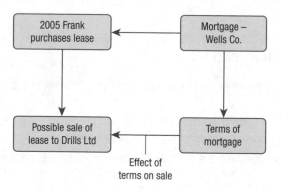

A printable version of this diagram plan is available from **www.pearsoned.co.uk/lawexpressqa**

Answer

[1] Do emphasise at the start of a problem on mortgages that it is equity that has laid down the fundamental principles.

[2] It is vital to stress the limits of the intervention of equity.

[3] Make sure that you explain exactly what this term means.

(a) A mortgagor owns the equity of redemption, and a fundamental principle of equity[1] is that there must be no unfair or unconscionable collateral advantage for the mortgagee. In *Alec Lobb (Garages) Ltd* v *Total Oil Ltd* [1985] 1 WLR 87, Ch D, it was held that, for equity to intervene, the transaction must not be merely 'hard or improvident' but 'overreaching and oppressive'.[2] A collateral advantage[3] is where, in addition to the return of the loan with interest, the mortgagee obtains an additional advantage, and this is an example as Frank is bound not only to repay the mortgage but also only to sell petrol and oil supplied by the mortgagee for a period of 30 years, which is 10 years longer than the mortgage term of 20 years. The principle is that this kind of stipulation operates as a 'clog on the equity of redemption' because, even after redemption, the mortgagor would not recover his property as it was before the mortgage, as it would still be bound by a tie to the mortgagee.

In **Biggs v Hoddinott** [1898] 2 Ch 307, CA,[4] the mortgagor agreed to sell only beer brewed by the mortgagee for five years, but this collateral advantage ceased on redemption of the mortgage and was upheld. In **Noakes & Co. Ltd v Rice** [1902] AC 24, HL, the tenant of a public house mortgaged a lease that had more than 26 years to run and agreed that, during this time, he would not sell any malt liquor other than that provided by the mortgagees. Moreover, this term would continue even though the mortgage was redeemed earlier and it was held void. The leading case is now **Krelinger v New Patagonia Meat and Cold Storage Co Ltd** [1914] AC 25, HL, where a firm of woolbrokers lent money on a mortgage that could be repaid at any time in the next five years. The mortgagor also agreed to give the mortgagee first refusal on all their sheepskins and to pay commission on any sold to a third party. This agreement was to last for the full five years. This collateral agreement was upheld on the basis that the agreement to give first refusal was, in fact, a separate agreement from the mortgage and so was not a clog on the right to redeem.

The requirement to sell only petrol and oil supplied by Wells Co. for a period of 30 years from the commencement of the mortgage lasts for 10 years after the mortgage has expired and it appears to be in the actual mortgage itself and so the principle in **Noakes & Co. Ltd v Rice** does apply. The only question is whether it can be argued that, in fact, this is a separate agreement from the mortgage. If so, it can be enforced. If not, it cannot. It is suggested that, on the facts, it looks like part of the actual mortgage and so is unenforceable, although this is a tentative conclusion, as we lack all the information.[5]

Another possibility is that this term might be struck down at common law as being an unreasonable restraint of trade,[6] as in **Esso Petroleum v Harper's Garage (Stourport) Ltd** [1968] AC 269, HL, where a tie requiring a petrol station to sell only a particular brand of petrol for five years was upheld but one for

[4] This paragraph deals with three cases, all of which have slightly different decisions on the facts. Make sure that you bring this out.

[5] We must apply the law to the question, but we cannot, on the facts, come to a definite conclusion. Remember that very definite conclusions are often a sign of weakness, not strength!

[6] This mention of another possibility will certainly gain you extra marks. Also point out that here we are dealing with common-law principles and so different considerations will apply. In particular, the emphasis will be on whether a stipulation is unreasonable and not whether it is unconscionable.

21 years was not. Note that the test here is unreasonableness and not unconscionability.

(b) The provision that, if Frank wishes to redeem the mortgage before the expiration of 20 years, he must pay a sum equal to five years' interest to Wells Co. involves the possible application of the equitable principle that, where postponement of the right to redeem is delayed to such an extent that the equity of redemption is valueless, then the mortgagor may be allowed to redeem earlier. Equity does not automatically strike down clauses preventing or hindering early redemption, as in **Knightsbridge Estates Trust Ltd v Byrne** [1939] Ch 441, CA,[7] where a mortgage for a term of 40 years could not be redeemed earlier. However, there, the parties were both commercial organisations experienced in these matters and the length of the term suited them. Here, Frank appears to be an individual dealing with what is, presumably, a large oil company. There is the additional factor that Frank has a lease for 21 years,[8] and there is a penalty against redemption earlier than 20 years. In **Fairclough v Swan Brewery Co. Ltd** [1912] AC 565, PC, the mortgagor was the tenant of a brewery which had a lease with 17 and a half years to run. A mortgage prevented redemption until six weeks before the end of the lease, and this was held to be void as, by the time the mortgage was ended, the mortgagor recovered nothing of value. Nevertheless, the courts today may decide that if there was no evidence of oppression, and as the agreement was a commercial one, it should not be set aside on the principle mentioned earlier in **Alec Lobb (Garages) Ltd v Total Oil Ltd** that, for equity to intervene, the transaction must not be merely 'hard or improvident' but 'overreaching and oppressive'.[9]

[7] This is a useful case to start with in answers on this area, but if a lease is involved you need to then mention *Fairclough* v *Swan Brewery*.

[8] Questions on mortgages often involve leases, and you need to check the length of the lease against the length of the mortgage.

[9] Note the emphasis on fundamental principles.

In this case, there is a period of one year between the redemption date of the mortgage and the end of the lease, but there is the additional factor not present in **Fairclough v Swan Brewery Co. Ltd** that Frank must pay a sum equal to five years' interest to Wells Co. if he wishes to redeem early. This could be viewed as a penalty for early redemption and so amount to a clog on the equity of redemption, and so be void. However, the courts today will look at the substance of the transaction, and we need to ask whether there was any bargain whereby, in return for paying this extra sum, there was a lower rate of interest, for example, in the early years of the mortgage. If not, then it is possible that, unless there is any reason that the payment of such a large sum can be justified, it is likely that it will be struck down as oppressive.

✓ **Make your answer stand out**

- Stress fundamental equitable principles.
- Consider the difficult decision in *Santley* v *Wilde* [1899] 2 Ch 474, CA, which appears to conflict with *Fairclough* v *Swan Brewery*.
- Mention the doctrine of restraint of trade.
- Show how slightly different facts led to different decisions.

! **Don't be tempted to . . .**

- Come to conclusions that are too definite.
- Fail to pick up the different decisions in this area – there are subtle distinctions among the cases.
- Miss the fundamental principles.
- Mention only one case per point: e.g. *Krelinger* v *New Patagonia Meat and Cold Storage*.

✒ Question 3

Critically consider the statement that the remedies currently available to a mortgagee need to be reformed to make them accord with the economic realities of the twenty-first century.

Answer plan

→ Introduction: why this topic is important.

→ Consider the following remedies of the mortgagee: action for debt, possession and sale, foreclosure.

→ In the case of each remedy, make sure that you state the essential statutory points clearly, and also any leading cases.

→ Evaluate the effect of the HRA 1998 and the *Horsham Properties* v *Clark* case.

Diagram plan

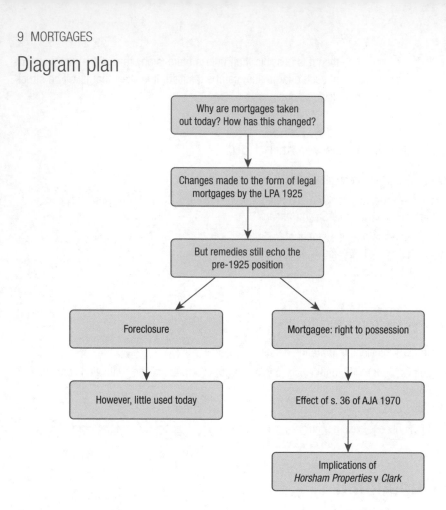

A printable version of this diagram plan is available from **www.pearsoned.co.uk/lawexpressqa**

Answer

[1] You need to make the point at the start that the problem is that the law has not moved on. However, do resist the temptation to give an account of the history of mortgages.

The reasons for which mortgages are taken out have changed over the years, but the form of a mortgage and, with it, the remedies available to a mortgagee against a mortgagor are rooted in history.[1] Mortgages were traditionally taken out to secure an existing debt, but today they are usually entered into because a person wishes to buy or lease a house or flat. However, the law of mortgages still contains echoes of the principle that applied before the Law of Property Act

[2] This gets the answer on the right lines at the start. You have avoided the temptation of taking the easier (but wrong) route of just listing the remedies, and instead you are engaging with the issue raised by the question.

[3] Note the precision of language here: it was not just any mortgage that gave the mortgagee the fee simple, but a first legal mortgage. If you are aiming for a 2.1 at least, this is the standard you must achieve.

[4] This concluding sentence is important: it shows that you are not just describing the law, but, as the question demands, looking at it critically.

[5] This is the kind of quote to include in an answer: it is easily recalled and makes the point exactly.

[6] Here, you are making a distinction between foreclosure and the right to possession. This is good exam technique: in each paragraph, always ensure that you are developing your answer and not just making the same point as before.

1925 (LPA 1925).[2] This was that a first legal mortgagee of a freehold[3] over the mortgaged property obtained a legal fee simple on creation of the mortgage. This is no longer the case, and the mortgagee's security is now a legal charge by deed over the mortgaged property, but the consequences of the mortgagee's holding of the fee simple remain.

The remedy traditionally available to the mortgagee was foreclosure. Where the mortgagee obtained the fee simple, this was logical. The courts declared that the mortgagor had lost the right to redeem the mortgage and so the mortgagee was left with the fee simple. Even though the form of mortgages has changed, this remedy of foreclosure still exists and, if it is used, the mortgaged property is vested in the mortgagee and the mortgagor has no rights to any surplus resulting from any sale. The drastic nature of foreclosure is mitigated, to some extent, by the rule that a court order is needed for a foreclosure and the courts can reopen a foreclosure order where, for instance, there is a marked difference between the value of the property and the amount lent. The result is that foreclosure has fallen into disuse. In *Palk and Another v Mortgage Services Funding Plc* [1993] 2 WLR 415, CA, Nicolls VC observed that 'So far as I am aware, foreclosure actions are almost unheard of today and have been so for many years. Mortgagees prefer to exercise other remedies. They usually appoint a receiver or exercise their powers of sale'. The question is then whether this remedy should still exist.[4]

The fact that mortgagees had the legal fee simple meant that the mortgagee was entitled to possession at any time after the creation of the mortgage, and this right is now, by section 87(1) of the LPA 1925, given to the legal chargee. Thus, Harman J observed in *Four Maids Ltd v Dudley Marshall Properties* [1957] Ch 317, Ch D that the right to possession arose 'before the ink was dry on the mortgage',[5] unless there was provision to the contrary in the mortgage deed, and in *Ropaigealach v Barclays Bank* [2000] QB 263, CA, Clarke LJ observed that 'I suspect that many mortgagors would be astonished to discover that a bank which had lent them money to buy a property for them to live in could take possession of it the next day'.

Unlike the foreclosure remedy, this right does have current practical implications, as it means that the mortgagee has the fundamental right to go into possession of the property without a court order[6]

(*Ropaigealach* v *Barclays Bank*). However, a mortgagee would normally go into possession without a court order only if the property was unoccupied, as section 6(1) of the Criminal Law Act 1977 makes it an offence for any person without lawful authority to use or threaten violence to enter premises if he knows that there is someone there who opposes his entry.

If a court order is sought, then, by section 36 of the Administration of Justice Act 1970 (AJA 1970), the court may, if it appears that the mortgagor will, within a reasonable period, be able to pay sums due under the mortgage, or remedy the breach of any other default arising under it:

(i)   adjourn the proceedings; or

(ii)   on giving an order for possession, stay or suspend execution of it or postpone the date for delivery of possession.

However, section 36 applies only where the property consists of or includes a dwelling house.[7]

The rule was that any arrears should be paid off in two years, but in *Cheltenham & Gloucester Building Society* v *Norgan* [1996] 1 WLR 343, CA,[8] it was held that the remaining term of the mortgage should be the starting point, and a number of relevant considerations were set out to assist courts in deciding what is a reasonable period to allow for repayment, such as how much the borrower can afford to pay, whether there are any temporary difficulties in making repayments and how long these may last, and the reason for arrears having accumulated.

Horsham Properties Group Ltd v *Clark* [2008] EWHC 2327 (Ch)[9] shows the significance of the mortgagee's right to possession and the limitations of section 36 of the AJA 1970. Under section 101 of the LPA 1925,[10] a mortgagee has the power to sell the mortgaged property when the mortgage money has become due (s. 101(1)(i)) or, by section 101(1)(iii), to appoint a receiver of the income from the property, which they did in this case. If the mortgagee had sought possession in pursuance of a sale under section 101(1)(i), then section 36 of the AJA 1970 would have applied. However, they appointed a receiver who then sold the mortgaged property by auction to Horsham Properties. Horsham's legal title to the property overreached that of the occupiers, the mortgagors, who were now simply trespassers. Instead, Horsham

[7] An important point to note if you get a problem question on this area. Note that section 36 will apply where a part of the property is used as a house and part for other purposes, e.g. a shop. See also section 39(2).

[8] Although this area is governed by statute law, there are important cases on the interpretation of the statutory provisions. Make sure that you know the main ones. You could construct an interesting answer by looking at the extent to which case law has attempted to move the balance more to the interests of the mortgagees.

[9] Up to this point the answer has described statute law and its interpretation by the courts. Here your answer takes off as it was and starts to earn you the marks for a really good pass. This is an important case which also involves the ECHR.

[10] Although not directly relevant here, you should remember that, whereas section 101 sets out when the mortgagee's power of sale arises, it is section 103 that sets out when that power is actually exercisable.

could rely on the mortgagee's right to possession, with the result that the mortgagors lost their home without a court order.

The mortgagor's claim that this result violated their right to the peaceful enjoyment of their possessions guaranteed by Article 1 of the First Protocol to the European Convention on Human Rights, as incorporated into UK law by the Human Rights Act 1998, was rejected as the loss of their home had occurred without any state intervention, and so Article 1 was not engaged.

[11] This is the kind of research detail that really adds to your marks.

This result was widely felt to be unsatisfactory and a private members' Bill, the Home Repossession (Protection) Bill, was introduced.[11] This would have amended section 101 of the LPA 1925 by ensuring that a mortgagee of a dwelling house could not exercise the power of sale without first obtaining an order of the court, and the court would be given substantially the same powers as those found currently in section 36 of the AJA 1970. However, it did not become law.

[12] As you read this paragraph, note how the central themes of this essay have been summarised and then right at the end the actual words of the question are brought in.

It seems clear that[12] the continuing presence of the archaic remedy of foreclosure, the right of the mortgagee to take possession at any time and the failure of the law to provide that there should always be a court order when possession is sought show that the quotation is justified and that the law of mortgages needs to be reformed to make it accord with the economic realities of the twenty-first century.

✓ Make your answer stand out

- Keep the idea of a critical approach in mind when looking at each remedy, and beware of the temptation to just describe it.
- See Greer, S. (2009) *Horsham Properties Group Ltd* v *Clark*. Possession – Mortgagee's Right or Discretionary Remedy? *Conv.* 516. Material from this extra discussion of the case will add value to your answer.
- Read also Wood, J. (2009) *Horsham Properties Group Ltd* v *Clark*: A Year On. *Coventry Law Journal*, 14(2): 31–6.
- Research current levels of mortgage repossessions.
- Look at the detailed analysis in *Cukurova Finance International Ltd* v *Alfa Telecom Turkey Ltd* [2013] UKPC 2 of the equitable jurisdiction of the court to relieve a person against the consequences of a seizure of their property. This could be as a result of default on a mortgage or on an ordinary debt.

> **!** **Don't be tempted to . . .**
>
> ■ Just describe the remedies.
> ■ Fail to mention case law.
> ■ Explain how the remedies relate to each other.
> ■ Miss the last point on the ECHR.

? Question 4

In 1993, Tony purchased a house, 'Southmead', for £200,000, of which £175,000 was provided by a loan from the Hanbury Building Society. Title to the property was unregistered. This loan was secured by a properly executed charge by way of legal mortgage over the property. The building society retained the title deeds as security for the charge.

In 1994, Tony created a charge over the property in favour of the Shark Building Society, to secure his overdraft, which then stood at £20,000. The charge also secured any other monies 'which the bank, in its absolute discretion, might advance'. This charge was protected by a Class C(i) land charge.

By 1995, the value of the property had increased to £250,000 and Tony borrowed £40,000 from the Friendly Building Society to finance some extensions to the property. This was also secured by a charge over the property.

In 1996, Tony borrowed a further £10,000 from the Nice Building Society, secured by a charge over the property, to fund the installation of double glazing.

In all the above cases, the charges were properly executed legal charges.

In 1997, the Shark Building Society made a further loan to Tony of £3,000.

The Friendly Building Society and the Nice Building Society did not protect their charges by registration at the time, but the Friendly Building Society did protect its mortgage by registration as a Class C(i) land charge in January 1998.

Tony is now bankrupt. His overdraft stands at £30,000 and all the loans are still outstanding. The house has decreased in value and is unlikely to realise more than £230,000 when sold after paying the costs of sale.

Explain the order in which the mortgagees will be paid if 'Southmead' is sold by one of the mortgagees.

How would your answer differ if title to the house was registered and the mortgages were registered at the time of their creation?

Answer plan

→ Identify that title to the property is unregistered and that all the mortgages are legal.

→ Distinguish between the rules applicable to protection of first mortgages from those applicable to second and subsequent mortgages, and apply these rules.

→ Identify the situation where tacking of subsequent mortgages may be possible, and apply the relevant rules.

→ Identify the situation where there are two possible rules governing priority of a mortgage, and apply the rules.

→ State and explain the rules on priority of mortgages in registered land.

Diagram plan

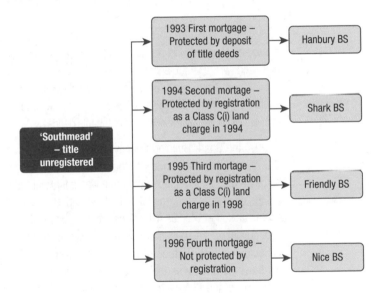

A printable version of this diagram plan is available from **www.pearsoned.co.uk/lawexpressqa**

[1] Although this is strictly a side issue, it does deserve a mention, as it shows the examiner that you were aware of this point.

[2] The rules on priority would differ if the mortgages were equitable, and so you need to check for this.

Answer

Title to the house is unregistered, and so the rules on priority of mortgages in unregistered land will apply. It is worth pointing out that if any of the mortgages had been created on or after 1 April 1998, this would have triggered registration of the property.[1] All the mortgages are legal and are properly executed.[2]

The first mortgage was taken out in 1993, for £175,000, in favour of the Hanbury Building Society. A legal mortgage is not registrable as a land charge and, instead, priority is secured by the retention of the title deeds.[3] As the Hanbury Building Society has done this, it will have priority over all other mortgagees and will be able to exercise its remedies as a mortgagee.[4] This means that it will probably take possession of 'Southmead' and sell it to recover its loan of £175,000. As the value of the property is £230,000, this means that, after the Building Society has deducted the costs that it has incurred in the sale, there will not be enough left to satisfy the claims of the other mortgagees.[5]

The charge over the property created in favour of the Shark Building Society was protected by a Class C(i) land charge at the time of its creation, and so it will be next in priority. This is because, by section 198(1) of the Law of Property Act 1925 (LPA 1925), registration constitutes actual notice of the charge to a purchaser and thus subsequent purchasers will take subject to this charge.[6] It is only what are termed 'puisne' mortgages, which are second or subsequent mortgages such as this one, that can be registered as first mortgages and, as we have seen, are protected by the retention of the title deeds by the mortgagee.

In 1997, the Shark Building Society made a further loan to Tony of £3,000, and the question is whether this can rank in priority to the charge created in 1994, even though it was not protected by a Class C(i) land charge. The charge taken by the Shark Building Society also secures any other monies 'which the bank, in its absolute discretion, might advance'.[7] The question is whether this clause allows the Building Society to 'tack' further advances onto this charge so that it also has the same priority as the actual charge. Tacking is dealt with by section 94 of the LPA 1925, which provides that a prior mortgagee (the Shark Building Society in this case) shall have a right to make further advances to rank in priority to subsequent mortgages:

(a) if an arrangement has been made to that effect with the subsequent mortgagees; or

(b) if he had no notice of such subsequent mortgages at the time when the further advance was made by him; or

(c) whether or not he had such notice as aforesaid, where the mortgage imposes an obligation on him to make such further advances.

---

[3] This point is often forgotten by students.

[4] You do not need to discuss remedies in detail, but it will add to your marks if you state the remedies briefly.

[5] Make a calculation at the start of the amounts owing against the value of the property.

[6] This is a very good example of how to gain extra marks. You could have stopped at the end of the first sentence, and that would have been correct, but we have continued and given the statutory authority for what we have said and its implications.

[7] When you see this wording, check further down the question to see whether there have been further advances.

In this case, there is no evidence of any arrangement with subsequent mortgagees under (a), and there is no reason why the subsequent lenders in this case should agree to the Shark Building Society having priority over their loan. Nor does (c) apply, as the wording of the charge does not impose an obligation on the Shark Building Society to make further advances, as it expressly states that it has an 'absolute discretion to do so'. However, (b) applies and the Shark Building Society can tack further advances onto the loan of 1994 until it has notice of any subsequent mortgages.

The problem is that the subsequent mortgages to the Friendly Building Society in 1995 and the Nice Building Society in 1996 were not protected by registration as Class C(i) land charges and, as we saw above, section 198(1) of the LPA 1925 provides that registration as a land charge constitutes actual notice of that charge. The Friendly Building Society did protect its loan by a charge in 1998, but the loan of £3,000 to Tony, which the Shark Building Society wishes to tack, was made in 1997. The conclusion must be that the Building Society can do so and that this loan will have priority over the two subsequent mortgages.

The final question is that of priority between the Friendly Building Society and the Nice Building Society. The mortgage to the Friendly Building Society was taken out in 1995 and that to the Nice Building Society in 1996. Neither was protected by registration at the time, but, as we have seen, the Friendly Building Society eventually protected its charge by registration in 1998. By section 4(5) of the Land Charges Act 1972, priority between charges that should have been registered as Class C(i) charges, which both of these are, is void against a purchaser for money or money's worth, and, by section 205(1)(xxi) of the LPA 1925, a purchaser includes a mortgagee.[8] Thus, as the charge to the Friendly Building Society had not been registered at the time of the mortgage to the Nice Building Society, the charge of the Friendly Building Society will be void against that of the Nice Building Society, and the Nice Building Society will have priority.

However, this point is not certain, and there is a view that the provisions of section 97 of the LPA 1925 mean that priority of mortgages shall rank in order of the date of their creation. In this case, as the mortgage to the Friendly Building Society was created first, it will have priority.[9]

It has never been decided with certainty which of these alternatives is correct,[10] but one powerful argument in favour of the application

[8] This is another example of a small point of extra detail that will increase your marks.

[9] You should watch for this point in any question on priorities between mortgages in unregistered land, as it is a very familiar one. The basic scenario is the one here: Mortgage A was created first, but, when Mortgage B was created, Mortgage A had not been registered. The application of section 4(5) of the Land Charges Act 1972 gives a different result to that if section 97 of the LPA 1925 is applied. The point is quite simple, but you need to be clear on it.

[10] The worst thing that you could do would be to come down definitely in favour of one alternative or the other.

of section 97 of the LPA 1925 is that it was included in the LPA specifically to deal with this point and, if it does not apply, then it is completely redundant. On the other hand, section 4(5) of the Land Charges Act 1972 applies to other interests in land.

If the title to 'Southmead' were registered and all of the mortgages were registered at the time of their creation, priority would be governed by this time and they would rank in priority accordingly (s. 48 of the Land Registration Act 2002 (LRA 2002)). Thus, the order would be: the mortgages granted to the Hanbury Building Society, the Shark Building Society, the Friendly Building Society and the Nice Building Society. The ability of the mortgagee to tack the mortgage is governed by section 49 of the LRA 2002, which has the same conditions as in section 94 of the LPA 1925, but it also adds another, which is that where the parties have agreed a limit up to which further advances can be made, tacking can take place up to that limit. This has not happened here.

✓ Make your answer stand out

- Consider in more detail the controversy over whether the order of priority between unregistered mortgages should in fact be governed by section 97 of the LPA 1925 and not section 4(5) of the Land Charges Act 1972. Another view is that the Land Charges Act 1925, the predecessor of the Land Charges Act 1972, was actually passed before the LPA 1925 and so it should prevail where there is a conflict, as here.
- Another argument in this debate is that the actual wording of section 97 of the LPA 1925 is that a mortgage 'shall rank according to its date of registration as a land charge pursuant to the Land Charges Act 1972'. Thus, section 97 only provides machinery for the operation of the Land Charges Act and so it is the Land Charges Act that should prevail.

! Don't be tempted to . . .

- Overlook that title to the land is unregistered.
- Overlook the question at the end, which asks what the position would be if the title were registered.
- Think that the mortgages should simply rank in priority according to the date of their creation and ignore the need to register second or subsequent mortgages as land charges.
- Fail to apply to the question all the possible cases when tacking of a mortgage can be allowed.

Question 5

In *Royal Bank of Scotland* v *Etridge (No. 2)* [2002] 2 AC 773, HL, Lord Nicholls contrasted the competing policy issues in cases where one party is asked to stand surety for the debts of another and, in particular, where a wife is asked to stand surety for the debts of her husband.

Consider what these competing policy reasons are and critically assess the extent to which the courts maintain a correct balance between them.

Answer plan

→ Give some context with an actual scenario, and you can then use this to demonstrate how the policy reasons could apply.

→ Set out the competing reasons and set out in Lord Nicholls' speech.

→ Explain the actual *ratio* of *Barclays Bank* v *O'Brien* clearly.

→ Critically consider the interpretation and development of the principle in *Barclays Bank* v *O'Brien* in later cases, especially *Royal Bank of Scotland* v *Etridge (No. 2)*.

→ Conclude by looking at possible future developments.

Diagram plan

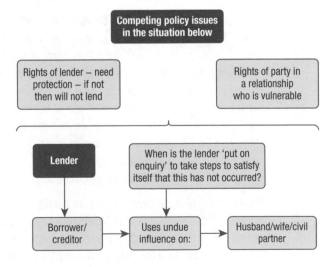

A printable version of this diagram plan is available from **www.pearsoned.co.uk/lawexpressqa**

Answer

Before we turn to the competing policy issues in this area, we need to be clear what a typical situation involves.[1] Suppose that the husband has a business that needs more capital. His main asset is the home that he owns with his wife. He persuades his wife, by undue influence, to agree to execute a document that mortgages the home in return for a loan. The wife in this case, in effect, stands surety for his agreement to repay the loan. The issue here is not undue influence itself. In this discussion it will be assumed that this has occurred. Instead, it is the extent to which the lender is affected by it.[2] The problem is that the lender in whose favour the mortgage deed was signed, typically a financial institution, will have no knowledge of any undue influence. Suppose that the husband defaults on the loan and the lender begins possession proceedings. The wife may say that her agreement was procured by the undue influence of her husband, but the lender may reply that that is a matter between her and her husband. This situation is now more common because, as Lord Browne-Wilkinson in **Barclays Bank Plc** v **O'Brien** [1994] 1 AC 180, HL[3] pointed out, wealth is now more widely spread, and a high proportion of privately owned wealth is invested in the matrimonial home. In addition, the majority of homes are now in the joint names of both spouses.

In his speech in **Royal Bank of Scotland** v **Etridge (No. 2**) [2002] 2 AC 773, HL, Lord Nicholls contrasted the competing issues in this area[4] as follows. He pointed out that 'a bank must be able to have confidence that a wife's signature of the necessary guarantee and charge will be as binding upon her as is the signature of anyone else on documents which he or she may sign'. If banks did not have this confidence then, as he pointed out, 'banks will not be willing to lend money on the security of a jointly owned house or flat'. This, in turn, would mean that homeowners would be unable to make economic use of their homes by raising mortgages on them.

On the other hand, he emphasised that 'the high degree of trust and confidence and emotional interdependence which normally characterises a marriage relationship provides scope for abuse. One party may take advantage of the other's vulnerability. Unhappily, such abuse does occur'. This, in effect, is what occurred in our scenario where

---

[1] In this opening sentence, you are telling the examiner that you are aware of the need to investigate the competing policy issues in this area, but first you are going to set them in context. Otherwise, your discussion could become too general and lack depth.

[2] There is no reason why you cannot give an account of the law on undue influence, but I suggest that if you explore the main issues in this question you will not have time for it! It is also worth bearing in mind that the principles in *Royal Bank of Scotland* v *Etridge (No. 2)* can also apply where there has been misrepresentation.

[3] Here, you are doing two things: introducing the case from which this area of law derives and giving more social context to support a discussion of policy issues.

[4] You must address these issues: the question does not ask for just a description of the law.

the husband exercises undue influence on his wife to persuade her to execute the document mortgaging their house.

[5] Although you have yet to address the question of competing policy issues here, you really do need to say this first, otherwise your essay could give the impression that the principle applied only to undue influence by husbands over wives.

Although Lord Nicholls referred to a scenario where a husband exercises undue influence over his wife, his speech makes it clear that the law can intervene where either a husband or a wife stands surety for the debts of the other, or where they cohabit, or even where there is no cohabitation[5] as in **Massey v Midland Bank Plc** [1995] 1 All ER 929, CA. Miss Massey, who signed the form, never cohabited with Mr Potts, but had a stable sexual and emotional relationship with him over many years, and they had two children. Since the Civil Partnership Act 2004, the categories will also include civil partners.

[6] This term will be used from now on.

The fundamental task of the courts is to find some legal relationship between the surety[6] wife, or whoever stands surety, and the lender so that, at some point, the creditor, such as the bank, can, as a consequence of that relationship, owe some legal liability to the surety. In the application of this, they must consider the competing policy reasons mentioned above.

[7] You could do some research and mention that this is not exactly notice as it is understood in cases involving the priority of equitable rights on a transfer of property.

The law derives from the speech of Lord Browne-Wilkinson in **Barclays Bank Plc v O'Brien**, who invoked the doctrine of notice[7] in determining the enforceability of securities by third-party creditors and outlined the circumstances in which a third-party lender will be 'put on enquiry'. When they arise, the lender will be fixed with constructive notice of the undue influence. Thus, balance between the interests of the surety and the lender is maintained by asking whether the creditor had notice: if so, he will be liable, and, if not, he will not be.

[8] It is vital to point out that the idea of notice in these cases is now not accepted. See Thompson (2003), especially pages 130–2.

However, use of the doctrine of notice was criticised, as 'notice' has traditionally referred to notice of a prior right but here it refers to the possibility of a right existing in the future – in this case, a right to set the transaction aside for undue influence.[8]

[9] It is vital that you make the connection between *Barclays Bank v O'Brien* and *Bank of Scotland v Etridge (No. 2)*: the general principle in this area derives from *Barclays Bank v O'Brien* but its present formulation comes from *Bank of Scotland v Etridge (No. 2)*.

The present law derives from **Royal Bank of Scotland v Etridge (No. 2)**,[9] where Lord Nicholls used the analysis of a tripartite transaction between creditor (i.e. the lender), debtor and surety. However, he retained the central notion that, in certain cases, a creditor can be put on enquiry and a transaction entered into as a result of undue influence may be set aside unless the creditor takes certain steps.

The House of Lords, in **Royal Bank of Scotland v Etridge (No. 2)**, then clarified the steps that the lender should reasonably be expected to take in satisfying itself that the security has been properly obtained:

(a) The lender must contact the surety and request that they nominate a solicitor.

(b) The surety must reply, nominating a solicitor.

(c) The lender must, with the consent of the surety, disclose to the solicitor all relevant information – both the debtor's financial position and the details of the proposed loan.

(d) The solicitor must advise the surety in a face-to-face meeting at which the debtor is not present. The advice must cover an explanation of the documentation, and the risks to the surety in signing, and emphasise that the surety must decide whether to proceed.

(e) The solicitor must, if satisfied that the surety wishes to proceed, send written confirmation to the lender that the solicitor has explained the nature of the documents and their implications for the surety.

[10] We need to come back to the policy issues here and apply them to what we have stated.

Thus, the crucial balance is maintained[10] between the interests of the surety and the creditor: if these rules are followed, the surety should have adequate protection and so the lender will be able to enforce its security. If they are not, then it will not be able to.

Is the lender responsible for the advice given? Lord Nicholls observed that the solicitor is not the agent of the creditor and that 'In the ordinary case, therefore, deficiencies in the advice given are a matter between the wife and her solicitor'. In this instance, the balance tilts towards the lender.

In *Banco Exterior Internacional* v *Mann* [1995] 1 All ER 936, CA, it was held that the solicitor could act for both parties, and Lord Nicholls in *Royal Bank of Scotland* v *Etridge (No. 2)* felt that, on balance, this rule should continue, as, although there was the possibility of a conflict of interest, there would be a significant increase in costs. However, he held that the solicitor must make it clear that, at this stage, he is advising the surety. Is this right?

There are still questions in this area that have not been settled, but it seems, especially in view of the lack of major litigation in this area since *Royal Bank of Scotland* v *Etridge (No. 2)*, that the balance may be right.

✓ Make your answer stand out

- Give a clear explanation of the *O'Brien* principle.
- Mention *HSBC Bank* v *Brown* [2015] EWHC 359 (Ch) on the steps that a lender should take.
- Consider Andrews, G. (2002) Undue Influence – Where's the Disadvantage? *Conv.* 456. This looks at the decision in *Royal Bank of Scotland* v *Etridge (No. 2)*.
- Consider Houghton, J. and Livesey, L. (2001) Mortgage Conditions: Old Law for a New Century?, in E. Cooke (ed.) *Modern Studies in Property Law*, Vol. 1. Oxford: Hart Publishing.
- Consider Thompson, M.P. (2003) Mortgages and Undue Influence, in E. Cooke (ed.) *Modern Studies in Property Law*, Vol. 2. Oxford: Hart Publishing. This gives a clear account of the law and of how it has developed, which many textbooks do not do.

! Don't be tempted to . . .

- Just describe the law.
- Spend a great deal of time on undue influence itself.
- Avoid explaining the link between the decision in *Barclays Bank* v *O'Brien* and that in *Royal Bank of Scotland* v *Etridge (No. 2)*.
- Disregard the conditions laid down in *Royal Bank of Scotland* v *Etridge (No. 2)* for the lender to observe.

Now take a look at the question below and attempt to answer it. You can check your response against the answer guidance available on the companion website (**www.pearsoned.co.uk/lawexpressqa**).

> You act for Cheaploans Ltd, a small firm of mortgage lenders. They normally seek an order for possession followed by an application for a sale when it is clear that a mortgagor will be unable to repay the loan that the mortgage secures. They have heard that there is also a remedy of foreclosure and they wonder how this differs from possession and sale, and whether it could be obtained by them when a mortgagor defaults.
>
> In addition, one of the principals in the business recently went on a course where the Human Rights Act 1998 was mentioned, and they ask for your advice on the impact, if any, that this could have on the remedies of mortgagees.
>
> Advise them.

www.pearsoned.co.uk/lawexpressqa

Go online to access more revision support, including additional essay and problem questions with diagram plans, and you be the marker questions, and to download all diagrams from the book.

10

Adverse possession

How this topic may come up in exams

This area is popular with examiners, as it contains material for detailed problem questions and also a number of topics for essays. Problems are likely to focus initially on the basic requirements for adverse possession, but then they can cover a variety of topics such as earmarked land, leaseholds, the mechanics of acquiring title by this method and the impact of the ECHR.

Essays may focus on whether it should be possible to acquire title by adverse possession at all, and perhaps on the social aspect, with an angle on urban squatting and homelessness.

In summary, this is an excellent area for all students and is especially good to score those vital extra marks on!

Before you begin

It's a good idea to consider the following key themes of adverse possession before tackling a question on this topic.

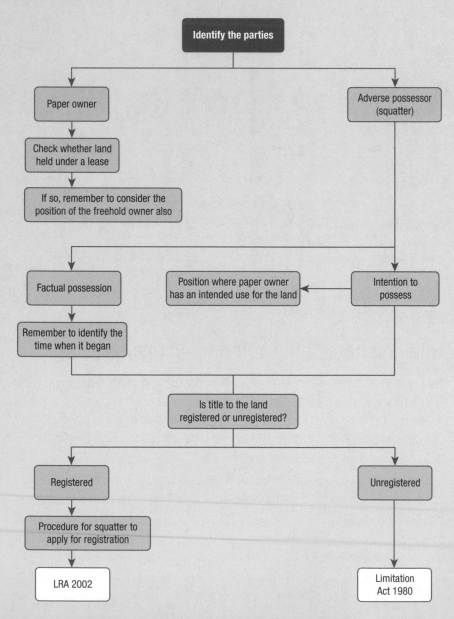

A printable version of this diagram is available from **www.pearsoned.co.uk/lawexpressqa**

❓ Question 1

In 2005, Steve started to develop a nature centre on several acres of derelict land by a stream. He cleared the bed of the stream, encouraged marsh plants to grow by the water's edge, planted trees and built shelters for wildlife. He drained the higher land and built a café for visitors. From 2007, he started charging for entry, although the land on which the nature centre is built would make it very difficult to fence it.

In 2014, solicitors acting for Angela, a wealthy recluse, who lives in a neighbouring house and has registered title to the land occupied by Steve, wrote to him, stating that he was trespassing on her land. Angela told Steve that she intended to build a small house on the land he is occupying for her carer to live in, but that this would be in the future. At present, she had no use for the land and would be happy to grant him a lease of it. Negotiations began between Steve and Angela, but they failed to reach any agreement.

In 2016, Angela transferred the title to her house and to the land occupied by Steve to her son, Mark, although she continues to live there.

It is now 2017, and Mark's solicitors have written to Steve, asking him to vacate the land as soon as possible. Steve seeks your advice.

Advise Steve on whether he might claim title to the land, and the procedures that he would have to follow.

Diagram plan

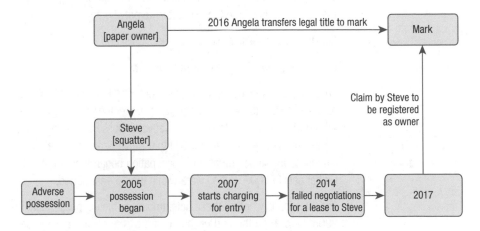

A printable version of this diagram plan is available from **www.pearsoned.co.uk/lawexpressqa**

Answer plan

→ Note that title is registered – calculate the period of adverse possession required: when did adverse possession actually begin?

→ Consider whether there was factual possession.

→ Continue by considering whether there was the intention to possess.

→ Note that some activities began in 2005 and others in 2007, and consider the significance of this.

→ Note that Angela has a future intended use for the land, and consider the significance of this.

→ Explain the position on the sale of the freehold by Angela to Mark

→ Explain the procedure under the LRA 2002 for the squatter to be registered.

Answer

Although there is no statutory definition of adverse possession, its essence is possession of land, which is inconsistent with the title of the true owner and which amounts to a denial of that title. In **Powell v McFarlane** (1977) 38 P & CR 452, Ch D, it was emphasised that there is a presumption that the owner of the land with the paper title is in possession and so, in any action based on adverse possession, the burden of proof is on the squatter[1] to prove both:

[1] This is an excellent way to start: you have set the answer in the context of who has to prove what.

(a) factual possession (*corpus possessionis*) and

(b) intent to possess (*animus possidendi*).

[2] You will need to apply the relevant procedures in the LRA 2002 to the question only when you have decided that there has been adverse possession for the requisite period. Why not draw a diagram and a timeline before you start on a problem question on adverse possession? Also remember to completely ignore the position where title is unregistered – this has no relevance.

These will be examined in detail later, but, at the outset, it is vital to note that, as title to the land is registered, under the Land Registration Act 2002 (LRA 2002), the period of adverse possession needed is a minimum of 10 years.[2] We are told that Steve began to develop the land in 2005, so presumably his occupation began then and he did further acts in 2007, but all were within the 10-year period.

The question is whether these acts amount to factual possession. In 2005, he cleared the bed of the stream by the centre, encouraged marsh plants to grow by the water's edge, planted trees and built shelters for wildlife. He also drained the higher land and built a café for visitors. In **Powell v McFarlane**, Slade J held that the adverse possessor must show that he has dealt with the land as an occupying owner. This is demonstrated by exercising control over the land.

[3] There are a vast number of cases on what constitutes factual possession. Rather than mention a lot of them, all making roughly the same point, it is better to state the principle of Slade J in *Powell v McFarlane* and then choose one case and apply one to the question.

[4] Controlling the means of access to the land by, e.g., fencing is a crucial issue and always deals with it carefully in an adverse possession question.

Thus, in **Williams v Usherwood** (1983) 45 P & CR 235, CA,[3] the Court of Appeal held that the enclosing of land by a fence, together with parking three cars and paving a driveway with decorative paving stones, the fitting of the door and building of fences, was conclusive evidence of factual possession.

Here, it is suggested that Steve's acts show that he has dealt with the land as owner with the exception of fencing.[4] Steve says that it would be very difficult to fence the area. In **Powell v McFarlane**, Slade J pointed out that clear evidence of establishing control is 'the locking or blocking of the only means of access' and, although Steve charges for entry, presumably access cannot be completely blocked. However, Steve obviously would have fenced the land if he could but for the nature of the land, and in **Red House Farms v Catchpole** (1977) 1 EGLR 125, CA, Cairns LJ said: 'The authorities make it clear that what constitutes possession of any particular piece of land must depend upon the nature of the land and what it is capable of use for.'

Moreover, it is suggested that Steve certainly has the intent to possess. This means the intention to exclude the whole world and the acts done showing factual possession, coupled with the fact that Steve clearly would have fenced the land if he could have done so, are, as it is suggested, sufficient evidence of this.

On the assumption that both these elements are satisfied, is Steve's claim affected by the negotiations between him and Angela for the grant of a lease? These were in 2014, and at that date Steve did not have the requisite 10 years' adverse possession. It is suggested that as the negotiations did not actually result in the grant of a lease, they amount merely to an acknowledgement by Steve of Angela's ownership and, as the House of Lords held in **J.A. Pye (Oxford) Ltd v Graham** (2005) ECHR 921, HL, what is required is not the intention by Steve to own but the intention to possess.[5] Had a lease actually been granted, then, as Steve would now be a tenant of Angela's, he could not have claimed title by adverse possession, because, as Ousley J pointed out in **Best v Chief Land Registrar** [2014] EWHC 1370, adverse possession involves 'possession as of wrong' and as a tenant his possession would not be 'as of wrong'.

[5] This is an absolutely basic point: make sure that you understand it and can apply it to questions.

On the assumption that Steve can claim, the fact that his claim is based on possession and not ownership is also relevant to Angela's continued intention to use for the land in future. In

[6] There is a good deal of earlier case law on this point, which might be relevant in an essay question but not in a problem that is concerned with what the law is now.

[7] This point often arises in exam questions where you are told that the paper owner is ill, away etc. This will not be relevant.

[8] Watch for whether the transferee is a purchaser (s. 29 of the LRA 2002 applies) or a donee, e.g. has acquired by inheritance (s. 28 applies). In this case, the matter seems doubtful, so consider both possibilities.

[9] If the land was not registered then, of course, the answer would be different: see the next answer.

[10] Students often completely overlook the fact that, at the end of an adverse possession problem, they will have to deal with the issue of overriding interests of occupiers. As a result, they often deal with this issue badly. Do not be one of them!

[11] A one-paragraph summary of the procedure is all that is expected at the end of a problem like this, with many issues.

Buckinghamshire CC v Moran [1989] 2 All ER 225, CA, the Court of Appeal held that the issue was the intention of the adverse possessor and not that of the paper owner.[6] Thus, Angela's future intentions for the use of the land will not bar Steve's claim.

If Steve claims, then the fact that Angela is a recluse and might not have taken steps to remove him does not affect Steve's claim, which could only be affected by an illness of Angela's which amounted to a mental disability[7] that meant that she was unable to make decisions on an actual application by Steve to be registered as proprietor (Sched. 6, Para. 8(2) to the LRA 2002).

If Mark bought the cottage from Angela in 2016, then, as he is a purchaser[8] under section 29 and section 30 of the LRA 2002 and this is a case where the title to the land is already registered,[9] he is bound by interests that fall under Schedule 3 to the LRA 2002. These include the interest of a person in actual occupation, as Steve is. However, Mark will not be bound if the interest is not within his actual knowledge at the time of the disposition nor could it have been discovered on a reasonable inspection of the land (Sched. 3, Para. 2).

However, from the facts given, and especially as Steve had erected a café on the land, Mark should have discovered his occupation and so will be bound by it.[10] However, Mark, as Angela's son, may have had the land transferred to him without consideration and is a donee. As such, he is bound by any rights in the land, and this includes rights in the course of being acquired by adverse possession by Steve (s.28 of the LRA 2002).

So, in conclusion, Steve can apply for registration and, on receipt of the application, the Registrar must give notice of it to Mark as the registered proprietor (RP) and to a number of others, including the owner of any registered charge over the property.[11] If Mark does not respond within 65 working days, Steve is entitled to be registered as owner of the estate. Mark may serve a counter-notice, which means that the matter is dealt with under Schedule 6, Paragraph 5, and, unless Steve can establish that he comes within one of three special circumstances, Steve's application is rejected. Mark has two years from this date to commence proceedings for possession. In fact, none of the three sets of special circumstances is relevant here.

✓ Make your answer stand out

- Include a further discussion of what constitutes factual possession and whether this is so here: a possible case to look at is *Purbrick* v *Hackney LBC* [2003] EWHC 1871 (Ch).
- Explain that when considering whether an adverse possessor has an overriding interest, he/she is treated as though they had an interest in the land. In one sense, the squatter has no interest in the land, as he or she is only a trespasser, but the law has given the squatter some recognition – see the Law Commission Consultation Paper (1998) No. 254, Paragraphs 5.42–5.54 and especially Paragraph 5.46.
- Note that in *Buckinghamshire CC* v *Moran* Slade LJ said that in some limited circumstances the paper owner's future intended for the land might be relevant. Research this and ask whether this could be the case here.
- Note *Wilkinson* v *Kerdene Ltd* [2013] EWCA Civ 44, a claim where title was unregistered and there were issues over acknowledgement of title and factual possession. The relevant period was 1974–90.
- Make a brief mention at the end that an argument that the law on adverse possession infringes the HRA 1998 would not succeed and why – *J.A. Pye (Oxford) Ltd* v *UK* (2005) ECHR 921 and *Ofulue* v *Bossert* [2008] EWCA Civ 7.

! Don't be tempted to . . .

- Deal with the mechanics of acquiring title under the LRA 2002 before you have decided whether there is adverse possession.
- Assume that Steve has factual possession – he almost certainly does, but state and apply the law!
- Overlook the fact that Angela is a recluse – in the end, it turns out not to affect the issue – but it could do so.
- Overlook the position on the transfer to Mark – do not assume that he is automatically bound or that he is not bound at all! Instead, leave yourself time to mention Schedule 3, Paragraph 2 to the LRA 2002.

❓ Question 2

For many years, Fred had used a field, Blackacre, under annual grazing licences, granted by Mike, the registered leasehold proprietor of the field. Mike held a 99-year lease and the freehold title is held by Robbie.

In 2000, Fred wrote to Mike to request the renewal of the licence. He also asked whether he might use the land more extensively than before. Fred received no reply. In the meantime, he did indeed use the field more extensively and he also replaced some of the boundary fences and the old gate.

In addition, Fred owned another field, Whiteacre, that adjoins Mike's land. When he bought Whiteacre in 2002, the seller, Teresa, told him that there had been a previous boundary dispute between her and Mike but that, as Teresa had heard nothing from Mike for some time, Teresa assumed that Mike was 'happy with the situation'.

It is now 2017.

(a) Fred wishes to make an application under the Land Registration Act 2002 to be regis-tered as leasehold owner of Blackacre.

(b) Mike has put boundary posts on Whiteacre, but Fred says that some of the land they enclose belongs to him.

How, if at all, would your answer differ if title to the land was unregistered?

Diagram plan

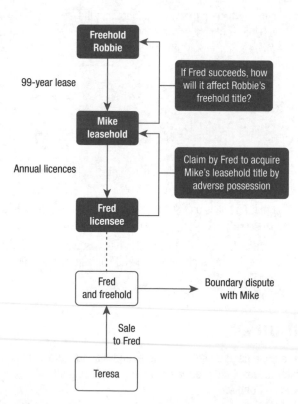

Answer plan

→ Identify the parties and their legal status – freeholder, leaseholder and licensee.

→ When did adverse possession begin?

→ Decide whether there is both factual possession and an intention to possess on the part of Fred.

→ Consider the relevance or not of the possibility that the land may be intended for another use in future.

→ Explain the procedure on an application under the LRA 2002.

→ Explain how Robbie, as the freeholder, would be affected by a successful application by Fred.

→ Explain the position if the title is unregistered.

Answer

(a) Fred is making a claim to be registered as the leasehold proprietor of a field where, at present, Mike is the leaseholder under a 99-year lease and the freehold title is held by Robbie. We shall first consider Fred's claim against Mike's leasehold title and then, if Fred does succeed against Mike, the effect that this will have on Robbie as the freeholder. The position if title to land is unregistered will be dealt with later.[1]

In ***Powell* v *McFarlane*** (1977) 38 P & CR 452, Ch D, it was emphasised that there is a presumption that the owner of the land with the paper title is in possession and so, in any action based on adverse possession, the burden of proof is on the squatter to prove both:

(a) factual possession (*corpus possessionis*); and

(b) intent to possess (*animus possidendi*).[2]

As title to the land is registered, under the Land Registration Act 2002 (LRA 2002), the period of adverse possession needed is a minimum of 10 years.[3]

Originally, Fred held the field under annual grazing licences and so no question of adverse possession can arise, as he did not have the intent to possess: he was there by the permission of the owner and so his possession was not inconsistent with Mike's title (***J.A. Pye (Oxford) Ltd* v *Graham*** [2002] 3 All ER 865, HL). Therefore any period of adverse possession will have begun in 2000, when Fred's licence expired.

[1] If you get a question on adverse possession involving a lease, you should first consider whether the claim will succeed against the leaseholder. The rules are the same as if the claim was to the freehold. Only if you consider that the claim might succeed need you go on to look at the effect on the freeholder.

[2] Never forget to mention these two points!

[3] Note the difference from the period where title is unregistered.

In **Powell v McFarlane**, Slade J held that factual possession is shown by the adverse possessor dealing with the land as an occupying owner in exercising control over the land, and he pointed out that clear evidence of this is 'the locking or blocking of the only means of access'. Here, factual possession by Fred is demonstrated by using the field more extensively and replacing some of the boundary fences and the old gate.

Fred can apply for registration after 10 years' possession, and here he may have 17.[4] The Registrar must give notice of the application to Mike, as the registered leasehold proprietor, and Robbie, as the registered freehold proprietor. Both can respond within 65 working days by serving a counter-notice and so, unless Fred can establish that he comes within one of three special circumstances set out in Paragraph 5(2) of Schedule 6 to the LRA 2002, none of which applies,[5] Mike has two years from the date of Fred's application to commence proceedings for possession.

If title to the land is unregistered, under section 15(1) of the Limitation Act 1980, the period of adverse possession is 12 years and Fred has achieved this.[6] The requirements of factual possession and intention to possess are the same as for registered land, and so Fred will then need to make an application to be registered as owner of the field. However, there are no provisions for Mike or Robbie to object, and so Fred is likely to become the registered owner.

Assuming that Fred does succeed in his claim, he will be registered as the new proprietor of the leasehold estate[7] (Sched. 6, Para. 1 to the LRA 2002). Thus, Robbie's freehold title is not affected by Fred's registration as the new leaseholder. Fred becomes, by operation of the LRA 2002, an assignee of the lease and is bound by all the covenants and any other obligations in it (Sched. 6, Para. 9(2) to the LRA 2002). If Fred wishes to succeed to the freehold, he will have to wait until Mike's lease has expired and then, assuming that Robbie or his successor in title takes no action either to grant a new lease or to evict him, he can then begin a new period of adverse possession against the freehold title.

The position is different if title is unregistered. Here, there is no statutory assignment of the lease to Fred, although Fred is entitled

[4] You need to identify very clearly exactly how long a period of adverse possession is required and how much there is in the situation.

[5] There is no point in saying any more than this, especially as you will have seen that in part (b) you will need to deal with this issue in more detail.

[6] It is easy to forget that if title is unregistered, the period is different – this is a basic point and you will lose marks if you get it wrong!

[7] This is a vital point, as the rest of this paragraph follows from it. Also, the position is different if title is unregistered.

to possession for the remainder of the term of the lease. Thus, Mike will remain liable on the lease (**St Marylebone Property Co. Ltd v Fairweather** [1963] AC 510, HL), and there is no privity of estate between Robbie and Fred. Thus, they cannot claim directly against each other. Of course, it may well be that Mike does not pay rent to Robbie, as he is no longer in possession, and, if so, Robbie will be able to take action against him for, for example, forfeiture of the lease, and this will end Fred's rights.[8] Moreover, if Fred breaches any of the covenants in the lease, Robbie may take action, not against him but against Mike, and so the lease may be forfeited. Moreover, as Mike is not a tenant, he cannot apply for relief from forfeiture.

Robbie may be unhappy that Fred is now in possession of the land, and the rent may be small and Mike may still be paying it, so that Robbie will be unable at the moment to take action to forfeit the lease. In **St Marylebone Property Co. Ltd v Fairweather**, it was held that the tenant might surrender the lease to the freeholder, who then has an immediate right to possession,[9] and so a surrender by Mike to Robbie would allow Robbie to seek possession against Fred who would, because Mike had surrendered the lease, be a trespasser. However, it is not clear what the dispossessed tenant has to surrender: in **St Marylebone Property Co. Ltd v Fairweather**, the House of Lords distinguished between the tenant's title to the leasehold estate, which the squatter had defeated, and his estate in the land, which he still held and which he could therefore surrender, but this seems a very fine distinction.[10]

(b) This is a boundary dispute between Fred and Mike, and Fred could apply to be registered as leasehold owner under Paragraph 5(4) of Schedule 6 to the LRA 2002. This requires that, for at least 10 years of the period of adverse possession ending on the date of the application, the applicant (or any predecessor in title) reasonably believed that the land to which the application relates belonged to him. Under section 98 of the Land Registration Act 2002, the date for deciding the question of reasonable belief is the day preceding the start of the proceedings. If so, then the applicant can apply to be registered at once. Here, Fred's belief dates from 2002, i.e. 15 years ago. In

[8] This section is a good example of the interrelationship between different areas of Land Law and why you should not leave out topics when revising. If you had left out leaseholds, you could not have said all this!

[9] Remember that this point is only relevant where title to the land is unregistered and the question involves adverse possession of a lease.

[10] This decision is controversial and so you will add marks if you say this and explain why it is controversial.

Zarb v *Parry* [2011] EWCA 1306,[11] it was held that the owners' belief that the land belonged to them was still reasonable as, although they knew that there had been a boundary dispute when they bought the property, they thought that it had been resolved. Fred could argue that Teresa's words that Mike was 'happy with the situation' made his belief reasonable. In *IAM Group Plc* v *Chowdrey* [2012] EWCA Civ 505 it was held that it might be reasonable in these cases to make enquiries of your solicitors when you buy the land to see whether there had been a boundary dispute; and, here, Mike could argue, in response to Fred's claim, that Fred should have checked when he bought the land. If title was unregistered, then Fred would simply be able to acquire title on the basis of 12 years' possession.

✓ Make your answer stand out

- Read the decision in *J.A. Pye (Oxford) Ltd* v *Graham* in detail, especially on the issue of the licence held by the adverse possessor.
- Criticism of the decision in *St Marylebone Property Co. Ltd* v *Fairweather* by Wade, H.W.R. (1962) Landlord, Tenant and Squatter. *LQR*, 78: 541.
- Mention that in *Chung Ping Kwan* v *Lam Islands Development Co. Ltd* [1997] AC 38, PC the Privy Council did not take the opportunity to comment on the decision in *St Marylebone Property Co. Ltd* v *Fairweather*.
- Explain that in *J.A. Pye (Oxford) Ltd* v *United Kingdom* (2005) 43 ECHR 43, ECtHR it was held that the unregistered land system was ECHR compliant, so explain why the new system under the LRA 2002 with its safeguards for the owner will also be compliant.

! Don't be tempted to . . .

- Forget the end of the question: remember also to deal with the position where title is unregistered.
- Omit to deal with whether there has been adverse possession before you discuss the position of Fred as against Mike, the leaseholder.
- Forget that adverse possession against the leaseholder does not affect the title of the freeholder.
- Omit, in (a), to set out the relationship between Fred, as the new tenant, and Robbie, the freeholder.

Question 3

Critically consider the statement that 'the law relating to adverse possession has been changed fundamentally by the Land Registration Act 2002': Cooke, E. (2003) *The New Law of Land Registration*. Oxford: Hart Publishing.

Answer plan

→ Explain what 'adverse possession' means.

→ Consider how the law was changed by the LRA 2002.

→ Contrast this with the position where title to land is unregistered.

→ Look at areas where the position was not altered by the LRA 2002.

→ Summing up – refer back to the question: evaluate whether the LRA 2002 made a fundamental change in the law or only the procedure for actually acquiring title.

Diagram plan

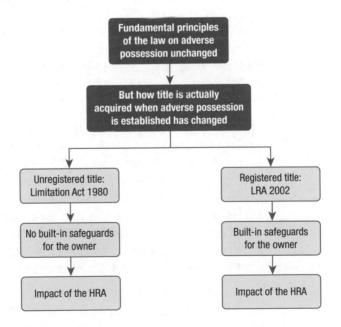

A printable version of this diagram plan is available from **www.pearsoned.co.uk/lawexpressqa**

Answer

[1] A fundamental point, but always worth remembering: start with a basic definition, which will save you time later.

[2] Do make it clear that the old law still applies to unregistered land.

[3] This is important, and you will lose marks if you rush in and explain the differences before clearing the ground and explaining the similarities.

[4] The Law Commission Consultation Paper is an excellent source of material, so put in quotes from it that assists your argument.

[5] This is a good example of what you should always search out for before the exam to boost your marks: a sound practical example that involves some research. It is guaranteed to impress the examiner.

[6] Take each point separately, and contrast the two systems.

[7] Superficially, the law seems to have tilted in favour of squatters, as the period is now only 10 years, but the actual mechanics of gaining title have actually tilted the law very much the other way.

The essence of adverse possession is that a person (the claimant, also popularly known as the squatter) by possession of land acquires title to it from the previous owner, who is known in this context as the registered or 'paper' owner.[1] The LRA 2002 made substantial changes to the law, which, as we shall see, have made it substantially more difficult to acquire title by this method. Before the new regime was introduced by the LRA 2002, the basic rules were the same for both registered and unregistered titles, and now these rules still apply where title to land is unregistered. Therefore, a comparison between them is still of practical importance.[2]

However, the basic requirements of claiming title by adverse possession, factual possession of the land with the intention to exclude others, apply in all cases.[3] The differences arise mainly when the adverse possessor has satisfied these requirements and actually wishes to make good his or her claim to the land. The fundamental point is that, as the Law Commission (1998) Consultation Paper, Land Registration for the Twenty-first Century, No. 254. http://lawcommission.justice.gov.uk/docs/lc254_land_registration_for_21st_century_consultative.pdf points out: 'Where title is registered, the basis of title is primarily registration then possession' (Para. 10.11).[4] It is, of course, the opposite for unregistered land.

Where title to land is unregistered, section 15(1) of the Limitation Act 1980 provides that the adverse possessor has to have 12 years of adverse possession. The paper owner's title is extinguished at once (s. 17 of the Limitation Act 1980) and the squatter has a new title. Thus, where the paper owner has taken no interest in the land, and may not even know that it is theirs, they will lose title with no warning. A good example is **Ellis v Lambeth LBC** (1999) 32 HLR 596, CA, where the council did not notice that the squatter was in occupation for more than 14 years and it lost title when the squatter claimed title.[5]

In contrast,[6] under the LRA 2002, there are considerable safeguards for the registered owner (see Sched. 6 to the LRA 2002, where the detailed rules are set out). Here, the squatter can apply to be registered after 10 years, unlike 12 years for unregistered land. However, this apparent shortening of the time required is deceptive.[7] If neither the registered proprietor nor anyone else served with notice, such

[8] This is a fundamental point and is the crucial change made to the law by the LRA 2002, and so you must stress it.

[9] You could, at this point and if you have time, give an example of how this could be so by looking at the law of estoppel and the decision in the important case of *Thorner v Major* [2009] UKHL 18, HL. See the Law Commission Report (2001) No. 271, Paragraph 4.40.

as a chargee, objects to the application by serving a counter-notice, then the squatter is entitled to be registered. However, the objection is simply a veto, as it does not have to be justified,[8] and, thus, there is no reason for a registered proprietor to lose title provided that he receives the application.

If the paper owner exercises this veto, he has two years in which to evict the squatter unless one of three situations set out in Paragraph 5 of Schedule 6 to the LRA 2002 applies. If so, the squatter is entitled to be registered after 10 years. These are:

(a) Where it would be unconscionable, because of an equity by estoppel,[9] for the registered proprietor (the paper owner) to seek to dispossess the squatter. This could be where an owner has allowed the squatter to build on land through a mistaken belief that the squatter is really the owner of it.

(b) Where there is a claim by a person with an independent right to registration, e.g. where the squatter is entitled to the land under the will or intestacy of the previous owner.

(c) Where the squatter already owns adjoining land and reasonably believes that the disputed land also belongs to him. This is intended to deal with cases where the boundary on the register does not match that on the ground.

[10] In effect, the first two were included to tidy up the law by providing a mechanism for registration in these cases.

[11] This is another fundamental point that the examiner will expect you to stress.

[12] This point is often missed by students, so a mention of it will gain a mark or two!

[13] Note the link with the basic point: where title is registered, the previous title is not extinguished, as in unregistered title, but the squatter succeeds to it. Emphasise this, as it will show the examiner that you are clear on the basic point.

Of the three cases above, the first two are, in a sense, unnecessary, as there is already a right to be registered as owner, which does not depend on 10 years' adverse possession.[10] It is the third case that will give rise to claims.

When the squatter is registered, it will be as the new registered proprietor of the estate against which he adversely possessed[11] (Sched. 6, Para. 9) and he takes subject to all existing legal and equitable rights in the land except registered charges[12] (Sched. 6, Paras. 9(2) and 9(3)). This is why a registered chargee is entitled to be served with notice of an application so that it can object.

Where the adverse possessor possesses against a leasehold title, the squatter acquires only the leasehold and not the freehold. If the claim succeeds, the adverse possessor will be registered as the new proprietor of the leasehold estate[13] (Sched. 6, Para. 1 to the LRA 2002) and he will become, by operation of the LRA 2002, an assignee of the lease and is bound by all the covenants and any other obligations in it (Sched. 6, Para. 9(2) to the LRA 2002).

If title is unregistered, there is no statutory assignment of the lease to the squatter, although he is entitled to possession for the remainder of the term of the lease. Thus, the disposed leaseholder will remain liable on the lease (**St Marylebone Property Co. Ltd v Fairweather** [1963] AC 510, HL). It was also held in this case that the tenant might surrender the lease to the freeholder, who then has an immediate right to possession. This will not apply where title is registered.

[14] Although the Court of Appeal has held, in *Ofulue v Bossert*, that UK adverse possession law does comply with the ECHR, an examiner would expect you to discuss this point in view of the extensive discussion of it in case law and academic articles.

Finally, is the law on adverse possession under either the registered or the unregistered system in breach of the ECHR?[14] Article 1 of the First Protocol says that 'No one shall be deprived of the peaceful enjoyment of his possessions except in the public interest and subject to the conditions provided for by law and the general principles of international law'. In **J.A. Pye (Oxford) Ltd v United Kingdom** (2007) 46 EHRR 1083, the Grand Chamber of the ECtHR held that UK law does not infringe the ECHR and found that adverse possession was a justified control of use of land rather than a deprivation of possession and this was within the margin of appreciation. In **Ofulue v Bossert** [2008] EWCA Civ 7, the Court of Appeal[15] held that this decision establishes that UK law complies with the ECHR. This decision was on the position where title was unregistered and it is even more likely that the law in the LRA 2002 where title is registered will be compliant with the ECHR with its safeguards for the paper owner.

[15] It is important to include this decision as well as that of the ECtHR mentioned above, as *Ofulue* v *Bossert* is, of course, that of the UK courts.

[16] You do not need a long conclusion, but do emphasise these two points as it rounds the answer off nicely.

In conclusion, the law on actually acquiring title by adverse possession has indeed changed fundamentally as a result of the LRA 2002, but the law on what is actually meant by adverse possession is very largely unaltered.[16]

✓ Make your answer stand out

- Look into the Law Commission's Consultation Paper (1998) No. 254, Paragraphs 10.4–10.78. Do not be daunted – there are only 33 pages on adverse possession! This was a consultative document and so you should search for it under 'Reports'.
- Look at the law of estoppel and the decision in the important case of *Thorner* v *Major*. See the Law Commission Report (2001) No. 271, Paragraph 4.40.

- Follow this with research into the actual Law Commission (2001) Report, *Land Registration for the 21st Century: A Conveyancing Revolution*, No. 271. http://lawcommission. justice.gov.uk/docs/lc271_land_registration_for_the_twentyfirst_century.pdf, part X1V. In particular, note the discussion, at Paragraph 14.69, of the decision in *Central London Estates Ltd* v *Kato Kaguku Co. Ltd* [1998] 4 All ER 948, Ch D where the land is leasehold, and how this decision influenced the final report.

- Mention the criticisms of *St Marylebone Property Co. Ltd* v *Fairweather* in Wade, H.W.R. (1962) Landlord, Tenant and Squatter. *LQR*, 78: 541. For an excellent analysis of the law on adverse possession, see Cooke, E. (1994) Adverse Possession – Some Problems of Title in Registered Land. *Legal Studies*, 14: 1.

- Look further at the discussion on whether the law on adverse possession is ECHR compliant – see, e.g. Kerridge, R. and Brierley, A.H.R. (2007) Adverse Possession, Human Rights and Land Registration: And They All Lived Happily Ever After. *Conv.* 71: 552.

! Don't be tempted to . . .

- Spend ages at the start just explaining what the general law of adverse possession is – the whole point is that this is generally the same whether title is registered or unregistered. Why not just say this?
- Set out the rules for both registered and unregistered land without comparing them.
- Ignore the difference between the registered and unregistered systems in cases where there is adverse possession against a leaseholder. This is one of the most significant differences between them.

📝 Question 4

In *J.A. Pye (Oxford) Ltd* v *Graham* [2002] 3 All ER 865, HL, Lord Browne-Wilkinson said that in cases of adverse possession the 'necessary intent is an intent to possess not to own and an intention to exclude the paper owner only so far as is reasonably practicable'.

Evaluate this statement in the context of the present law of adverse possession.

Answer plan

→ Explain exactly what Lord Browne-Wilkinson meant in the quotation.

→ Evaluate the significance of the squatter only needing to show an intention to possess.

→ Consider the implied licence theory – how it evolved and was applied in the cases.

→ Explain that the implied licence theory is no longer good law.

→ Mention the attempt to resurrect this theory in *Beaulane Properties* v *Palmer* and explain why it did not succeed.

Diagram plan

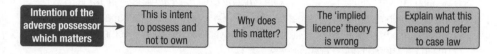

Intention of the adverse possessor which matters → This is intent to possess and not to own → Why does this matter? → The 'implied licence' theory is wrong → Explain what this means and refer to case law

A printable version of this diagram plan is available from **www.pearsoned.co.uk/lawexpressqa**

Answer

[1] Note that this introduction has identified two issues: the focus on the intention of the adverse possessor and not the owner and then precisely what intentions the adverse possessor must have. You should then follow this theme through the essay.

This statement of Lord Browne-Wilkinson in **J.A. Pye (Oxford) Ltd v Graham** [2002] 3 All ER 865, HL was intended to banish from the law of adverse possession what he called the 'heretical and wrong' view that the intentions of the owner of the land are relevant and to emphasise that it is the intention of the adverse possessor that counts. Furthermore, the adverse possessor does not have to intend to own the land, but only to possess it.[1]

[2] This is not only a valuable point to make in relation to adverse possession, but also shows cross-subject knowledge – here, of the law on easements and profits. This always impresses examiners.

[3] The main thrust of this question is about the implied licence theory, but, before you mention it, you should also mention this point, as you will lose marks if you do not.

The fact that the adverse possessor (usually referred to as the squatter) does not have to intend to own the land is, in a way, a statement of the obvious, as in many, if not most, cases the squatters are squatting on land that they know is not theirs. In other cases, the squatter may at first honestly believe that it is his, as in the case of a boundary dispute, and in others the squatter may not have any intention at all except to occupy land that no one else happens to be occupying. Thus, in **Best v Chief Land Registrar** [2014] EWHC 1370 (Admin), Ouseley J pointed out the fundamental difference between acquisition of an easement or a profit by prescription and adverse possession: prescription involves 'possession as of right', based on the presumed intention of the landowner to grant title, while adverse possession involves 'possession as of wrong'.[2] This is shown by the decision in **J.A. Pye (Oxford) Ltd v Graham** itself, where the squatter had held the land under a licence agreement that was not renewed, and so at this point his possession became adverse.[3] Clearly, he did not intend to own the land at that time, as he knew that it belonged to the

[4] This case and the next one are not well known and so this shows good research detail, which will gain you marks.

[5] Now you can come to the main area of this question.

[6] It is important that you look back at what the law was here, as the point of Lord Browne-Wilkinson's remarks was that the law had been wrong and it was right to change it.

[7] You are earning extra marks by mentioning this case as well as *Leigh* v *Jack*.

[8] This case follows from *Wallis's Cayton Bay Holiday Camp v Shell Mex and BP* as it shows the change in attitude.

licensor. Similarly, in **Williams v Jones** [2002][4] EWCA Civ 1097, a tenant successfully claimed adverse possession after he continued to possess the land after rent had been neither paid nor sought for many years. The point was that it was the tenant's continued possession that counted. However, the requirement of possession adverse to the paper owner was emphasised in **Clowes Developments (UK) Ltd v Walters** [2005] EWHC 669 (Ch), where permission was under a licence originally granted to another member of the family and then continued. Thus, as there was no possession as such, the claim to title by adverse possession failed.

Lord Browne-Wilkinson's emphasis on the intention of the adverse possessor also means the exclusion of the 'implied licence' theory[5] that the claimant is assumed to have been given an implied licence to use the land because his actions were not inconsistent with an intended use by the owner. The effect of this was that if the possessor's actions *were* inconsistent with the owner's intended use then there could be no adverse possession, and this made the success of a claim to adverse possession dependent on the intentions of the owner. Thus, in **Leigh v Jack** (1879) 5 Ex D 264, CA, it was held[6] that where possession did not affect plans which the paper owner had for the future use of the land, the possessor could not begin to acquire adverse possession (i.e. the period of years required would not begin to run) until his use did conflict with those plans. Thus, where land was vacant but was earmarked for future use, an adverse possessor who occupied it could not be in adverse possession until either the owner abandoned his plans or the claimant did acts that made those plans impossible. In **Wallis's Cayton Bay Holiday Camp Ltd v Shell-Mex and BP Ltd** [1974][7] 3 All ER 575, CA, the defendant owned land in the middle of a field in which it intended to erect a garage. The rest of the field belonged to Wallis, who, for over 12 years, also farmed the defendant's land. The defendant then abandoned plans to erect a garage because a proposed road was not going to be built. It was held that Wallis had not acquired title by adverse possession, because time could only run from when the defendant abandoned its plans for the road. In effect, whether there was adverse possession was held to depend on the owner's state of mind.

This rule was rejected by the Court of Appeal in **Buckinghamshire CC v Moran** [1989] 2 All ER 225, CA.[8] A strip of land had been reserved by the council for a road diversion for many years, although nothing separated the strip from the adjoining house that the claimant had bought in 1971. He padlocked the only access to the strip and exercised complete control of it until 1985, when the council sued to recover it. It was held that he had demonstrated an intention to possess the plot that overrode the council's future intended use of it. The Court of Appeal held that the issue was the intention of the adverse possessor and not that of the paper owner. Here, the possessor was well aware of the future intentions of the council, but that was not the point. However, Slade LJ did accept that, in some circumstances, knowledge of the paper owner's future intentions for the use of the land may be relevant, e.g. if it indicates that the possessor does not intend to use the land so as to interfere with the paper owner's future intended use of the land, there will not be the requisite intention.

[9] This case brings the story up to date. You should by now have gained crucial marks by mentioning the four main cases on this point. In addition, you should stress the general point made by Lord Browne-Wilkinson that there is only a requirement to exclude the paper owner as far as is reasonably practicable. This then leads you on to earn marks by explaining that in some cases it may be that the existence of an intended use for the land by the paper owner may prevent adverse possession. You are thinking ahead about where the law might develop, and this will earn you marks.

This was confirmed by Lord Browne-Wilkinson in *J.A. Pye (Oxford) Ltd v Graham*, HL by emphasising that only an intention to 'exclude the paper owner only as far as is reasonably practicable' is needed. Thus, provided that the owner is excluded in order for the squatter to establish factual possession that will be enough. He did observe, however, that where the adverse possessor is aware of some special purpose for which the owner needs the land, and the use made by the adverse possessor does not conflict with that use, then that may 'provide some support' for a finding that the adverse possessor did not intend to possess but only had an intention to occupy until it was required by the paper owner. Thus, the door is left open for such a claim as in *Wallis's Cayton Bay Holiday Camp Ltd v Shell-Mex and BP Ltd*, but on the basis of the adverse possessor's intention and not any presumed intent by the owner.[9]

[10] This is another example of a case that is no longer good law – but as this is an essay question that asks you how the law has developed, you need to mention it.

It should be added that in *Beaulane Properties v Palmer* [2005] HRLR 19, Ch D, the High Court sought to reintroduce the implied licence idea in order to make the relevant legislation, section 75 of the Land Registration Act 1925, compliant with the Human Rights Act 1998.[10] It did this by holding that, as the squatter's action in that case was not inconsistent with any use or intended use of the land by the owner, his possession of it was not adverse. This put the emphasis back on the intentions of the owner. However, in *J.A. Pye (Oxford) Ltd v United Kingdom* (2007) 46 EHRR 1083, it was held that UK law is compliant with the Human Rights Act 1998 anyway – a view confirmed in *Ofulue v Bossert* [2009] UKHL 16 – and so it is clear that *Beaulane Properties v Palmer* is no longer good law.

✓ Make your answer stand out

- Mention that the fundamental question here is about possession of land, and that English law has always emphasised possession of land and not title.
- Read a detailed article on the *Buckinghamshire* case: Harpum, C. (1990) *Buckingham County Council* v *Moran. CLJ*, 23.
- Have a look at Tee, L. (2000) Adverse Possession and the Intention to Possess. *Conv.* 113 and then read a different view in Harpum, C. and Radley-Gardner, O. (2001) Adverse Possession and the Intention to Possess: A Reply. *Conv.* 155.

! Don't be tempted to . . .

- Just set out the facts of the cases and do not relate them to any theme.
- Fail to trace the evolution of the law through the cases.
- Leave out the possible effect that the Human Rights Act 1998 might have had on this area – but in the end did not have.

📝 Question 5

'The decision in *Best* v *Chief Land Registrar* supports the proposition that the law of adverse possession is no more than a primitive taking of land by theft.'

Critically consider this statement, illustrating your answer with decided cases and taking into account recent developments in the law relating to adverse possession.

Diagram plan

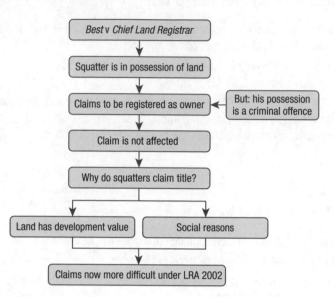

A printable version of this diagram plan is available from **www.pearsoned.co.uk/lawexpressqa**

Answer plan

→ Explain the decision in *Best* v *Chief Land Registrar* not only on its own facts but also in relation to the wider issues raised by this question.

→ Then go beyond this case and look at the law of adverse possession more generally, in order to evaluate the question of whether adverse possession is indeed no more than the taking of land by theft.

→ Take care to mention the importance of the changes made by the LRA 2002.

→ Set out different points of view on whether there should be a law of adverse possession at all.

→ Look at actual issues – different types of squatting.

→ End by coming back to the actual issue raised in the question.

Answer

[2] It is vital that you address the policy reasons that lie behind the law on adverse possession and that you do this at an early stage in your answer, as this question is not about the fine details of the law but is asking you to look more widely.

[3] We have not mentioned the result of the case, as it would have distracted from the main argument. In fact, the litigation arose from an application by Best to register title – the first step in the procedure under the LRA 2002.

[4] At once we have got away from a mechanical recital of the law and are addressing the issues in the question.

[5] This kind of research detail makes your answer much more vivid. The law of adverse possession is full of interesting stories – research some for your exam.

There is a particular issue raised in this question – the significance of the decision in **Best v Chief Land Registrar** [2014] EWHC 1370 (Admin) – but this needs to be related to the general question of whether, if indeed adverse possession is no more than, in effect, legalised theft of land, claims to acquire title by adverse possession should be allowed at all.[1]

Best v Chief Land Registrar concerned the possible application to the law of adverse possession of section 144 of the Legal Aid, Sentencing and Punishment of Offenders Act 2012. This came into force on 1 September 2012 and creates the offence of squatting in a residential building where the defendant 'knows or ought to know' of his or her trespassing. The High Court held that the fact that a person is committing an offence under section 144 does not mean that they cannot claim title by adverse possession under the Land Registration Act 2002 (LRA 2002). A major reason for this decision was the policy consideration[2] that, in the words of Ouseley J, legal ownership of land must not be 'left uncertain in the face of long possession to which there had been no adverse reaction'. Moreover, there was no evidence that Parliament, in passing the Legal Aid, Sentencing and Punishment of Offenders Act 2012, had intended to alter what he called 'the delicate and comprehensive regime under the LRA 2002'.

Thus, this decision shows that, to some extent, the courts do uphold the notion that the law of adverse possession is theft of land. Ouseley J pointed out in this case that adverse possession is indeed 'possession of wrong' and here the squatter knew that the land was not his, and committed a criminal offence by squatting there, but could still claim title.[3] It is important, before deciding whether the law of adverse possession is just, to distinguish between different reasons why squatters may claim title and so commit 'theft' of land.[4]

Buckinghamshire CC v Moran [1989] 2 All ER 225, CA involved a claim to a small strip of land that had been annexed to a garden, and the squatter was a wealthy Lloyd's broker who appeared in lists of the richest people in the UK;[5] and in **J.A. Pye (Oxford) Ltd v Graham** [2002] 3 All ER 865, HL, 25 hectares of development land, worth 'untold millions with planning consent', was claimed by adverse possession. Auchmurty, R.S. (2004) Not Just a Good Children's Story:

A Tribute to Adverse Possession. Conv. 68: 293 remarks, that, in the late nineteenth century, adverse possession claims often involved 'disputes over the boundaries of railway land, which offered such a fruitful field for litigation that no railway company seems to have been exempt'. In ***Best v Chief Land Registrar***, Mr Best was a builder who found out that the property was empty as the owner had died and so entered the property and refurbished the house, intending to make it his permanent home. The fact is, though, that he knew that it was not his, had paid nothing for it and had indeed 'stolen' the land.

Cobb, N.A. and Fox, L. (2007) Living Outside the System? The (Im) morality of Urban Squatting after the Land Registration Act 2002. Legal Studies, 27: 236 point out that 'In social and political discourse in this country, however, the term tends to be associated specifically with the deliberate [author's italics] occupation of empty residential buildings in metropolitan areas'.[6] In ***Ellis v Lambeth LBC*** (1999) 32 HLR 596, CA, a group of squatters successfully claimed a council house worth £200,000. Moreover, Cobb and Fox point out that the Law Commission (2001) Report, Land Registration for the 21st Century: A Conveyancing Revolution, No. 271. http://lawcommission.justice. gov.uk/docs/lc271_land_registration_for_the_twenty-first_century. pdf recognised that unlawful occupation of property may arise from acute housing needs, and the Commission expressed 'understandable sympathy' with squatters in cases where they took possession of empty properties when they were desperate for a home. However, Cobb and Fox argue that the Commission bypassed this issue by claiming that most cases of squatting involved 'the landowner with an eye to the main chance, who encroaches in his or her neighbour's land' (Para. 2.70). In fact, Cobb and Fox argue that urban squatting does serve a social purpose, and they quote statistics showing that there were 78,000 families living in temporary accommodation and properties lying empty that could potentially offer 600,000 new homes: ODPM (Office of the Deputy Prime Minister) (2002) More than a Roof: A Report into Tackling Homelessness. London: ODPM.[7] Thus, the argument of land theft is countered by the defences of necessity and social purpose and stewardship of the land. The Law Commission (Para. 14.4) instead thought that cases involving acquisition of title to council housing by adverse possession represented a loss to the public purse and this was wrong. Cobb and Fox argue that 'Any stewardship duty should include a fundamental obligation to engage in an

[6] This is a very important point to make: if most cases of squatting involved boundary disputes between neighbours, would the topic arouse the same passion?

[7] This kind of question really does need you to mention some statistics. These ones are especially telling.

appropriate degree of supervision over empty land' and point to Lambeth Council's housing department not merely forgetting that it owned certain properties but actually losing them. Thus, in *Ellis* **v** *Lambeth LBC* the council did not notice that the squatter was in occupation for more than 14 years. By contrast, Neuberger J in *J.A. Pye (Oxford) Ltd* **v** *Graham*[8] considered that it was 'Draconian to the owner, and a windfall for the squatter, that, just because the owner has taken no steps to evict a squatter for 12 years, the owner should lose 25 hectares of land to the squatter with no compensation whatsoever'. The context was different, as he was speaking of development land and not housing, but the argument is the same.

[9] Note the structure of this answer very carefully. We could have started with the point that we are making now, about the details of the law and how it has changed with the LRA 2002. However, the danger of this is that we would have spent too much time on this and not enough on the policy issues, which is what will gain the marks.

In the end, the view that one takes on the merits of having a law allowing title to be acquired by adverse possession depends on the view that one takes on the purpose of land itself and the obligations of owners towards their land. What is clear is that the new regime introduced by the Land Registration Act 2002 (LRA 2002) has made claiming title in this way much more difficult.[9] Under the previous law, which still applies where title to land is unregistered, it is where the squatter has been in factual possession of the land for 12 years (s. 15(1) of the Limitation Act 1980) with the intention to exclude others. At that point, the paper owner's title is extinguished at once and the squatter has a new title. Thus, where the paper owner has taken no interest in the land and may not even know that it is his, as in *Ellis* **v** *Lambeth LBC*, he will lose title with no warning. In contrast, under the LRA 2002, the squatter applies to be registered after 10 years but the paper owner then has two years in which to evict the squatter unless one of three situations applies, in which case the squatter is entitled to be registered after 10 years.

[10] In the conclusion you need, as always, to come back to the issue raised in the question.

Although there is no doubt that the law of adverse possession is indeed theft of land,[10] there is a difference between where homeless people squat in a house and where there is a dispute between wealthy landowners simply seeking to realise development value of land. The law needs to strike a balance so that claims based on adverse possession are still possible while providing safeguards to protect the legitimate rights of the owner. The question is whether the LRA 2002 gets that balance right.

✓ **Make your answer stand out**

■ Read Davison-Vecchione, D. (2014) To Make a House a Home: *Best v Chief Land Registrar*. Conv. 78: 351.

■ Read in full the articles cited in this essay – especially that by Cobb and Fox (2007), which is exceptionally full and detailed.

■ Look at the position in other jurisdictions – there is a helpful summary in Cooke, E. (2003) The New Law of Land Registration. Oxford: Hart Publishing.

■ Read Radley-Gardner, O. (2007) *Good-bye to Pye*. Web Journal of Current Legal Issues, which gives a very clear account of the Pye saga and offers some reflections on the impact of the ECHR on the law of adverse possession. However, you should note that this article was written before the decision of the Court of Appeal in *Ofulue* v *Bossert* [2008] EWCA Civ 7.

❗ **Don't be tempted to . . .**

■ Just describe the law – this question is about the policy behind the law, and if you do not recognise this in your answer, you will probably fail on this question.

■ Leave out, on the other hand, any mention of the actual legal position.

■ Omit to stress the effect of the changes made by the LRA 2002, which make it more difficult to acquire title by adverse possession.

■ Leave out a mention of the ECHR's attitude.

@ **Try it yourself**

Now take a look at the question below and attempt to answer it. You can check your response against the answer guidance available on the companion website (**www.pearsoned.co.uk/lawexpressqa**).

> Consider what needs to be proved in order to establish a claim for adverse possession of freehold land, and assess how this differs from where the land is leasehold.

www.pearsoned.co.uk/lawexpressqa

Go online to access more revision support, including additional essay and problem questions with diagram plans, and you be the marker questions, and to download all diagrams from the book.

A mixture
of questions

How this topic may come up in exams

In Land Law, as in other areas of law, it is a mistake to assume that actual legal issues necessarily fit neatly into the categories where they appear in textbooks. Examiners recognise this and, accordingly, they set questions that cut across subject divisions. This also has the added benefit (or burden, depending on whether you are a teacher or student) of ensuring that students do not confine themselves to only certain subject areas when revising, but need to revise the whole syllabus. There have already been questions in earlier chapters that have involved knowledge of more than one area but where one particular area was the main one. In this chapter, however, you will find a genuine mix.

Before you begin

It's a good idea to consider the following key themes before tackling a question that ranges across a variety of topics in Land Law.

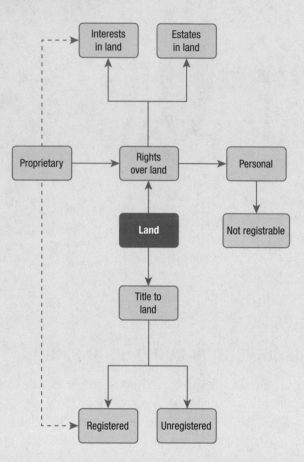

A printable version of this diagram is available from **www.pearsoned.co.uk/lawexpressqa**

🖋 Question 1

'The 1925 legislation was at best only a partial success in bringing property law into the modern era'.

Critically comment on this view.

Diagram plan

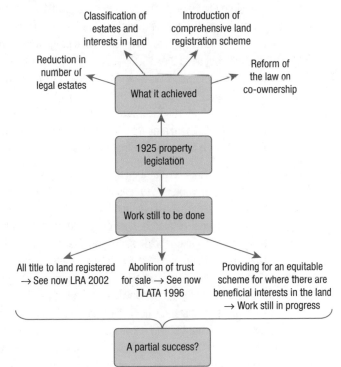

A printable version of this diagram plan is available from **www.pearsoned.co.uk/lawexpressqa**

Answer plan

→ Take up the words of the question and say briefly what your view is. This gives the essay a theme.

→ Identify the 1925 property statutes.

→ Consider the reduction in the number of legal estates.

→ Then go on to consider interests in land and distinguish between legal and equitable interests.

→ This takes us to third-party rights in land and the distinction between registered and unregistered land.

➡ Consider co-ownership and the problems where the legal estate was vested in tenants in common.

➡ Mention of trusts for sale under the 1925 legislation and the changes made by TLATA.

➡ End by going back to the words of the question.

Answer

The statement that the 1925 property legislation was, at best, only a partial success in bringing property law into the modern era seems a harsh criticism of what was an ambitious programme. The legislation of 1925 contained the following six statutes:[1] the Law of Property Act (LPA), the Land Registration Act (LRA), the Settled Land Act (SLA), the Land Charges Act (LCA), the Trustee Act (TA) and the Administration of Estates Act (AEA). This essay will concentrate on the first four, as the Trustee Act concerns trust law and the Administration of Estates Act deals with probate and other matters.

[1] Do not be misled into thinking that the only property legislation of 1925 was the Law of Property Act!

It is often forgotten what the legislation achieved.[2] First, section 1(1) of the LPA 1925 greatly simplified the law by introducing the idea of the estate owner who alone had the right to convey the legal estate. It reduced legal estates to two: an estate in fee simple absolute in possession (legal freehold estate) and a term of years absolute (legal leasehold estate). The holder of a legal estate in land which is in fee simple absolute in possession has the right to use the land for an infinite time and thus to convey that land to another. Before 1925, land might, for instance, be held under a life interest where the owner did not have the right to convey it as he held it only for his life. Not only this, but all land must have an owner in fee simple[3] and so all land must have an estate owner with the right to convey it. It is easy to forget what an advantage this is. All the other rights, such as life interests, can still exist but only in equity under a trust.

[2] It is important to achieve a balance in your answer: look at what the 1925 legislation did achieve and balance this against any perceived defects.

[3] Having used the full 'fee simple absolute in possession' to start with, you can then revert to the shorter fee simple.

The LPA classified all other rights over land as interests in land with a division between estates, whether freehold or leasehold, which described the rights of the actual estate owner, and interests, which are rights which third parties have over another's land. Thus, a right of way over another's land is an easement and is an interest in land.

There was, and still is, a further division between legal and equitable interests in land. Suppose that Jack has a restrictive covenant over

John's land that prevents John from building on his land.[4] John then sells his land to Richard. Is Richard bound by Jack's restrictive covenant? A restrictive covenant is an equitable interest in land and so Richard will be bound only if he is a purchaser in good faith of the land without notice of that covenant. How do we show that he is without notice? That will be a factual question, and there is much case law on it.[5] Turning to the land that John has sold to Richard, suppose that Teresa has a right of way over it, created by deed. This will be an easement and will be a legal interest in Richard's land. Legal interests bind all the world, including Richard.

Suppose that Richard has bought the land unaware of either Jack's covenant or Teresa's easement. To prevent this from happening, a lengthy investigation of title is needed. The obvious solution is to have a register on which interests are entered.[6] This was first proposed in 1739, but it was not until the Land Registration Act 1925 that a comprehensive scheme came into force. However, registration of title to land was not made compulsory in all areas until 1990 and even now there is a good deal of unregistered title.

Where title is unregistered there is a register of land charges a – kind of mini-land registration system set up by the Land Charges Act 1925, which was replaced without any changes of substance by the Land Charges Act 1972. If an interest is registrable as a land charge, as with registered land, a purchaser will take subject to it and, if it is not registered, it cannot bind a purchaser. If an interest is not registrable as a land charge, whether a purchaser is bound depends on whether it is legal or equitable, and the same rules as stated above apply.

Meanwhile, in 2002, the Land Registration Act 2002 was passed, which replaced the 1925 Act, and, while keeping the essential structure, itself a tribute to the 1925 Act, changed details such as a reduction in the number of overriding interests, which continue to bind purchasers of land even though not registered. One question is whether they should remain.[7]

The 1925 legislation also dealt with co-ownership of land. Before 1925, it was possible for title to land to be held by tenants in common with undivided shares. So, many people could hold shares in the legal title to, for example, a small house, and, as the consent of all of them would be needed to a sale, it could be practically impossible to sell. Here, the LPA 1925 made a welcome change by simply providing, by section 1(6), that 'A legal estate is not capable of subsisting or of being created

[8] You cannot be expected to recall lengthy extracts from statutes verbatim, but do try to recall the essentials such as this.

[9] You do need to say something on other areas in order to give this essay balance, and a mention of trusts for sale is a good and clear example.

[10] Another simple example helps here.

[11] You need to mention this type of point: since 1925, there have been enormous social changes that could not have been foreseen, and it ties in nicely with the conclusion.

[12] Note that, in one sentence, we have touched on two areas and so picked up marks: the law on co-ownership and overriding interests.

in an undivided share in land'.[8] Now, where there are co-owners of land, the legal title must be held by joint tenants and there can be no more than four (s. 34(2) of the LPA 1925). There can still be tenancies in common, and indeed they are often found, but they can only exist in equity under a trust of land. Once again, we see the policy of the 1925 legislation in pushing back interests into equity, as with life interests, mentioned above. Where the title is held by joint tenants, survivorship applies and, as joint tenants own no individual share, they cannot leave any part of their joint tenancy by will, nor does it pass under the intestacy rules. Instead, it passes to the surviving joint tenants.

Finally, the Settled Land Act 1925 provided that, where land was held on trust, it was held on a trust for sale.[9] Although, by section 25 of the LPA 1925, there was an implied power to postpone sale, it was the duty of the trustees to sell unless they unanimously agreed to postpone sale (**Re Mayo** [1943] Ch 302, Ch D). This made no sense in modern conditions. Suppose that Tim and Tom decide to buy a house to live in,[10] but the legal title is in the name of Tom, although Tim made substantial contributions to its cost. They bought the house to live in and not to sell but Tom has a duty to sell. It took until the Trusts of Land and Appointment of Trustees Act 1996 for the law to change and now, by section 4 of that Act, trusts for sale are trusts of land.

If we consider the position as it was in 1925, we can say that, at that time, the legislation was a success – and not just a partial one. It is easy to criticise it with the benefit of hindsight and, for example, the great expansion in co-ownership could not have been foreseen,[11] where one of the parties may not be a legal owner of the home but has contributed to the purchase price. This has led to an enormous amount of case law (see **Jones v Kernott** [2011] UKSC 53) together with an emphasis on the rights of occupiers as overriding interests under land registration rules.[12]

✓ Make your answer stand out

■ Do not go into too much detail on any one area – this question covers so much that you really have to make a selection and resist the temptation to write all that you know!

■ There is some good material on the history of Land Law and the events leading up to the 1925 legislation in Simpson, A.W.B. (1986) *A History of the Land Law*. Oxford: Oxford University Press.

- Keep a theme running through your answer – i.e. from estates in land to interests in land to registered land to unregistered land, etc.
- Keep the focus on the 1925 legislation – it is easy to stray into other areas.
- If you have time, mention that the Trusts of Land and Appointment of Trustees Act 1996 prevented the creation of new strict settlements. Why did it do this?

! Don't be tempted to . . .

- Give a summary of the 1925 legislation without commenting on it.
- Go into great detail on certain areas, e.g. write at length on overriding interests which is not justified in this type of question.
- Start the answer without having a very clear idea of what areas and themes you will be looking at. If you do not, you will find that you just wander from point to point and the essay will be very disjointed.

🖎 Question 2

De Veloper Ltd is interested in purchasing a large piece of land extending to 250 acres with registered title. It intends, subject to planning permission, to build a mixture of residential units and light industrial buildings on it, but before going ahead, requires advice on the following matters that have come to light in the course of its preliminary enquiries:

(a) It has learned that, for about the last eight years, Sid, a market gardener, has occupied an area of land of about 5 acres, which he has partially fenced off. At the moment, De Veloper Ltd has no immediate use for the land and, as Sid is at least taking care of the land, is inclined to allow him to stay.

(b) Some of the houses that De Veloper Ltd wishes to build will be overlooking the sea, with splendid views. However, there is a strip of land between the land on which De Veloper Ltd wishes to build and the sea, and this could itself be built on. If so, the view would be destroyed. Is there any way in which De Veloper Ltd can make sure that this view is preserved?

Answer plan

→ Note that the land has registered title and that our clients have not yet bought it.

→ Situation (a) – possible adverse possession claim if Sid is allowed to stay – solution – grant of lease/licence.

→ Situation (b) – consider whether an easement is possible – if not, look at the possibility of a restrictive covenant and how it can be made binding on subsequent owners.

→ Finish with a brief mention of the possibility of planning permission in (b).

Diagram plan

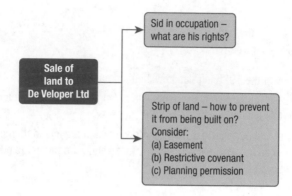

A printable version of this diagram plan is available from **www.pearsoned.co.uk/lawexpressqa**

[1] As always, it is vital to check this first.

[2] Don't forget this basic point.

[3] This is an important practical point, often overlooked in answers to questions on adverse possession: if the seller sells and there is an adverse possessor on the land, then why not sue the seller?

[4] This is important: watch for whether the transferee is a purchaser (s. 29 of the LRA 2002 applies) or a donee, e.g., has acquired by inheritance (s. 28 applies).

Answer

The first point to note is that title to the land that De Veloper Ltd is interested in buying is registered.[1] Moreover, the fact that it has not bought the land means that we need to advise the company on both the practical consequences of buying the land with any existing rights and also how, in view of those rights, it can best protect its position.

(a) The first point is that Sid is, at the moment, a trespasser,[2] and so can be ejected by the owner. De Veloper may do this when it acquires the land, although it would be better advised to require the present seller to do so. If the sale goes through and Sid is still on the land, the seller is in breach of his implied covenant to give vacant possession and so can be sued by De Veloper for damages, or it can rescind the contract.[3] If De Veloper goes ahead and buys the land, it will be a purchaser,[4] and this is a

[5] A good point of detail: if the land was not registered, then, of course, the position would be different, as De Veloper would be making an application for first registration.

[6] Note: only 'may be' and not 'is' in actual occupation. This picks up the point, in the next paragraph, that Sid may not be in occupation as he does not have control of the land.

[7] This shows a confident answer that will impress the examiner – as Sid's occupation is known to the buyer, the buyer will obviously be bound and so there is no point in setting out the rest of Schedule 3, Paragraph 2(c).

[8] You can find this information in the *Land Registry Practice Guide 5: Adverse Possession* (2010).

case where the title to the land is already registered.[5] Thus, under sections 29 and 30 of the Land Registration Act 2002 (LRA 2002), it will be bound by interests that fall under Schedule 3 to the Act. These include the interest of a person in actual occupation, which Sid may be.[6] However, De Veloper would not be bound if the interest is not within its actual knowledge at the time of the disposition, but, here, it does know of it.[7]

We are told that De Veloper is inclined to allow Sid to stay. If it does so without taking steps to regularise the position, Sid may have a claim, after 10 years, to be registered as owner of that part of the land that he has possessed, on the basis that he has been in actual possession of the land and that he has the intention to possess. In **Powell v McFarlane** (1977) 38 P & CR 452, Ch D, Slade J held that the adverse possessor must show that he has dealt with the land as an occupying owner. This is demonstrated by exercising control over the land and, as Slade J pointed out, clear evidence of this is 'the locking or blocking of the only means of access'. We are told that Sid has partially fenced off the land. When he applies to be registered, the Land Registry will carry out a preliminary check to see that the claim is founded on reasonable grounds, and it may be that it deems this not to be so.[8] Moreover, the lack of complete fencing may also mean that Sid is not a person in actual occupation for the purposes of Schedule 3 to the LRA 2002.

We are told that one reason why De Veloper is happy for Sid to remain is that it has no immediate use for the land that he is possessing. However, what counts is whether Sid had the intention to possess. In **J.A. Pye (Oxford) Ltd v Graham** [2002] 3 All ER 865, HL, Lord Browne-Wilkinson said that the view that the intentions of the owner of the land are relevant was 'heretical and wrong'.

The best course would be for De Veloper to grant Sid a lease or a licence, as the grant of either would debar any claim by Sid based on adverse possession, as his possession would then not be adverse to the owner. Thus, in **J.A. Pye (Oxford) Ltd v Graham**, it was accepted that the period for which the claimant held under a licence did not count towards the period of adverse possession.

If De Veloper does not do any of these things, after 10 years' adverse possession, Sid may apply to be registered as the freehold owner of the land he has possessed. If this application gets beyond the preliminary stage (see above), it is then served on De Veloper, which will have 65 working days to object by serving a counter-notice. Having done this, it has a further two years in order to take steps to evict Sid by, at the very least, commencing eviction proceedings.

(b) It appears that the land that De Veloper does not wish to be built on does not belong to it, and so the only way would be to get the owner of this land to agree either not to build on it or, possibly, not to build at more than a certain height. De Veloper may consider acquiring an easement over this land, but, in fact, a right to a view cannot be claimed as an easement because one of the characteristics of an easement is that it is capable of being the subject of a grant[9] (see **Re Ellenborough Park** [1955] 3 All ER 667, CA) and in **Aldred's Case** (1610) Co Rep 57, KB, it was held that a view cannot be the subject of a grant as it cannot be precisely defined.

Instead, it should be advised that it should seek the agreement of the owners to enter into a restrictive covenant that would give De Veloper an equitable interest in this land and could be protected by a notice under section 32 of the LRA 2002. Obviously, De Veloper will wish the covenant to be binding on successors in title to the original covenantor, and it was held in **Tulk v Moxhay** (1848) 1 H & Tw 105, HC that, in equity, a covenant can bind subsequent owners on certain conditions. This rule was refined in subsequent cases so that it only applied to negative covenants.[10] In **Haywood v Brunswick Permanent Benefit Building Society** (1881) 8 QBD 403, CA, Brett LJ referred to covenants 'restricting the use of the land' and this is a good working definition of a negative covenant.[11] The benefit of this covenant could be expressly annexed to each plot sold by De Veloper, so that each owner could sue for breach.[12]

If the covenant was breached, De Veloper would be able to seek an injunction to restrain this, but it should be pointed out that injunctions are equitable remedies and, as such, are granted at the discretion of the court. Thus, damages could be awarded instead to compensate for the loss of the view, which would not be so satisfactory.

A final thought is that if the owners of the adjoining land obtain planning permission[13] to build houses, this will not discharge the covenant and they will still be liable on it (**Re Martin's Application** (1988) 57 P & CR 119, CA at 124).

[9] You could go through the other characteristics of an easement as well, but why? It is obvious that this right cannot be an easement, so just make this point and move on.

[10] Although the actual covenant in *Tulk* v *Moxhay* was negative, the decision was not confined to positive covenants – this restriction came later, as we have explained.

[11] An average answer would simply refer to 'negative' covenants and leave it there. However, this answer goes one step further and looks more closely at what 'negative' means.

[12] Don't forget this point: if the burden of the covenant can be made to run, the benefit must be made to as well, otherwise there will be no one who can take action for any breach.

[13] An excellent example of some lateral thinking that will impress the examiner. If our clients can get planning permission for their development, why can't their neighbours? Hence, this point.

✓ Make your answer stand out

- This question has a strong practical element – so any evidence of ability to think as a land lawyer in practice will add to your marks!
- Go to the Land Registry website (https://www.gov.uk/government/organisations/land-registry) and look at the *Land Registry Practice Guide 5: Adverse Possession* (HM Land Registry, 2010) – it is extremely clear and helpful, especially where the question has a practical slant, as here.
- Could any of the reasons mentioned in Schedule 6, Paragraph 5 enable Sid to be registered at once? Possibility of estoppel? Unlikely, but perhaps worth a mention.
- Mention exactly how the benefit of covenants can be annexed to the land.

! Don't be tempted to . . .

- Overlook that title to the land is registered.
- Overlook the significance of De Veloper being purchasers and whether Sid's rights are binding on them.
- Just deal with the adverse possession point. Instead, think of how the owners can solve their problem by granting a lease or a licence.
- Stop at the point where you have said that there cannot be an easement, in the question concerning a right to a view: again, take it further and look at other possibilities.

Question 3

Mike owned a freehold factory building with registered title. He needed extra funds and so, in 2012, he arranged a mortgage with Cheeploans Ltd. In 2015, Mike became unable to make the repayments on the mortgage and so Cheeploans Ltd wish to possess the building in order to sell it. However, they now find that the building is also occupied by Arthur, Mike's son, who runs a small business from it and who can prove that he contributed half the purchase price when Mike bought it.

Advise Cheeploans on their position with regard to Arthur's occupation.

Would it make any difference to your answer if:

(a) Cheeploans Ltd knew of Arthur's existence before they granted the mortgage, but insisted that Arthur sign a document stating that Cheeploans Ltd would not be bound by any rights that Arthur had in the property.

(b) Legal title was in the name of Mike and his wife, Sally, who both took out the mortgage.

(c) Although title was in Mike's name only, the mortgage advance was released by Cheeploans Ltd to Mike at a later date, at Mike's request.

Diagram plan

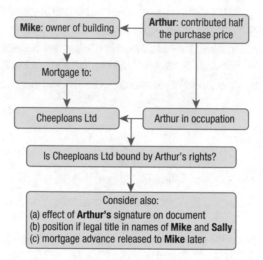

A printable version of this diagram plan is available from **www.pearsoned.co.uk/lawexpressqa**

Answer plan

→ In the main situation, note that Cheeploans Ltd are purchasers.

→ Explain that Arthur has a beneficial interest, but it seems not to have been registered.

→ Does Arthur's interest override? State and apply the relevant parts of the LRA 2002.

→ In (a), knowledge of Arthur's interest will not affect Cheeploans Ltd, but has he consented to their interest having priority over his? Or was his consent procured by undue influence?

→ In (b), state and apply the overreaching provisions.

→ Will the overreaching provisions still apply? Note dicta in *Shami* v *Shami*.

Answer

[1] These must be your initial two points: first, you need to establish that title is registered, as this affects the rest of your answer. You then need to mention that a mortgagee is a purchaser. Many students miss these points: not only do they lose marks, but they also lose the chance to get their answer off to a good firm start.

[2] Always subdivide your answer on overriding interests of occupiers into these two points.

[3] You will get bonus marks for knowledge of the ways in which a beneficial interest may be claimed, but go no further than this, as it is clear that Arthur does have a beneficial interest.

[4] This is the crucial link: if he is not in actual occupation, there is no point in applying Schedule 3, Paragraph 2.

[5] Although it is actually obvious from the facts that these two exceptions will not apply, you do need to investigate them.

Title to the land is registered and so the provisions of the Land Registration Act 2002 (LRA 2002) will apply. The creation of the mortgage by Mike in favour of Cheeploans Ltd means that it is a purchaser,[1] as, by section 205(1)(xxi) of the Law of Property Act 1925 (LPA 1925), the expression 'purchaser' includes a mortgagee.

Although Arthur's interest is not registered, he may have an overriding interest that binds Cheeploans Ltd. This will be under Schedule 3, Paragraph 2, which deals with when a purchaser can be bound by the overriding interest of an occupier. There are two questions: (1) does Arthur have an interest?; and (2) was he in actual occupation at the time of the disposition?[2] The disposition here will be the creation of the mortgage.

The property is registered in Mike's sole name and so Arthur's interest will be equitable, on the basis that, by virtue of his payment of contributions to the purchase price, Mike holds the property for himself and Arthur under a trust, thus giving him a beneficial interest in it. As Arthur's interest arose by way of contributions to the purchase price, there is certainly a resulting trust (**Dyer v Dyer** (1788) 2 Cox Eq Cas 92, Exch), and it could also be argued that there is a constructive trust under the principles laid down, by the House of Lords, in **Stack v Dowden** [2007] UKHL 17.[3]

Arthur is clearly in actual occupation at the time of the disposition, as we are told that he runs a small business from the building. We then apply Schedule 3, Paragraph 2 to the LRA 2002,[4] which deals with the two cases when a purchaser will not be bound by the overriding interest of an occupier:

(a) If Arthur's occupation would not have been obvious on a reasonable inspection of the land. There seems to be no question of this, as we are told that he runs a small business from the building.

(b) If Arthur failed to disclose his rights over the property when he could reasonably have been expected to do so. There is no evidence that Cheeploans Ltd ever asked Arthur if he had an interest in the property, and indeed that they knew he even existed, and so this will not apply.[5]

[6] There is no need to pursue this further: clearly, this conclusion will affect all three parties, but you are simply asked whether the purchaser is bound by an overriding interest, and you have answered that they are.

[7] This is a very basic, obvious point, but you must get it right!

[8] Although the facts of this case are different and so not relevant, the principle is the same.

[9] The crucial point is that you have spotted that Arthur is Mike's son. This should then lead you to ask questions about the transaction.

[10] Your identification of this point is crucial, as you are showing that you are not just applying the law unthinkingly.

[11] You do not need to outline what the steps are: this is only one part of the question and we are given no information to enable us to decide this issue.

As neither of these applies, Cheeploans Ltd will be bound by Arthur's interest as an occupier.[6]

The fact that Cheeploans Ltd knew of Arthur's existence before they granted the mortgage is not relevant because, unless an interest overrides, as we suggest that it does here, a purchaser will not be bound by a prior interest unless it is registered[7] (s. 29(1) of the LRA 2002). However, Arthur has signed a document stating that Cheeploans Ltd would not be bound by any rights that Arthur had in the property. Thus, Cheeploans Ltd could argue that Arthur has consented to the mortgage and so is bound by it, as in *Paddington Building Society v Mendelsohn* (1985) 50 P & CR 244, HC.[8]

However, Arthur is Mike's son and as signing his consent to the mortgage appears not to be to his financial advantage, he might claim that his signature is voidable on the ground that Mike has procured his signature by undue influence.[9]

There are two issues; whether Mike exercised undue influence over Arthur to gain his consent to the mortgage and, if he did, then whether Cheeploans Ltd were put on enquiry so that they took reasonable steps to ensure that Arthur did in fact give his consent freely.

We do not know whether Mike did exercise undue influence over Arthur, but in *Royal Bank of Scotland v Etridge (No. 2)* [2002] 2 AC 773, HL, Lord Nichols said that where there is a relationship of trust and confidence between two people and there is a 'transaction which calls for some explanation', undue influence can be presumed. We do not know whether there was such a relationship between Mike and Arthur and it may be that the mortgage was to Arthur's advantage as it enabled him to stay in occupation of the building. On the other hand, the creation of the mortgage created a charge on the property that was not to Arthur's advantage.

Even if undue influence is presumed, it will not affect Cheeploans Ltd's ability to enforce the charge created by the mortgage unless they are put on enquiry. It is suggested that, on the facts, they may be, as, although Arthur is not actually standing surety for Mike's debts under the mortgage, he is affected by it.[10] If that is so, Cheeploans Ltd are under a duty to take the steps outlined by Lord Nichols in *Royal Bank of Scotland v Etridge (No. 2)*. If they did not,[11] and undue influence is either proved or can be presumed, Arthur will not be bound by his signature and so his rights will override those of Cheeploans Ltd.

[12] If you see that a question involves a sale by two or more owners, it is likely that it will involve overreaching.

If the legal title was in the name of Mike and his wife, Sally, who both took out the mortgage, my answer would be different, as the sale by two owners means that Arthur's rights would be overreached even though he had an overriding interest.[12] Overreaching occurs here when section 2(1)(i) of the LPA 1925 applies and the provisions of section 27 of the LPA 1925 are complied with. The effect is that if capital money arising on a sale (the mortgage advance) is paid to two trustees or a trust corporation, any interests of beneficiaries in the property are overreached and exist only in the proceeds of sale. Where there are two or more co-owners then they are trustees and so overreaching can operate (*City of London Building Society* v *Flegg* [1987] 3 All ER 435, HL).

If title was in Mike's name only, Arthur's interest would normally override the rights of Cheeploans Ltd as explained above. However, it may be that if the mortgage advance was released by Cheeploans Ltd to Mike at a later date at Mike's request, even if the sale is by only one owner, then the rights of beneficial owners such as Arthur are overreached.

[13] This is an interesting and controversial point, and you would miss these marks altogether if you had not kept up to date.

In *State Bank of India* v *Sood* [1997] Ch 276[13] it was held that a valid disposition by two (or more) trustees can overreach beneficial interests even where no capital monies arise – for example, where the mortgage is taken out to secure future lending under an overdraft. This was then extended by *obiter* remarks in *Shami* v *Shami* [2012] EWHC 664 (Ch) to say that if no capital money arises on the sale, beneficial interests are overreached even where the sale is by one owner. The argument is that as the requirement for two trustees is in section 27 of the LPA 1925, this does not apply when no capital monies are payable. The logical consequence is that one trustee can overreach under section 2(1) when no capital monies are payable. However, this was only *obiter* and is a startling result, as all that one legal owner need do to sell free of beneficial interests is to receive payment for the property or the mortgage advance later.

✓ Make your answer stand out

- Refer to recent discussion on what actual occupation means under Schedule 3, Paragraph 2 of the LRA 2002.
- Point out that, as title is already registered, this is a subsequent registration and, as such, is governed by Schedule 3, Paragraph 2 and not by Schedule 1, Paragraph 2, which would apply if this was a first registration. Research this point.
- Read and use the article by Dixon, M. (2014a) *Land Law.* on the implications of the decision in *Shami* v *Shami* on overreaching.
- Point out that there is an argument that the overreaching provisions are incompatible with the European Convention on Human Rights (e.g. Art. 8), but that, in *National Westminster Bank Plc* v *Malhan* [2004] EWHC 847 (Ch), Morritt VC indicated *obiter* that he did not agree.
- Note the strange case of *AIB Group (UK) Plc v Turner* [2015] EWHC 3994 (Ch), where the overreaching point was apparently overlooked.

! Don't be tempted to . . .

- Write all about land registration law or mortgages – this question is about specific issues in these areas.
- Write about unregistered land as well. This would be dreadful!
- Fail to identify what right Arthur has before you apply the LRA 2002.
- Assume that, just because Arthur seems to have consented to the mortgage, he is bound by it.

@ Try it yourself

Now take a look at the question below and attempt to answer it. You can check your response against the answer guidance available on the companion website (**www.pearsoned.co.uk/lawexpressqa**).

> Quiet Days Ltd owns a number of rest homes in the south of England. They are concerned about two matters and ask your advice:

a. They have a number of long-term residents who have self-contained accommodation, although they have meals provided, and who benefit from the back-up care services provided, as well as from those of the resident manager. Two of them are unable to look after themselves and should really be in accommodation where their needs can be better provided for. Quiet Days Ltd will, of course, need to handle any question of terminating their accommodation sensitively, but, as a preliminary point, it would like to know whether these residents do have leases over their accommodation. All relevant details are in writing.

b. One of their homes is on land where there is a covenant that prevents any building more than 30 metres high. Quiet Days Ltd wish to erect an extension that is 35 metres high. The covenant was made with the previous owners of the land, Loud Sounds Ltd, and was taken for the benefit of the owners of 'The Laurels', a house nearby. Can this covenant be enforced against Quiet Days Ltd?

www.pearsoned.co.uk/lawexpressqa

Go online to access more revision support, including additional essay and problem questions with diagram plans, and you be the marker questions, and to download all diagrams from the book.

Bibliography

Andrews, G. (2002) Undue Influence – Where's the Disadvantage? *Conv.* 456.

Auchmurty, R.S. (2004) Not Just a Good Children's Story: A Tribute to Adverse Possession. *Conv.* 68: 293.

Bandali, S.M. (1977) Injustice and Problems of Joint Tenancy. *Conv.* (NS) 41: 243.

Bogusz, B. (2011) Defining the Scope of Actual Occupation under the LRA 2002: Some Recent Judicial Clarification. *Conv.* 75: 268.

Bogusz, B. (2014) The Relevance of Intentions and Wishes to Determine Actual Occupation: A Sea Change in Judicial Thinking? *Conv.* 78: 27.

Bridge, S. (2009) Prescriptive Easements: Capacity to Grant. *CLJ*, 68(1): 40.

Bright, S. (2000) Leases, Exclusive Possession and Estates. *LQR*, 116: 7.

Bright, S. (2012) The Uncertainty of Certainty in Leases. *LQR*, 128: 337.

Bright, S. and McFarlane, B. (2005) Proprietary Estoppel and Property Rights. *CLJ*, 64(2): 449.

Cobb, N.A. and Fox, L. (2007) Living Outside the System? The (Im)morality of Urban Squatting after the Land Registration Act 2002. *Legal Studies*, 27: 236.

Cooke, E. (1994) Adverse Possession – Some Problems of Title in Registered Land. *Legal Studies*, 14: 1.

Cooke, E. (2003) *The New Law of Land Registration*. Oxford: Hart Publishing.

Cooke, E. (2009) To Restate or Not to Restate? Old Wine, New Wineskins, Old Covenants, New Ideas. *Conv.* 448.

Cooke, E. (2012) *Land Law*. Oxford: Oxford University Press.

Cork Committee (1982) *Insolvency Law and Practice*. Cmnd 8558.

Cowan, D. and Hunter, C. (2012) 'Yeah but, no but' – *Pinnock* and *Powell* in the Supreme Court. *MLR*, 75(1): 75–91.

Davis, C.J. (1998) The Principle of Benefit and Burden. *CLJ*, 57(3): 522.

Davison-Vecchione, D. (2014) To Make a House a Home: *Best* v *Chief Land Registrar*. *Conv.* 78: 351.

Dawson, I. and Dunn, A. (1998) Negative Easements – A Crumb of Analysis. *Legal Studies*, 18: 510.

Dewar, J. (1986) Licences and Land Law: An Alternative View. *MLR*, 741.

Dixon, M. (2009) Proprietary Estoppel: A Return to Principle. *Conv.* 260.

Dixon, M. (2014a) *Land Law*. Abingdon: Routledge.

Dixon, M. (2014b) Editorial: Reaching Up for the Box in the Attic. *Conv. instead and Property Lawyer*, 78: 165.

Dixon, M. (2016) Mortgages, Co-owners and Priority: Some Basics. *Conv. instead and Property Lawyer*, 80: 81

Douglas, G.F., Pearce, J. and Woodward, H. (2008) Cohabitation and Conveyancing Practice: Problems and Solutions. *Conv.* 72: 365.

Etherton, T. (2008) Constructive Trusts: A New Model for Equity and Unjust Enrichment. *CLJ*, 265.

Etherton, T. (2009) Constructive Trusts and Proprietary Estoppel: The Search for Clarity and Principle. *Conv.* 73: 104.

Gardner, S. (1987) Equity, Estate Contracts and the Judicature Acts: *Walsh* v *Lonsdale* Revisited. *Oxford Journal of Legal Studies*, 7(1): 60.

Gardner, S. (1993) Rethinking Family Property. *LQR*, 109: 263.

Gardner, S. (2004) Quantum in *Gissing* v *Gissing* Constructive Trusts. *LQR*, 120: 541.

Garner, J. (1977) Severance of a Joint Tenancy. *Conv.* 77.

Gray, K. (2002) Land Law and Human Rights, in L. Tee (ed.), *Land Law, Issues, Debates, Policy*. Uffculme: Willan Publishing.

Gray, K. and Gray, S.F. (2005) *Elements of Land Law* (4th edn). Oxford: Oxford University Press.

Greer, S. (2009) *Horsham Properties Group Ltd* v *Clark*. Possession – Mortgagee's Right or Discretionary Remedy? *Conv.* 516.

Haley, M. (2008) Easements, Exclusionary Use and Exclusive Principles: The Right to Park. *Conv.* 72: 244.

Harpum, C. (1990) *Buckingham County Council* v *Moran*. *CLJ*, 23.

Harpum, C. and Radley-Gardner, O. (2001) Adverse Possession and the Intention to Possess: A Reply. *Conv.* 155

Hayward, A. (2016) Common Intention Constructive Trusts and the Role of Imputation in Theory and Practice. *Conveyancer and Property Lawyer*, 80(3): 233–42.

Hill-Smith, A. (2007) Rights of Parking and the Ouster Principle after *Batchelor* v *Marlow*. *Conv.* 71: 223–34.

HM Land Registry (2010) *Land Registry Practice Guide 5: Adverse Possession*. https://www.gov.uk/government/publications/adverse-possession-of-1-unregistered-land-and-2-registered-land#guide-mark-0

Hopkins, N. (1996) The Trusts of Land and the Appointment of Trustees Act 1996. *Conv.* 267.

Houghton, J. and Livesey, L. (2001) Mortgage Conditions: Old Law for a New Century?, in E. Cooke (ed.), *Modern Studies in Property Law*, Vol. 1. Oxford: Hart Publishing.

Howell, J. (2002) Subterranean Land Law: Rights below the Surface of Land. *Northern Ireland Legal Quarterly*, 53: 268.

Hudson, A. (1984) Is Divesting Abandonment Possible at Common Law? *LQR*, 100: 110.

Junor, G. (2008) Warning – Parking Problems Ahead (*Montcrieff* v *Jamieson* Applied). *SLT*, 1: 1–2.

Kerridge, R. and Brierley, A.H.R. (2007) Adverse Possession, Human Rights and Land Registration: And They All Lived Happily Ever After. *Conv*. 71: 552.

Law Commission (1989) *Transfer of Land, Trusts of Land*, No. 181. www.bailii.org/ew/other/EWLC/1989/181.pdf

Law Commission (1991) *Transfer of Land: Land Mortgages*, No. 204 www.bailii.org/ew/other/EWLC/1991/204.html

Law Commission (1996) *Landlord and Tenant: Responsibility for State and Condition of Property*, No. 238. http://lawcommission.justice.gov.uk/docs/lc238_landlord_and_tenant_responsibility_for_stake_and_condition_of_property.pdf

Law Commission (1998) Consultation Paper, *Land Registration for the Twenty-first Century*, No. 254. http://lawcommission.justice.gov.uk/docs/lc254_land_registration_for_21st_century_consultative.pdf

Law Commission (2001) Report, *Land Registration for the 21st Century: A Conveyancing Revolution*, No. 271. http://lawcommission.justice.gov.uk/docs/lc271_land_registration_for_the_twenty_first_century.pdf

Law Commission (2002) *A Discussion Paper, Sharing Homes*, No. 278. http://lawcommission.justice.gov.uk/docs/lc278%281%29_sharing_homes_discussion_paper.pdf

Law Commission (2004) *Termination of Tenancies for Tenant Default*, No. 174. http://lawcommission.justice.gov.uk/docs/cp174_Termination_of_Tenancies_Consultation.pdf

Law Commission (2007) Report, *Cohabitation: The Financial Consequences of Relationship Breakdown*, No. 307. http://lawcommission.justice.gov.uk/docs/lc307_Cohabitation.pdf

Law Commission (2008) Consultation Paper, *Easements, Covenants and Profits à Prendre*, No. 186. http://lawcommission.justice.gov.uk/docs/cp186_Easements_Covenants_and_Profits_a_Prendre_Consultation.pdf

Law Commission (2011) Report, *Making Land Work: Easements, Covenants and Profits à Prendre* (LC 327). http://lawcommission.justice.gov.uk/docs/lc327_easements_report.pdf

Lovelace, I. (2014) Public Law and Art. 8 Defences in Residential Possession Proceedings. *Conv*. 78: 245.

Lower, M. (2010) The Bruton Tenancy. *Conv*. 74: 38.

Luther, P. (2004) Fixtures and Chattels: A Question of More or Less. *Oxford Journal of Legal Studies*, 24: 597.

MacMillan, C. (2000) A Birthday Present for Lord Denning: The Contracts (Rights of Third Parties) Act 1999. *MLR*, 63(5): 721.

McFarlane, B. (2009) Apocalypse Averted: Proprietary Estoppel in the House of Lords. *LQR*, 125: 535.

Martin, J. (2012) *Hanbury & Martin: Modern Equity*. London: Sweet & Maxwell.

Matthews, P. (2009) The Words Which Are Not There: A Partial History of the Constructive Trust, in C. Mitchell (ed.), *Constructive and Resulting Trusts*. Oxford: Hart Publishing.

ODPM (Office of the Deputy Prime Minister) (2002) *More than a Roof: A Report into Tackling Homelessness*. London: ODPM.

Omar, P. (2006) Security over Co-owned Property and the Creditor's Paramount Status in Recovery Proceedings. *Conv.* 70: 157.

Pascoe, S. (2000) Section 15 and the Trusts of Land and Appointment of Trustees Act 1996 – A Change in the Law? *Conv.* 315.

Pritchard, A.M. (1987) Beneficial Joint Tenancies: A Riposte. *Conv.* 273.

Radley-Gardner, O. (2007) Good-bye to *Pye*. *Web Journal of Current Legal Issues*.

Roberts, N. (2012) The *Bruton* Tenancy: A Matter of Relativity. *Conv.* 76: 87.

Rotherham, C. (2004) The Property Rights of Unmarried Co-habitees: A Case for Reform. *Conv.* 268.

Scottish Law Commission (1998) *Discussion Paper, Real Burdens*. No. 106. www .scotlawcom.gov.uk/index.php/download_file/view/94/127/

Simpson, A.W.B. (1986) *A History of the Land Law*. Oxford: Oxford University Press.

Sloan, B. (2009) Estop Me if You Think You've Heard It. *CLJ*, 68(3): 518.

Stevens, R. (2004) The Contracts (Rights of Third Parties) Act 1999. *LQR*, 120: 292.

Tee, L. (2000) Adverse Possession and the Intention to Possess. *Conv.* 113.

Televantos, T. and Maniscalco, M. (2015) Proprietary Estoppel and Vendor Purchaser Constructive Trusts. *CLJ*, 74(1):27

Thompson, M.P. (1987) Beneficial Joint Tenancies. *Conv.* 29.

Thompson, M.P. (2001) Do We Really Need Clogs? *Conv.* 502.

Thompson, M.P. (2003) Mortgages and Undue Influence, in E. Cooke (ed.), *Modern Studies in Property Law*, Vol. 2. Oxford: Hart Publishing.

Wade, H.W.R. (1962) Landlord, Tenant and Squatter. *LQR*, 78: 541.

Wallace, H. (1990) The Legacy of *Street* v *Mountford*. *Northern Ireland Legal Quarterly*, 41: 143.

Wilkinson, H. (1991) Farewell, Ladies Must We Leave You. *Conv.* 251.

Wood, J. (2009) *Horsham Properties Group Ltd* v *Clark*: A Year on. *Coventry Law Journal*, 14(2): 31–6.

Index

INDEX